PRACTICALLY INVESTING

Smart Investment Techniques Your Neighbour Doesn't Know

COREEN T. SOL, CFA

iUniverse LLC
Bloomington

PRACTICALLY INVESTING
SMART INVESTMENT TECHNIQUES YOUR NEIGHBOUR DOESN'T KNOW

Copyright © 2014 Coreen T. Sol, CFA.

All rights reserved. No part of this book may be used or reproduced by any means, graphic, electronic, or mechanical, including photocopying, recording, taping or by any information storage retrieval system without the written permission of the publisher except in the case of brief quotations embodied in critical articles and reviews.

iUniverse books may be ordered through booksellers or by contacting:

iUniverse
1663 Liberty Drive
Bloomington, IN 47403
www.iuniverse.com
1-800-Authors (1-800-288-4677)

Because of the dynamic nature of the Internet, any web addresses or links contained in this book may have changed since publication and may no longer be valid. The views expressed in this work are solely those of the author and do not necessarily reflect the views of the publisher, and the publisher hereby disclaims any responsibility for them.

Any people depicted in stock imagery provided by Thinkstock are models, and such images are being used for illustrative purposes only. Certain stock imagery © Thinkstock.

ISBN: 978-1-4917-2202-2 (sc)
ISBN: 978-1-4917-2204-6 (hc)
ISBN: 978-1-4917-2203-9 (e)

Library of Congress Control Number: 2014901189

Printed in the United States of America.

iUniverse rev. date: 1/28/2014

*This book is dedicated to Jakob, Eiden and Sofia
"Mommy, are you done writing yet?"*

prac·ti·cal·ly
\\'prak-ti-k(ə-)lē\\

adverb
1. Virtually; almost
2. In a practical manner; likely to succeed or be effective in real circumstances; feasible

Merriam-Webster Dictionary ®

CONTENTS

	Acknowledgements	xi
	Introduction: Great Investing Isn't Rocket Science	xv
1	Stop Making Investment Mistakes	1
2	Stocks Will Fight Inflation	27
3	Bonds, James Bond	55
4	Alternative Investments: The New Frontier	81
5	Be Careful With Mutual Funds and Other Pooled Products	113
6	This Investment Account Will Change Your Life	147
7	What's Wrong with My Retirement Plan?	175
8	Professionals Are Not Created Equally	201
9	An IPS Will Save Your Bacon	235
	Conclusion: Final Steps	239
	Glossary	241
	About the Author	267

ACKNOWLEDGEMENTS

If it weren't for the gaggle of compatriots and friends who contributed moral support, opinion and conjecture, this would never be a ready work. Thank you to the Women's Investment Clubs and especially Mary, whom I've prevailed upon for content and review. I'm indebted to my fellow CFA® charterholders with whom I've happily spent a week each May for the last several years proliferating ideas over bar stools and coffee shop tables around the world. Many of them graciously offered to lend their voice to this project. Douglas for your sound advice and lastly, for the patience of my children who know how important this is to me, thank you.

PRACTICALLY INVESTING

Introduction

Great Investing Isn't Rocket Science

> Man's mind and spirit grow with the space in
> which they are allowed to operate.
> —Krafft A. Ehricke, rocket-propulsion engineer

There have been far too many investors over the years, who've slid their broken investment statement across my blotter, asking if I can fix it.

As a whole, the experience of Canadian investors has been abysmal as if we weren't really investing at all: as if we were practically investing, instead of investing practically. Over the last couple of decades, since I began managing money, the number of investors that I've met whose portfolios haven't grown a penny beyond their own deposits, is staggering. More recently, through one of the most tumultuous investment cycles, complete with cold cloths and sleepless nights, couples have been driven to conflict and retirees back to the workforce. If the last financial crisis left your fingernails gnawed to the quick or forced you out of retirement, you're in good company.

As a whole, we are on the leading edge of really understanding our financial world. The recent development of **behavioural finance** is more evidence of that. This study of how people behave around money with alarming consistency, is teaching us that our markets are an extrapolation of collective human emotion, predictable in nature. Armed with this emerging information, the profession of investment analysis and forward motion in managing economics, the ebb and flow of money is more manageable and understandable than it has ever been. By harnessing these developments, you can use this awareness and these tools to make a small shift in the things you're already doing and discover, with very little effort, how to make your money work effectively for you.

For the last twenty-some-odd years, I've worked with hundreds of private wealth clients and institutional investors, successfully building and managing their investments. As a portfolio manager (PM), clients rely on my expertise and experience to handle all of their day-to-day financial decisions and the overall stewardship of their assets. Through this book, you will gain the years of experience that I offer my clients directly.

I began this project by writing down a few truths about investing, only to find topics tumbling onto the pages haphazardly, as I burst at the seams. Eventually, that transitioned into organized chaos and finally, chronology. This introduction similarly evolved from versions of cathartic chastisement for the wrongs of the world, to the introspective, calm satisfaction of eventually finding a voice. I've written a dozen introductions, ranging from professional rants to motivational speeches but at the end of my exhaustion and an ever-closer release date, my indulgence is close to spent.

The investment industry as a whole is evolving. Back in the early 1940s, great investment thinkers began a heated debate about whether security analysis was more art or science. During that time, investment pioneers, including Benjamin Graham, gave birth to the idea that financial analysts should form a profession. In order to do so, practitioners must be subject to a measurable testing program and structured, if not scientific, processes. According to *The Gold Standard: A Fifty-Year History of the CFA Charter*, the ensuing decades witnessed a myriad of constructive arguments among practitioners until June 1959, when financial analysts finally adopted a professional status. The proposal, led by Ezra Solomon of the University of Chicago, set out to certify financial analysts through a curriculum and written standards.

Today, the CFA Institute continues to test investment professionals around the globe through a series of three post-graduate, self-study examinations focused on security analysis and ethics, in order to obtain the charter. The organization works to impact market integrity all over the world. With more than 115,000 professionals entitled to use the Chartered

Financial Analyst® designation in more than 137 countries across every continent, the CFA Institute's objectives are "raising standards of professional excellence in the industry; championing ethical behaviour in investment markets; serving as a respected source of knowledge in investment markets; and creating a strong global community of investment professionals." I obtained my CFA® charter in 2002, an achievement that I hold in high esteem.

Economic understanding and development is making great strides, as well. Never before have citizens seen such high correlations between asset classes and profound financial intervention worldwide than since the financial disaster of 2008. Fiscal and monetary policy makers are collaborating among countries and formulating decisions based on tried and untried economic policies founded on the lessons of the 1930's economic depression. The moral hazard of this profound and consistent intervention is yet to unfold, but in the meantime, volatility has dropped to creepy levels encouraging risks in areas that may have offered less sure footing in the past. New opportunities for exploitation abound for the wise and fearless.

From the perspective of real people who are working, raising children, saving, investing and living, what really matters is whether enough meat and potatoes are on the table, whether our children can fulfill their dreams and that there is relative calm and predictability in our retirement years. The lessons taught in the plethora of self-help financial planning books have been all-for-not, if our squirrelling away results in nothing but vapid reserves with barely enough to squeak by on in retirement. How could it be that savings diligence didn't pay off over the last couple of decades? Too many investors are wallowing in directionless portfolios, hoping for a strike of good luck. And yet, this isn't rocket science. Investing should be easier and more rewarding. If you have the keen sense to tuck some money away, it's time for you to start reaping the rewards for that.

Most of my clients are professionals, retirees and business people who have already been saving for several years. From a content perspective, this book covers a wide range of topics: some technical in nature and some anecdotal. In the same way that I speak to my clients, I offer the straight-up facts and then follow it up with examples and stories to make it more approachable and useable. So, if at first you don't quite grasp the jargon, read on. You will.

Also, the chapters are each broken up into sub-categories and stories, some of which may be more or less applicable to your life. Ultimately, you will either want to know the most effective ways to select and work with a professional advisor or how to effectively invest on your own. In every case, you will discover how a simple Investment Policy Statement (IPS) can save your bacon.

Although this book serves out a generous helping of the knowledge I have gained from working in the investment industry for over 20 years, the information contained within is not investment advice, nor is it capable of taking into account your own specific circumstances. One thing you are about to learn from *Practically Investing* is that you have to do your homework. If, by the end of the book, any of the products or strategies you have read about sound appealing, I urge you to seek out an investment professional who can help you explore whether those products and strategies are right for you.

Also, the organizations that I work with now and in the past represent a wide body of individuals and opinions. I'd like to point out that the views set out in this book are well-researched from sources that I believe are credible and reliable, and that the conclusions of my work may not be those held by the respected organizations that I work with now or those that I have worked with in the past.

Note: Words set in **bold** are defined in the glossary at the back of the book.

Chapter 1

Stop Making Investment Mistakes

> It was when I found out I could make mistakes
> that I knew I was on to something.
> —Ornette Coleman

Not Quite a 12-Step Program

We all make mistakes and, as with every hangover, we emphatically and fruitlessly vow never to do it again. But I promise that you will. The end.

Just kidding.

Innate human tendencies were meant to help us survive the wilderness, not make investment decisions. And yet, those are the tools we rely on today for complicated reasoning. No wonder investing hasn't been seamless. Not totally wrong, but not totally right either. Recognition and acknowledgement are the first steps in any 12-step program for change. You don't know what you don't know, and if you aren't aware in the first place, you can't make a decision to affect change. If you soberly knew a way to make intelligent investment decisions, you would. If it only took a bit of understanding to be more profitable, you'd do that too.

This is not a book telling you to spend less and save more, but one that provides all smart things to do while you are saving and once you have a nest egg. Whether you read it cover to cover or you select individual sections that will help you when you need them most, I hope you will keep a well-worn copy next to your investment account statements.

Play it Again, Sam

Both men and women harbour **cognitive biases** that influence our behaviour. The way each of us reacts is alarmingly predictable and consistent. *Predictable* and *consistent*. The good news is that you're not alone. The propensity to make errors with money and investing is well documented through a growing body of study called **behavioural finance**.

Luckily, **cognitive biases** are nothing more than tricks and shortcuts that our brains use to help us make quick decisions and be more efficient in our lives. Unfortunately, these pre-fab decision trees don't necessarily add value to the financial outcomes at hand.

The plight of the human condition leaves no one behind. Over the years, these biases have taken hold regardless of race, education, gender or socioeconomic status. Decision errors are made and repeated with great regularity. Rational financial decisions are much easier to make once you understand the reasoning behind these biases and are able to recognize the predispositions. If you're already entrenched in the belief that each of us operates as a free decision maker, you won't need convincing that experience is the sum of mistakes that we don't need to repeat. Ultimately, it would be ideal to enhance your financial situation with the least amount of effort on your part. To do that, we need to lay out some groundwork.

Decision errors are made and repeated with great regularity. Rational financial decisions are much easier once you understand the reasoning behind these biases and you are able to recognize the predispositions.

Possibly the most important piece to understand is the notion that investment markets are efficient. This idea gained popularity in the 1950s. To be brief, the **efficient market hypothesis** maintains that stock market prices are random and fair. Essentially, it contends that there are enough rational people buying and selling **stocks** and other **securities** that the market will determine a fair price simply through the buying and selling of the securities. If the price are too high, no rational person would buy. If it's too low, no one would sell.

When stock prices get out of whack, sellers eagerly dump overpriced securities, driving prices down, and buyers then snap up underpriced ones with earnest, forcing fair values. Imagine a passerby frantically rapping on your door, offering to purchase the gargoyle peering over your eaves for twice what you bought it for. You'd be a fool not to sell it. The passerby must have different information about the value of the statue of course, or she rationally would not purchase the ugly beast against her financial best interest. If there were a crowd outside your home, some selling gargoyles and some buying, you could reasonably assume that the average agreeable price of the transactions represents a **fair market value** for the statues.

The second part of the **efficient market hypothesis** (you'll have a few great phrases to throw around the coffee shop by the last chapter!) is that the prices of stocks and bonds reflect all information that buyers and sellers have. For example, when a company announces its earnings, the investing public analyzes the new information (very quickly!) to determine the **fair market value** of the **shares**. Assume that the company's reported earnings came in lower than expected. Obviously, investors who value the share price relative to the earnings would sell the shares at current levels. You'd be as much a fool as the homeowner with the gargoyle not to. In turn, the sheer interest in selling the shares at the inflated levels and the diminished interest in buying the relatively high priced shares drives the share prices lower on the market. Once the shares are at the fair market value, the opportunity to profit on the difference no longer exists.

This oversimplification is to illustrate what drives market prices up or down. In practice, there are multiple facets affecting the perceived value of any stock, bond or gargoyle, much of which is disputed among market participants. For every transaction, there's someone willing to buy and someone willing to sell at an agreed price, both believing that it's good value and that the **counterparty** is a little crazy. That's what's fun about this. The differences of opinion are what keep markets humming and prices continually adjusting to find the fair value. It's been said that

*For every transaction, there is someone willing to buy and someone willing to sell at an agreed price, both believing that it's good value and that the **counterparty** is a little crazy.*

it's only a fair trade when both parties consider the other to have received the better deal.

In real life, it's more complicated than just analyzing new earnings information every 3 months. Consider the influences of global economic growth, new competitors, interest rates and changes in the price of supplies or wages that can fluctuate minute by minute. Beyond the hard data, subjective factors equally influence the prices of everything. The complexity of analysis is as thick and deep as there are opinions. There are at least two opposing viewpoints every time a transaction happens. Sometimes a stock will trade at a price that is 10 times the value of the earnings **per share** and sometimes at a price that is 16 times. It's the aggregate opinion that determines who is right and who is less right.

What the efficient market hypothesis doesn't account for is that people are not always rational. Just ask any divorce lawyer.

At first glance, the theory makes sense, but what the **efficient market hypothesis** doesn't account for is the fact that people are not always rational. Just ask any divorce lawyer. Despite this fissure, the theory's premise doesn't need to be thrown out with the bathwater. It's a reminder that we do not operate like machines. You can't simply install an update to fix a programming bug.

Since people are at the helm of these trading decisions, the market itself is subject to collective human errors. This notion can be extrapolated to entire economies. In general, economic cycles are built on stages of cumulative human errors. When people collectively feel exuberant or fearful, or they do something in concert the way a cohort (like the baby boomers) might, the economy follows. When everyday folks feel wealthy as their bonus rolls in higher than expected, their annual house assessment jumps, their RRSP statement climbs again this month or their high-flier stock doubles, jubilance spills over into spending habits. If the majority of people feel this way and behave this way, the economy expands or continues expanding.

The cycle of optimism and euphoria leading to greed, fear and capitulation, giving way to hope and building back to optimism, drives the expansion and contraction of our financial world in a market cycle of collective human emotion.

I trust that you've already made the leap to see that the reverse is also true. When you hear nothing but solemn news reports of financial collapse and economic deterioration, or the value of your RRSP has been chopped in half and you can't sell your real estate, people naturally start reigning in spending. With all that depressing news, who feels like a shopping spree anyway?

The cycle of optimism and euphoria leads to greed, fear and capitulation, giving way to hope and building back to optimism. It drives the expansion and contraction of our financial world in a market cycle of collective human emotion.

Your actions and your neighbours' actions send a ripple effect throughout your community, city and province, compounding the issue. If you own a business, you may find yourself cutting costs, reducing marketing efforts and inventories, and possibly laying off staff. And so, we have market cycles driven by waves of human behaviour, some of which is rational and some of which is emotional.

Takes One to Know One

The following illustrations set out several common **cognitive biases** that have been working against you all of these years and the reasons that our hardwiring is naturally and irrationally applied to how we look at money. The reasons for why your attempts haven't worked in the past are not shocking. Simply by being aware of where the trouble lies and understanding some very interesting and goofy things that people do consistently, you suddenly become able to approach money differently than you have in the past. By realizing what can go wrong, you are in a position to impact your financial successes.

Hindsight is Not Foresight

Of course, anybody could have predicted the collapse of the fourth-largest U.S. investment bank, Lehman Brothers, which reported assets of $635 billion when it filed for bankruptcy protection, and Merrill Lynch & Co. agreed to be sold to Bank of America Corp. a week after the U.S. government bailed out other major U.S. financial institutions, on

September 10, 2008. Mollenkamp, C. et all. (2008, Sept. 16). Lehman Files for Bankruptcy, Merrill Sold, AIG Seeks Cash. *Wall Street Journal*. Weren't your assets all cashed in before that happened? Your financial advisor must have known that it was going to happen! Why didn't he sell out your account beforehand? Or at least once the bankruptcy was announced?

The truth is that no one knows until they know. Once they know, so does everyone else. (If I start sounding too much like Dr. Seuss, just kick me under the table.)

With the speed of information today, share prices are affected almost immediately. Moreover, the initial correction is often overdone. When dramatic news is first released, there is often an overreaction resulting in a sell-off that may be more than warranted. In this case, the price drop is followed by a rebound as cooler heads prevail. If you want to see how accurate your foresight is, there's a simple way to find out. I told you this was going to be easy, didn't I?

Grab a small piece of paper and pen or pencil. Write down the closing value of the Canadian **stock market index** (**S&P/TSX**) for this Friday. You can find today's value by visiting www.tmx.com.

Simple!

Over a short period of time, surely you can tell where the market is going. If you don't know by how much, you'll at least know the direction with some certainty! (Note the sarcasm.)

Ah, but you're not a professional, you say.

Interestingly, Chartered Financial Analyst® societies all over the globe hold an annual Forecast Dinner. I've been involved with these events in Kelowna, B.C., as a board member since 2003. Every year, pre-eminent investment professionals are invited from all over North America to our little community of 125,000 people. They are asked to foretell the level of the **S&P/TSX**, the Dow Jones Industrial Average (DJIA), a **long** stock and a **short** stock (which we will cover in chapter 2) on the upcoming December 31. The following year they're invited back to defend their predictions in a roast format usually reserved for comedians or retiring guests of honour. It's an obviously impossible task for the incumbents and a great deal of fun for everyone else.

Instead of using your intuition about the direction of the market, step back, take a deep breath and dust off your good ol' **Investment Policy Statement (IPS)** that you wrote in more sober times. An IPS is a document that you will hear much about over the pages ahead, outlining how your investment decisions will unfold. If you haven't done so yet, there are wagers out that you'll have something in writing before you finish the last chapter. Realize that your appetite for risk (a.k.a. **volatility**) will change during different market conditions so it's important to write your IPS during times of stability in your life, when no major changes are on the table and when markets are relatively steady. Then stick to it.

The details of an IPS is explained in detail in chapter 9, dedicated to establishing one, why and what it contains. In the meantime, it's suffice to say that when markets become volatile, emotions often get in the way of a good plan. Treat them as **lagging indicators.** A lagging indicator is something that tells you what is going to happen after it already happened. Ironically, not kidding.

> "Rebalancing and Investment Policy Statements—that is the key: IPSs written in calmer, rational times which dictate the frequency and timing of rebalancing is paramount. Buying **equities** after a major market decline is often the toughest exercise for retail clients but inevitably is the best thing to do. Having an IPS that you review annually with your Investment Professional is a crucial document. Sign and date this together to make it 'official.' Humans have an innate tendency to have their actions match their words. What actions will I take if the market declines by 20%? Figure this out before it happens."
> —John Stubbs, Director, Wealth Management, Richardson GMP Ltd.

IPSs work. Write what you believe and how you wish to invest in black and white. Revisit it often.

Like shampoo instructions: lather, rinse and repeat.

Unleashing the Dogs

I love my family, but sometimes, personal relationships get in the way of asserting professional philosophies. When my father insists on holding a stock position, who am I to say no?

I now practice **discretionary portfolio management** for a bucket full of reasons, but a main motivation is to eliminate **entry-level biases.** Having discretion means that in addition to saving people from their biases and emotions, I can act quickly and efficiently during times of volatility. Instead of calling each client to convince them of the current course of action, I'm able to pull the switch and act in accordance with their IPSs and the prevailing market conditions.

A 'dog' is a beloved term used to describe a bad investment, as in, "this portfolio has gone to the dogs." It's an alarmingly common belief that if you don't sell anything that is down, you aren't really losing money! While this logic is rewarded when you own good quality, suitable investments during temporary drops in the overall market, it's never rewarded when you hold onto a bad investment that continues to drop in value or one that has no hope of recompensing you. Trying to convince someone who grips this notion with white knuckles and the strength of an army is like blowing out an electric light bulb. No one is better for the effort. If an investor only sells the stocks that appreciate in value and refuses to sell those that drop, eventually the investor has nothing left but a portfolio dogs. I've seen these beauties.

Behavioural finance researchers have also labeled this problem. **Anchoring** is when you assign a value to something based on information that is irrelevant or even random. Prudent investors build decisions on whether to buy, hold or sell a security based on the relevant economic information, their investment objectives and suitability of the position within those parameters. Past information and irrelevant facts, including a historic price for the security, are not part of the process. With the error of **anchoring**, people have an inclination to consider either the price paid for an investment in the past, the price at which it peaked (regretting not selling it) or some other irrelevant information. These are powerful motivators to keep the stock for completely irrational reasons.

> "There is nothing more destructive to a portfolio than allowing deteriorating companies to grow into outsized losses. Have the fortitude to admit mistakes early, move on and reallocate your capital to better investments. Be able to also recognize when your biggest winners have run their course and despite still being great companies are no longer great investments. Simply, have a well-defined sell discipline and follow it. It's the difference between having a successful investment **strategy** and one that is not."
>
> —Clark Linton, CFA, Portfolio Manager, Raymond James Ltd.

If you're still not convinced, just remember that it never matters what you paid for an investment. If it no longer fits your investment strategy, it has deteriorated in quality or there are better opportunities for that capital, forward-looking investors will sell. Period. Whether it's up, down or equal to the price originally paid should never be a determining factor in whether to continue owning an investment. Your original investment price only matters when you're calculating the tax on the investment. Nothing more.

If you need an emotional firewall between you and your biases, hire a **discretionary Portfolio Manager (PM)** to take control of these decisions. Discretionary portfolio management, where the manager makes all of the daily decisions strictly based on your objectives, eliminates the subjectivity keeping you from dumping those dogs.

The tricky part is knowing when it's a dog and when it isn't.

Cocktail Party Investing

I love cocktail parties, but they were a lot more fun during the '90s. Perhaps that's because I had less white and more blonde in my hair, the rock bands were better or the stock market was a bit less directionally challenged. Chiming in with the *tink-tink* of ice in a Bombay tonic, the stories of parabolic dot-com returns or recounting the latest press release from Bre-X brought out the competitive nature in everyone. Recently, one of my clients admitted buying Bre-X on May 3, 1997, two days before an independent mining company reported there was virtually no gold in Busang.

"And I don't even gamble," she admitted.

According to a timeline published by CBC News on July 31, 2007, a former stockbroker named David Walsh formed Bre-X in 1988. It wasn't until 1992 that a partnership was formed with geologist John Felderhof and a second geologist, Michael de Guzman, was hired. Initially, the shares of Bre-X traded at less than $1. Over the next 3 years, Bre-X announced gold reserves on their Busang property in Indonesia could contain 30 million ounces of gold. Analysts across many investment firms raised their buy targets and price projections, and the shares hit $200 in 1996 with a **stock split** on a 10-to-1 basis. Eventually the company had a **market capitalization**—or total market value—of over $6 billion.

Concurrently, Bre-X again upped its expectations to a whopping 71 million ounces of gold, only to be trumped 2 days later by a comment from Walsh that the Busang deposits may be as much as 200 million ounces. What an absolutely fantastic outcome, worthy of another glass of Champagne, if you were one of the early adopters of the sales pitch.

Imagine the excitement that stockholders containing their thrill shared when the most recent company report increased estimates from 39 million ounces of gold to 47 million and the complementary share price surged. Real or not, if you sold at those share prices, you would have made a gargantuan profit. In February 1997, Bre-X and Freeport-McMoRan reached an agreement to develop the property, each with its own interest and a slice going to the Indonesian government. Concurrently, Bre-X again upped its expectations to a whopping 71 million ounces of gold, only to be trumped 2 days later by a comment from Walsh that the Busang deposits may be as much as 200 million ounces. What an absolutely fantastic outcome, worthy of another glass of Champagne, if you were one of the early adopters of the sales pitch.

On March 12, 1997, Freeport announced that its own tests turned up only minor amounts of gold and demanded to speak with the geologist de Guzman later in the month. On March 19, 1997, de Guzman fell to his death from a helicopter over the Indonesian jungle. The perfect ending to the drama would have been the suicide note reportedly found but the better story was about his possible murder. Even Hollywood wouldn't write the ultimate clincher: if de Guzman had faked his own death.

There are two things that I want to point out. Firstly, most of us have been guilty of falling for a great story. It happens all the time. Independent analysis is the only way to turn **speculation** into investment and even then, you may not have much on which to base a prudent decision. Without numbers, risk is wholly a matter of the gut.

*A **stock split** is when a company decides to multiply the number of shares outstanding without changing the equity in the company. If you hold 300 shares and the stock splits on a 2-for-1 basis, you will own 600 shares each valued about half of your original shares.*

Secondly, despite the Bre-X story being one of fraud, investors in the company were no less speculators than those who bought unproven Internet stocks with a shattering **Price to Earnings** ratio. Buyer beware. When every other vase costs $5, why is this one $48?

The lesson in all of this is that there are no new paradigms. When pundits start stating that it's different this time, look around you for evidence of a bubble ready to pop. Eventually, everything reverts to normal levels. It's-different-this-time means that it isn't.

The best way to avoid getting caught up in the cocktail party story is to have a story of your own. Write down your objectives and believe in them. An IPS is a fantastic way to ensure you maintain your discipline and goals. Write it down in black and white, and read it from time to time, especially when emotional, disastrous or unusual events happen. Then stick to it.

I may be redundant, but repetition is effective.

Fear is an Emotion, Not a Stock Indicator

With the advent of the dot-com crash in the early part of the millennium, the **Asset Backed Commercial Paper (ABCP)** fallout in 2006, followed by the big hit everyone took in 2008, a decade of profoundly volatile markets have taken their toll. Within those events, certain patterns emerged. There is no science behind it and these observations are based purely on anecdotal evidence. That being said, it's with alarming consistency that clients tend to call their Investment Advisor (IA) to liquidate their entire portfolio within 3 or 4 days of the lowest level that stocks reach when the markets drop. Literally, the bottom of the market.

If I receive 3 phone calls of distress and inability to sleep, I know that we must be near or at the crux of capitulation.

Today, it's less often that I receive calls directly from clients panicking, yet the phenomenon prevails. If I receive three phone calls of distress and inability to sleep, I know that we must be near or at the crux of capitulation.

This is when an investment professional earns the money you pay him. He reaches back into his quiver and pulls out the compassion and rationality arrows and a copy of your written IPS. Having the black and white pages before you while undergoing an emotional event like a stock market tumble, is an excellent reminder of your goals in more sober times. Your second line of defense is having a professional whom you trust, with the steady hand of objectivity to pull the trigger or not. That is why trust is so important.

What are the very last things you should consider doing when you're swimming in emotion? Shoot a gun, end a relationship or buy and sell assets. The time to address the quantities that you have in risky assets is when stock prices are flying high. In 20 years, I have NEVER received a phone call from a client asking to reduce his equity exposure when his stocks are up 25%, yet that is exactly the time to do that if you wish to reduce your volatility. The problem is, no one minds volatility when the direction is up. The time for asset allocation decisions is when the world is calm, volatility is low and emotions are in check. When you make those decisions, write them down.

In 20 years, I have NEVER received a phone call from a client asking to reduce his equity exposure when his stocks are up 25%, yet that is exactly the time to do that if you wish to reduce your volatility.

Tactical asset allocation is the disciplined approach of taking profits on predetermined, periodic dates, from investments that are overweight in your portfolio, and investing the excess money into those that have less money allocated to them. Positions become overweight almost always due to their outperformance over your other investments. Positions proportionately shrink in your portfolio due to either a contraction in their market value or the outperformance of your other investments.

> "A good plan violently executed now is better than a perfect plan executed next week."
> —General George S. Patton

Generals make decisions for the collective good based on strategies to win the war, not fight the battle. **Tactical asset allocation** works because it replaces emotional decision making with structured decision making. The human input is in the selection of securities you wish to invest in, but once you've decided where to put your money and how much to have in each security, the **tactical asset allocation** process dictates the rebalancing of those investments, ever after. Obviously, you aren't going to throw good money into bad investments but if your security selections are still sound, reconstituting investments that dry out relative to your other holdings, is a good idea. If your portfolio holds a collection of companies or **exchange-traded funds (ETFs)** representing various markets or types of investments you wish to retain, this calculated strategy could eliminate the impact of fear from your investment decisions.

This is no easy task, but without other barriers in place to divert emotional decisions during volatile conditions, it's an alternative to consider. If you don't believe that you make emotional decisions, ask yourself if market conditions were ever a deciding factor, preventing you from contributing to your RRSP in any year. If you answer yes, more structure will increase your returns.

If you don't believe that you make emotional decisions, ask yourself if market conditions ever prevented you from contributing to your RRSP. If you answer yes, a more structured approach will increase your returns.

There will be days that you'll need to garner every ounce of strength you have to sell some of those investments that are doing well and buy the ones that aren't. Without the conviction of tactical processes, it can be heart wrenching to sell the darlings that are making you look good to buy the ones that are ugly for the moment. It goes against our natural inclination to let the winners run, smile and reflect on your good decision to buy them in the first place. Keep in mind that investment professionals are here to increase and protect your investments.

Implementation of **tactical asset allocation** is easy. On a monthly, quarterly or semi-annual date, reset the amounts you have invested in equities, fixed income, **alternative strategies**, cash, real estate, etc. Or, if you have an entirely stock portfolio, rebalance the amount in each of the stocks that you hold or the ETFs in your account. For a balanced portfolio where you want to maintain 35% of your investment in bonds, 50% in stocks and 15% in alternative assets, sell the positions that have exceeded those percentages and buy the ones that no longer meet the quantities that you want to hold. Without blinking an eye, tactically sell the excess securities and buy more of the insufficient ones, with the proceeds.

Alternative strategies differ from traditional investment portfolios either by investing in non-traditional investments (other than stocks, bonds, etc.) or by executing the investment strategy in a non-traditional fashion (shorting, arbitrage, etc.).

Similarly, you could review your portfolio for instances where a single security has outperformed or underperformed compared with rest of your holdings. Tactically sell the excess shares of the company that has performed well and purchase additional shares of the one that needs to be beefed up to an equal level within your account, with the cash. It's prudent to have written guidelines for your portfolio to help with this process. Establish how much of your portfolio you want to allocate in each type of investment in your IPS. Set out the steps you'll take and when to take them, so that when it comes time to act, you know exactly what to do. Don't let fear override your IPS instructions. Taking emotion out by adding structure is a small shift that can change your results. Act differently than the way that didn't work before.

Like Buckley's, it tastes terrible, but it works.

Mental Accounting to Zero

The term **mental accounting** isn't a particularly intuitive phrase but it's been coined to describe another common, faulty way of thinking. If you've ever categorized your assets into buckets based on the use of the funds, the source of the funds or some other arbitrary division, you're guilty of it.

Folks who receive an inheritance are prime candidates. People sometimes attach emotion to money based on the source from which it came, often leading to **mental accounting**. Problems arise if you segregate those funds from other assets, treating them in a radically different manner from your global investment strategies. While the detrimental nature of this irrational approach to money may not be immediately obvious, consider the person who stashes spare change in a wide-mouth mason jar behind the cookbooks, with "Vacation Fund" handwritten in purple Sharpie, yet they carry credit card debt at 21% interest.

Investment issues come into play when an investor is tempted to divide his assets into different risk categories rather than formulate a concerted investment approach. If he assigns different risk levels to each of his accounts or if he requests that part of his assets be invested differently than the rest of his money, he has fallen into a trap that can work against him. In one case, new clients came into my office and announced they had set aside $125,000 to be kept in ultra-safe money market funds. They went on to affirm that this structure was in order to fund the first five years of their retirement income, at $25,000 per year. This couple planned to retire five years hence. With their remaining assets, they were happy to invest in a moderately aggressive, balanced investment approach including **equities**, **fixed income** and alternative strategies.

The problem was that the first bucket of funds did not reflect their rational overview of investing for the medium and long term. For their long term strategy, they were comfortable holding a variety of good quality, diversified asset classes that would grow over time and appreciate in concert with inflation yet for their medium term strategy, they held their assets hostage in cash, depreciating in value with the rate of inflation. They were crippled by their fear of loss, deciding to separate five years of income, doing as much harm to their purchasing power as stuffing blue $5 bills into their sock drawer.

Their fears were justified, of course. They'd been socking away (excuse the pun) money for decades with nothing more than their original capital to show for it. Combine that with a few catastrophic years in the stock market and a looming retirement date (another emotional event) and presto…**mental accounting**.

In another example, a different set of clients stated they had a conservative investment approach but that they were willing to gamble with 10% of their assets. Yes, you read that correctly. I've taken the word "gamble" verbatim from our interview. In fact, I've heard other terms and phrases in similar contexts including, "Vegas it," "my lotto ticket," "all my other stuff is safe" and the like.

Mental accounting is irrational. Your investment strategy should be inclusive of all your investable assets. Your right arm is not more aggressive than your left. Your RRSP, **margin** or cash account, Tax Free Savings Account (TFSA), etc., should all be part of your overall plan. The only reason these accounts are separate is the government rules for tax shelters, and holding higher taxed investments within a sheltered account makes tax-sense.

If you're a conservative investor, there's no rational reason to speculate. Zero. None. Not even in that stock that the guy you know, who knows a guy, who knows another guy, who said it will make you rich and only you and a few others can get in at the ground floor. If you're a moderate or growth investor, there's no rational reason to keep large portions of your investments out of your investment strategy or in cash over the long or medium terms.

If you have significant pending liabilities or planned payment dates, it is entirely rational to align maturities or terms with certain investments in your portfolio. This is called **liability matching**. Pension funds often use this strategy. They will have specific securities mature or come due when they need funds available to be paid out each year. Similarly, you can apply this strategy to an annual Registered Retirement Income Fund (RRIF) payment so that the cash is available when you need it and the rest of your portfolio can remain invested, alleviating volatility fears around your payment dates. This strategy is substantially different from holding part or your entire portfolio hostage, in cash, for extended periods of time.

Buy and Hold at Your Own Risk

Remember the good ol' days when you could buy a **blue chip stock**, just hang onto it and never imagine selling it? Wasn't "Buy and Hold" the marketing tag line for a major mutual fund company at one time?

If you think buy and hold is the way to produce good returns, take a look at some of the early components of the Dow Jones Industrial AverageTM (DJIA), a standardized stock index in the United States. Today the only company that is still listed in the index is General Electric. The American Tobacco Company disseminated due to antitrust action in 1911. The North American Company broke up in 1946 and the United States Leather Company dissolved in 1952.

The fact is, the world changes at an exponential pace in the contemporary age of technology. Remember Northern Telecom, better known as Nortel? The Canadian darling of the '90s Internet boom was an optical equipment maker, including routers. In the early days of the technology explosion Nortel was spun off to shareholders of the **bellwether, orphan and granny company**, Bell Canada Enterprises (BCE). Being that BCE was a widely held stock, the majority of equity investors in Canada received Nortel shares either directly or within other investments. If you owned a mutual fund in 1998 or invested in stocks over that period of time you likely owned Nortel, one way or another.

Two years prior to its spin-off from BCE, Northern Telecom transformed from an electronics subsidiary to a global, multiprotocol switching and optics manufacturer, through acquisitions and business developments in the early 1990s. By the time BCE spun off the shares of Nortel, the **speculation** of Internet and Internet related companies was orbiting out of sight. Eventually reaching a peak of over $124 per share, many investors contemplated buying more when it had dropped below $20, then $18, then $10. Finally, at 47 cents, the company ceased operations and under bankruptcy protection, endeavoured to sell off assets.

> *"History never repeats itself, but it often rhymes, to borrow from Mark Twain's famous quote...a piece of advice which rings just as true in today's financial market as it ever has. A robust understanding of history reveals nothing is really new...perhaps just another colour. While this will not prevent us from making some financial missteps in life, it will help us to avoid life altering, portfolio destroying mistakes and to be wise enough to elude the 'this time is different' trap!"*
>
> —Scott Ross, CFA, Portfolio Manager,
> RBC Dominion Securities

Frankly speaking, there are too many dynamic variables, market altering developments and complete upheavals to buy and close your eyes. Eastman Kodak, Blockbuster, Yellow Pages Group and others have tried desperately to reinvent themselves or have all but gone the way of the wagon wheel. Once considered **blue chip** companies with strong **dividends**, in many cases, are worthless today.

Despite these obvious ramifications, the buy and hold strategy (the term strategy used loosely, in this case) also doesn't work when a market moves sideways. **Oscillating markets** that move up and down within a limited band, still offer opportunities to increase your account value by being selective but overall doesn't produce much. Actively managing your holdings even when the aggregate market plateaus is the only way to reap rewards.

Diversification Won't Save You

The last half of 2008 was an extraordinary lesson for market participants for many reasons beyond the red handprint across our cheeks, as we were all gobsmacked with losses. In 1990 Harry M. Markowitz won the Nobel Memorial Prize in Economic Sciences for his work in **Modern Portfolio Theory**. This theory looks at the risk–return trade-offs and the effects of **diversifying** between **low correlated** assets to predict the best possible portfolio in a period of uncertainty. Essentially, the theory contends that if you design a portfolio among various investments that behave differently at different times, there is a set of mathematically ideal portfolios that extract the most return for the minimum amount of **volatility**. That's good, right? When your stocks are up and your bonds are down, by blending the two investments (or more), you create a result of the highest possible return for flattest roller-coaster ride.

Low correlated assets behave differently from one another so combining them in one portfolio flattens the overall volatility.

Based on this work, contemporary portfolios are designed on the practical notion of achieving the highest return for a given amount of **volatility**. Investing in multiple types of assets that have **low correlation** to each other seems as pragmatic as the old "don't put all your eggs in one basket" adage. If you have $100,000, don't buy just one stock. Buy several stocks scattered among various sectors, in multiple countries. While you're at it, buy some bonds, too, and spread them among a bunch of corporate and government issuers with a variety of maturity dates. Add a diverse selection of other non-correlated investments to the mix and Bob's your uncle. Don't forget gold, silver and real estate.

This was roughly the time when alternative strategies or **hedge funds** became a retail phenomenon. Many of these portfolios claimed to extract **absolute returns,** indicating positive performance regardless of how much the benchmark portfolio is up or down. In contrast, **relative returns** are the conventional measure of performance for traditional portfolios. When the stock market drops in value traditional portfolios, including long-only mutual funds, feel that they are doing well by dropping in value less than the market.

Buy several stocks scattered among various sectors, in multiple countries. While you're at it, buy some bonds, too, and spread them among a bunch of corporate and government issuers with a variety of maturity dates. Add a diverse selection of other non-correlated investments to the mix and Bob's your uncle.

Other hedge fund strategies simply claim to produce returns that aren't correlated (behaved differently) to traditional investments. Early adopters of these alternative strategies added them to their traditional portfolios as a means to dampen the effects of **volatility** when the going gets tough.

Well, the going did get tough. In 2008, we witnessed the worst financial crisis since the Great Depression of the 1930s. What we learned from this exercise is that **liquidity** is the great equalizer in the same way that we all put our pants on one leg at a time. When markets freeze and investors need cash to meet **margin calls** and trust is eroded between **counterparties**, cash is king and everyone sells everything. When everything is sold, the price of everything is driven down and securities behave the same under these conditions regardless of what they are.

That is when correlation is the same for everything: close to a perfect one-to-one relationship.

Down.

Individuals who had borrowed to invest in stocks found themselves on the other end of a mafia style telephone call, receiving instructions to come up with cash to cover their **margin** and meet their debt obligations or be forced to sell their stocks at the prevailing, brutally low prices.

When there is no liquidity, everything drops significantly in value as investors rush to the red-lit exit signs. All the baskets slam together simultaneously, crushing all the eggs at once.

Without cash in reserve and not wanting to sell stocks at post-apocalyptic prices, many leveraged investors were forced—reluctantly—to liquidate other investments. Naturally, they turned to anything that hadn't dropped or had dropped less than their annihilated stock portfolios. This widespread concerted reaction forced good quality assets to drop in value even though they were unaffected otherwise by the current crisis. Coupled with the lack of otherwise normal buying activity in the market, all assets around the world were crushed to ruinous prices.

During normal market conditions, **diversifying** among a variety of investments that behave differently (**low correlated** asset classes) is a reasonable way to reduce the fluctuations in your portfolio. Since the investments act differently during normal times, one being up and the other down, the averages iron out the overall changes in the portfolio value. It's during those unexpected and extreme events, called **tail events** by statisticians because they're so far from normal, that diversification is rendered ineffective.

Real estate developers and investors could not sell battered investments in the **illiquid markets** because there were simply no buyers. Everyone was in the same field trying to dig up cash and wiggle out of their cement boots. To compound the issue, many investors who had borrowed (heavily in some cases) against those beleaguered investments, had to sell other assets to satisfy loan payments. They were literally selling anything that they could find a buyer for, in order to pay interest and **margin calls**. When all of the cash that was in the market was withdrawn and those who held cash hoarded it, our financial deck of cards came crashing down. When there is no liquidity, everything drops significantly in value as investors rush to the red-lit exit signs. All the baskets slam together simultaneously, crushing all the eggs at once.

Diversification has other issues beyond catastrophic illiquidity events, however. The world is getting smaller, trading is becoming increasingly automated and technology delivers information and execution at lightning speeds. The opportunity for diversification is ebbs away with time as our investment options narrow. When the volume of information increases and businesses become necessarily integrated, the ability to find true diversification diminishes.

Consider a company operating in the Canadian oil sands of Alberta. With international trade expanding; improved operational efficiency of shipping and transportation; more homogenous pricing; increased accessibility to information regarding the amount of oil available, refined and stored; and concerted usage worldwide, the share price of that Canadian company suddenly becomes remarkably affected by the same supply and demand inputs as any other oil company anywhere on earth. So the ultimate effectiveness of diversification becomes less and less beneficial over time as our world becomes more interactive.

As we move toward fewer opportunities for traditional diversity, more innovative approaches continue to emerge. Be aware when building a strategy for yourself and consider the relationships between your investments. You have to become a skilled pharmacist to your investments, ever watchful for drug interactions between holdings.

Robbing Peter to Pay Paul

Seeking high distributions on investments for their own sake is perilous. This faulty investment stance is prevalent in Canada for two reasons. Overwhelming demand is the first. Our aging population's insatiable appetite for monthly cash flow during retirement has driven the market for income bearing investments to overinflated levels. Mutual fund companies and the corporate financing departments of banks across North America are tripping over themselves to come up with investments that provide monthly income for investors. Investment manufacturers are developing just about anything to spit out a monthly payment to meet this huge and growing interest. In the wake of creative financing, a variety of financially crafted products have appeared with ill devised structures that offer little transparency. In many cases, these businesses and structures have no business distributing income at all.

If you made $12,300 one month, $614 the next and $4250 the following, how difficult would it be to pay your $6000 rent? Imagine the life of a commissioned real estate agent who gets paid only when a home sells. You have 6 homes listed and if they sell, you stand to earn net commissions of $76,000 in the year. That is pretty decent if it weren't for the unknown payment. Your monthly bills are predictably due regardless. In the same way, these enterprises with volatile income easily cut off a slice of the earnings in robust months and on average, the income is enough to satisfy all of the payments. With a few lean months in a row, it can get a little tricky, forcing management to become crafty. Moreover, distributing much needed cash during a marginal month of production or a severe period of loss could easily injure an otherwise healthy business.

The moral hazard of giving investors double-digit income every month is that they come to expect it. On Halloween 2006, the government revoked the favourable tax structure that made those distributions possible, setting the stage to eradicate the proliferation of **income trust units**. Retirees addicted to the high income streams were reduced to desperately tapping their two fingers on the inside of their left elbow to activate a vein of cash flow.

Income trust units were first popularized in the early 1990s, beginning with Koch Pipelines and others. Initially exploited by resource businesses, trust structures utilized a tax loophole that allowed the distribution of pre-tax operating income to unit holders. The funds retained their original qualities as **capital gains**, interest or dividends and were channelled to the unit holders to be taxed in their hands directly, instead of being taxed at the corporate level and again as dividends in the hands of shareholders.

Since the income is only taxed once, Canada Revenue Agency (CRA) collects fewer dollars, keeping more money in the hands of Canadian spenders. The issue with these distributions is that they were set at unprecedented high levels. Unfortunately, resource companies operate with volatile income driven by fluctuating commodity prices. Also, they're often in expansionary growth phases and need a great deal of capital to expand operations, develop mines and fields and find additional resources which deplete over time. Income-bearing investments are ideally suited to mature, stable businesses rather than growth-oriented ones that need money and have unstable earnings.

Retirees addicted to the high income streams were reduced to tapping their two fingers on the inside of their left elbow to activate a vein of cash flow.

In a perfect world, businesses with unstable income coupled with a need for ongoing new capital should reserve cash to supply their operations and stabilize their funding needs. Yet, the benefit of distributing pre-tax capital to investors is too enticing. Together with the huge appetite of retirees for cash flow, it's like throwing shrimp into a pool of piranhas. Attracting investors is part of the objective of raising share prices and capital, so when these businesses need cash for projects, they opt to issue a new round of shares to the salivating market instead of holding onto their own revenues and pay taxes on them. Moreover, some creative accounting began meeting cash distribution shortfalls by handing out new shares or trust units instead of using accumulated money from operations. This continues to dilute the value of the enterprise over time to existing share and unit holders.

Remember that the finite resources from which the company derives its profits may deplete, as well. So while the unit holder is paid handsomely each month, the value of the investment can erode over time. Prior to the federal government's announcement, the high levels of cash distributed by these **trusts** created a false ideal of payout ratios for non-mature businesses.

This isn't true of all income trust units and is less true of those remaining in the market today but the precedence of elevated distributions have left a wake of expectation in their path. Investors have a lingering taste of unsustainable cash flow being paid to them. Even today, I still hear people insisting that they should buy a particular stock or security because it has a *high payout*. Shockingly, there is little or no regard for the affect of that payout on the share price. When a business does not have the earnings to make these distributions, yet it continues to do so, the share or unit price will drop. Guaranteed.

Compare the earnings of the company to the amount that it pays out each quarter and how stable that margin between the two is. If the business earns widely variable earnings and pays out a high distribution, this is dangerous. If it has a stable and growing distribution and only pays out a fraction of the company's earnings, this is the safest scenario. When a company pays out more than what it earns, there is an obvious erosion of value over time and the share price will eventually reflect this, one way or another.

Recall that when a company doesn't pay out any money and it retains those earnings within the company, reinvesting them in its business (or keeping part of that cash in its coffers) the value of the company and the shares should increase, all else being equal. As an investor, you could sell some shares to fund your financial needs, rather than expecting dividend income. Capital gains have a 50% income tax inclusion rate. So for every $1 of income, you only include 50 cents in your tax return. In contrast, dividends from Canadian corporations have a **gross up amount** and tax credit, which makes them more heavily taxed than capital gains for tax payers with higher income.

Although I personally prefer to hold companies that pay a distribution of some kind, in some cases those that retain a portion of their earnings to reinvest in their own business or to stabilize cash flows reflect better management practices. What is better for the company is in turn better for the shareholder.

Prospect Theory

Imagine you're faced with this choice. Situation A is to accept a guaranteed loss of $3000 or situation B is to accept an 80% chance of losing $4000? Which would you choose? Did you select A or B?

You likely chose B.

When people are faced with losses, they prefer the chance that they will not lose anything instead of pragmatically limiting their losses. Similarly, when asked if they would rather have a guaranteed $3000 or an 80% chance of getting $4000, most people again choose the second option for the higher reward even though there is a risk that they will receive absolutely sweet nuthin'. Surprisingly, the gamble for a higher return seems to offset the 20% chance of walking away with nothing but lint in your pocket. When probabilities are low, most people blush away the risk in favour of the larger gain option.

We feel reasonably lucky.

This may not sound like an issue at first glance, but consider a similar scenario of loss. Imagine the chance of losing an additional $1000 or 25% more money in the 80/20 scenario. The rational decision should be to limit the absolute loss rather than to accept the risk of a greater forfeiture. Human nature, however, has a built-in hopefulness that we will land on the unlikely 20%, as low as that probability may be.

Irrationality can sound reasonable until you examine it. These are illustrations where no real money is at stake, merely a decision in imagination-land. The stakes change dramatically though, once you have skin in the game. When real cash is on the line, **loss aversion** is even more pronounced. Also, the effect of recent memories of significant loss amplifies these irrational changes in behaviour.

An easy way to prove this is to look at online theoretical stock portfolios versus ones that are actually funded with cold, hard cash. The theoretical versions don't really matter because nothing real is at stake, and your willingness to *try* an investment strategy that may be dramatically higher risk is more likely than if your hard-earned money could slip away with the trade.

Understanding how we think about these options is the first step to limiting your exposure to this irrationality. Tempting as it may be, limiting your losses, even if they're absolute, is the best route in high probability situations.

Extrapolation

One of the more useful, dangerous mind tricks is the natural ability to predict near term events using **extrapolation**. Without being able to extend our current understanding of the world in the next moments, we could not function. It's necessary for our very survival that we hold the ability to project or extend our current experiences into the future to be able to plan and make everyday decisions.

Epic powder day. Blue bandana across your facial extremities. Nothing but vertical in front of you. You inhale and go. The skis crest the first vault and position into the next exhale. There's no fight as each glide between firm mounds drive your heels to push off for the next carve. The repetition isn't exact but you understand the depth of the snow and how light or sticky it is, intuitively. The next turn you make is extrapolated from the last.

Valuable information from recent experience guides your next move. This unconscious preconception to link near future events to near past events acts as a guide for what's upcoming. Enjoy the functionality of how it works but be aware of the double blacks. Extrapolation is useful. When it comes naturally, be careful where you use it. Physical, autonomic experiences aside, it can get you into trouble when applied to investing.

Despite the common disclaimer on portfolio returns cautioning us that past performance is not an indication of future returns, convention is to adjudicate the merits of investment options on that very set of facts. Industry insiders call this "chasing performance". They may go so far as to forecast new deposits to their portfolios based on their most recent returns. Unfortunately, if a certain style or investment method has performed well in current market conditions, it's more likely to underperform (not to be confused with declining in value) in the future as market conditions change.

The other problem with being human is the propensity to weigh recent experiences more heavily in our expectations of what will happen next, than distant past experiences. If you're driving on a winding road in wet conditions, this is a useful tool. When you're experiencing the exponential rise of some of your shares, you might assume that they'll keep rising, when the more rational computation should include the growing risk that they'll retreat as the price rises higher.

Awareness is the key. If you're in a severely depressed market that has dropped week after week after week, realize that there is a bottom and the moment you're tempted to capitulate is likely the moment the human condition has similarly driven other investors to feel the same. Their execution on that emotion exhausts the downward spiral and the market is at or near the bottom of the cycle. Hold on and wait until sober heads prevail. Recognize the emotional content and the reasons that the market is being irrationally oversold.

Chapter 2

Stocks Will Fight Inflation

> I will tell you how to become rich. Close the doors. Be fearful when others are greedy. Be greedy when others are fearful.
> —Warren Buffet

Take Stock

Investing in stocks is interesting, hopeful, exciting, profitable, euphoric, concerning, arduous, frustrating, treacherous, agonizing and distressing, in that order. There's a trick to keeping emotions in check especially through major economic events. When the boat starts rocking, coaching yourself to keep your eye on the horizon is not just a nice soliloquy. Steadying your gaze and maintaining a forward perspective will help navigate the rough seas when other investors are bailing. You will, nevertheless, be better off with a stronger boat built with a few key fundamentals.

Successful investing isn't rocket science. Over the next few pages, you'll begin to garner a meaningful understanding of practical stock investment strategies. Not stock tips, but guidelines and underpinnings that you can apply to sound portfolio management.

Let's get 'er done.

Going Public

At some point in everyone's investing life, comes the temptation to get a piece of a highly publicized **initial public offering (IPO)**. In recent memory, several iconic social media companies issued public shares for the first time, sending investors clamouring for their piece of the pie thinking that it was a lottery ticket of some kind. Investing in **new issues** is not as straightforward as it may appear. Due to the fact that these companies have never been required to file public documents or announce their earnings, visibility of the company's financial information and historic trends aren't as robust as for companies that have been public for years. Moreover, a company's IPO issue price can be tricky to nail down. Guessing where the market will ultimately trade the stock when it's released is part analysis, part art and part magic.

Guessing where the market will ultimately trade the stock when it's released is part analysis, part art and part unknown.

There are other nuances that investors should know. For example, the IPO for Facebook, Inc., was only filed in the U.S. Thus Canadians were relegated to aftermarket purchases once the shares began trading on the NASDAQ stock exchange. You couldn't have participated in Facebook's IPO shares as a Canadian regardless of how much money or how many connections you had, as they were only offered through U.S. dealers.

People often ask if they should buy shares of an IPO thinking it could be a good investment to flip and make a profit. Conventionally, corporate financiers (the folks who bring **new issues** to market) aim to price brand new shares just below where they think they'll trade. This gives investors an incentive to support future IPOs and issuers have an easier time garnering support for additional **new issues**. If investors have a profitable experience they're more likely to participate in new shares when the company comes back to the **capital markets** to raise more money. Sometimes the analysis of where the shares will trade in the market is totally off the mark and in some cases, the issuers become too greedy.

In the final week leading up to the IPO of Facebook, 84 million shares were added, bringing the total up to 421 million shares. They also increased the price range from $28–$35 per share to $34–$38 per share according to Reuters on May 16, 2012. That's as much as $840 million more and prices the stock in the 99 times trailing earnings range, not substantially dissimilar to **Price to Earnings** ratio for other high flying internet companies, including Apple Inc. and Google. The famed Harvard student who started the company was the primary private shareholder prior to the IPO. Mr. Mark Zuckerberg retained more than half of the voting rights and wrapped his arms around an estimated $15 billion of cool cash once the deal was done.

The final price decision on **new issues** is a balance between rewarding new shareholders for their support while maximizing the amount the company receives from the offering. In an over-hyped market like the iconic social media company created, one would expect some hefty upside from the $38 starting point. Ironically, within the first two days of public trading, the shares closed below the issue price. Initial investors lost money right out of the gate.

Conversely, the principals involved with LinkedIn Corporation agreed to issue their initial public shares at $45. Remember that the absolute share price is not important; rather, the proportion of the business that each share represents is what gives it value. When the shares of LinkedIn began trading, they opened at $83 per share, blew way past $100 and settled the day at $94 per share. The investors who purchased the shares on the IPO before they hit the market were pretty happy campers.

A company will convert from private ownership to public for two reasons: access to capital markets as a source of financing and for the private shareholders to monetize their investment in the company. Private company shareholders often have a good deal of money tied up in the company since it was their own capital that was used to build the business. Getting that money out to be used for other purposes is monetizing an investment. By becoming a publicly traded company, the owners of the private entity sell part of their interest to withdraw some of their invested capital. At the same time, this also reduces their exposure to the business because they own a smaller portion of the company. Moreover, once the shares are listed on an exchange, they're able to more of their public shares in the future should they wish to become less involved with the business or extract additional capital for other purposes. I smell a retirement plan.

In some cases, the company issues public shares to add cash to the coffers for business expansion or operational funding. When new shares are issued, the ownership of the company becomes diluted, but the additional cash can increase the value of the business if those funds are invested in the enterprise. Regardless of the reasons that funds are raised in a public offering, the trade-off for access to capital markets is the regulatory reporting and accountability to public shareholders like you and me.

A company will convert from private ownership to public for two reasons: access to capital markets as a source of financing and for the private shareholders to monetize their investment in the company.

Typically, publicly traded companies are owned by a wide variety of people who buy and sell the company's shares. The shares are listed on one or more of the major stock exchanges, providing transparency for investors through reporting, regulation and greater **liquidity** through availability on the public market. New investors can purchase shares of the company on the stock exchange where the market participants determine the value of the shares simply by demand (or lack thereof) for a particular company's stock. If the market determines that the shares are too expensive, there is no demand, therefore driving the price down. Recall from chapter 1 that efficient markets allow the buyers and sellers to decide the fair price of any stock, security or gargoyle and that opportunities to sell something that is overpriced or buy something that is underpriced are where you can make extra profits beyond the growth of a company's income.

A **stock** is one piece or **share** of a business. The terms **stock** and **common shares** are synonymous, used interchangeably. If you purchase 500 shares of a company that has 5000 shares issued and outstanding, you've become the proud owner of 10% of the company's business.

Earnings and other financial details of the company are broken down to reflect the amounts on a per share basis. It's easier to compare apples to apples by dividing them into equal standardized pieces. Since each share represents a proportional interest in the company, it makes sense to break down the financial details that way, as well.

The shareholders are the owners of the company. Each shareholder has a claim on a proportion of the equity and earnings of the business, divided equally among the number of shares. So, in the previous example, if the company makes a million dollars, you make $200 per share on your investment. Not literally, but in terms of the profitability of the company.

What management actually distributes to shareholders as dividends is another story.

You get this! The office at the end of the hallway is yours.

Buy Low/Sell High

"I just hold on if the market is volatile. I only trade stocks in my portfolio when the market is going up," boasted the fellow sitting on the other side of my desk, as if his secret to trading stocks in a rising market was a crafty trick. Note the sarcasm in that. He missed the clairvoyant sell-before-the-market-drops stuff but he was proud of his skill-set, nevertheless. He believed that trading stocks when the market rises somehow produces the increased value of the portfolio, when *holding* rising stocks (rather than trading them back and forth) will probably do as good a job, if not better. There are no trading commissions if you aren't buying and selling.

Further, during market downturns, he easily blamed the decline in his portfolio value on the market rather than the investor at the helm since he was passive during those periods of **volatility**. Perhaps scapegoating should have been a topic in chapter 1.

Regardless of the hobbyists' sense of omnipotence during **long bull markets** (where a game of darts is a darn fruitful stock selection process!), a sound analysis strategy is a saving grace in any market. Successful investing doesn't just come from amplifying returns on the upside and protecting a portfolio on the down. The true test is being able to produce returns when markets oscillate non-directionally. There are opportunities in every market to make a positive return beyond market timing and throwing darts. Here are the pieces you need to do just that.

Analysis is the cornerstone of investing. Understanding the value of a security and whether it's trading above or below that value is the difference between investing and speculating.

Analysis is the cornerstone of investing. Understanding the value of a security and whether it's trading above or below that value is the difference between investing and **speculating**. Just because a stock is being traded on the market at a certain price, does not mean that its price reflects the value of the company, per share. Therefore, the first step is to determine what the stock is worth. This is the price at which the stock is expected to trade once all of the altering facts are brought to light and the information has been digested by all of the people who trade its shares.

There are a variety of basic, traditional measures of value that provide some footings. **Price to Earnings ratio (P/E)**, **Price to Book ratio (P/B)** and **Price to Cash Flow ratio (P/CF)** are good starting points to determine a stock's real value. These are nothing more than simple ratios developed to find comparable standards among similar businesses.

P/E is used to determine whether the share price is too high or too low compared with the relative earnings per share of the company. This measure is always used in comparison with something else. Is the P/E for this company higher or lower than another company or the average P/E for this type of business or even the entire market? By comparing the P/E among peers, you can better understand how a company ranks in terms of its earnings, relatively speaking. There may be good reasons for one company to trade at a higher P/E than another, but common sense prevails. Levels that are way out of whack will come into line with peers at some point. It's interesting to consider what the market may be telling you when this kind of anomaly transpires. A P/E that is at historically high levels may indicate an anticipation of higher earning growth for the economy aggregately or for the company specifically. Or it may be something else entirely which you are left to your own devices to figure out.

*The term **bellwether** refers to the practice of placing a bell around the neck of a castrated ram (a wether) leading his flock of sheep. While out of sight, the sound of the bell is a directive on the whereabouts of the flock. When earning season begins, the **bellwether** stock is that of the largest (typically industrial) companies who report their earnings. Analysts look to these reports as an indication of how subsequent reports will come in under or over expectations.*

Consider the price of a share divided by the cash flow of the company per share. The **P/CF** provides standardized comparison of top-line revenue streams with the market value of the shares. Similarly, the **P/B** measures the market price of the shares compared with the balance sheet assets, also on a per share basis. All of these ratios are interesting but you cannot take them into account on their own. They are most useful as a benchmark for approximate levels. The best way to evaluate a business in which you're considering investing is to draw up an Excel spreadsheet and compare the stock ratios with those of peers and other businesses you're interested in, or against other **bellwether stocks**. Even as an exercise, it will get you used to various values and how they compare with each other and change during various market cycles. Exceedingly low ratios may indicate the shares are oversold or there is trouble with the company. You need to determine which. High levels point to over-exuberance or anticipated expansion of growth, or both.

Beyond the basic ratios, populating your matrix with various other characteristics can help draw out the best companies by mining for specific traits. If, for example, an investment analyst increases what she believes a company's earnings will be over the next three to twelve months, the IAs in that firm increase their interest in buying the shares. When the demand for anything increases, the price logically trends up. Additionally, upward revisions of a company's earnings mean that prospects are improving for a company or the sector in which they operate. There may be a change in management direction, positive economic conditions or some other catalyst that makes the investment interesting. Consider other qualitative factors including the company's consistency in its earnings, growth profile, business development, acquisition plans, innovation and dividend policy. Some of these can be quantified in your spreadsheet.

CAGR, pronounced [kay-ger], (as in kegger - a bash at which party-goers drink beer from a keg) is an acronym referring to a company's Compound Annual Growth Rate. It measures how much the earnings of a company are growing over a specific period of time, like 5 or 10 years. It's an indication of the company's health and how well it's managed. Growth rates on their own aren't all they appear to be, however. Evaluating a growth rate in relation to other value metrics is wise. For example, the PEG divides a company's PE ration by it's growth rate in order to compare companies with various growth rates.

All of these subjective measurements attempt to quantify and standardize analysis. As much an art as a science, analysis integrates tangible as well as intangible characteristics to define or discover undervalued companies that have fallen through the cracks by the mass investors.

Dividends Aren't Just for Grannies

Companies that pay dividends often outperform those that do not, over time. Think of it this way. If a company retains all of its extra money to reinvest back into new company projects, their best project ideas will likely be a good use of the cash they earn. By the time management exhausts those first few ideas, I swear that with three kids, I have a few of my own opportunities that would be more fruitful than their leftover, tertiary projects. It's probably obvious by now that this line of work comes with the moral hazard of the constant, ongoing analysis of everything in life.

As a shareholder I'd like management to keep money to invest when they have plans that will produce good returns but at a certain point, paying a dividend to shareholders is the best use of that cash since shareholders also have investment options.

There are often good places to put money. Putting some or most of the free cash flow generated from the business into the hands of investors - who can create even more wealth from healthier opportunities - is a great solution. Moreover, companies that pay regular distributions attract more investors given the heavily weighted demographic of cash flow junkies in the midst of a North American retirement. That being said, it's wise not to discount the benefits of investing in companies that don't pay dividends. There are reasons to hold both.

From an investor's point of view, owning stocks with a dividend policy makes a great deal of sense unless the company has a high growth profile, all else being equal. Despite the fact that eligible Canadian dividends paid into taxable accounts are usually more expensive to receive than capital gains for those in the highest marginal tax brackets, they attract fewer taxes for most taxpayers in the lower brackets. Receiving dividends regularly can help to stabilize portfolio values and allow investors to fund their lifestyle or reinvest periodically in a market that offers opportunities.

On the flip-side, aggressively expanding businesses have a high burn rate. It's practical in these cases to retain all or most of their earnings for projects and operating expenses. Retained earnings are put back to hard work, increasing the share price and your investment.

Take the pragmatic approach. Consider what line of business the company is in and determine whether it's a burgeoning sector such as technology; a mature and stable market such as pipelines; or one that is on the decline, like hard-wired telephony. Let common sense weigh in. Keep an eye out for companies that typically increase dividends over time or elect to pay out special, one-time or extra dividends. Increasing dividends reflect management's confidence of continued, stable growth and as dividends increase, the share price typically follows suit.

The second consideration is to ensure that the earnings can support the amounts paid out. It may sound like an obvious prospect but the number of companies that pay distributions higher than what they can afford would surprise you. Many times, this is due to a change in their business cash flow and management's reluctance to adjust dividends downward for fear that they will lose shareholders. For this reason, some end up paying distributions as shares instead of cash, which ultimately dilutes the value of the shares that you already own. More shares on the market means that the earnings of the business are divided among more shareholders, each of whom receives a smaller piece of the pie.

Dividends are usually paid on a quarterly basis but some companies elect to declare and pay dividends monthly, semi-annually or annually. When planning to buy or sell shares, be aware of when dividends are doled out as there are no standard distribution or shareholder of **record dates** for these transactions. In order to participate in the distribution of a dividend, the shares must have settled in your account before the **ex-dividend date**. Typically, **settlement** for **common shares** and preferred shares is 3 business days after the trade or transaction date.

Most Canadian dividend paying public companies offer an automatic Dividend Reinvestment Program (DRIP). Dividends are automatically reinvested in additional whole shares of the company for an amount equal to the nearest number of the company's shares on the day the dividend is paid. This is an excellent way to force dollar cost averaging, a strategy of investing on a scheduled, periodic basis.

Ethics and Reasons to Buy Coach Handbags

The discussion at the January Women's Investment Club meeting in Kelowna was lively. At each meeting we discuss two recent stock additions to the portfolio, hot economic topics and some aspect of financial planning. On this occasion, the first part dominated our discussion. The all-consuming topic circled around ethical investing of the recent addition to the portfolio. Why did we buy it?

Well, the answer was the same as it was for any stock we invest in. It fit in the quantitative model and after analysis, was deemed to be a good investment. It was immaterial that some of the club members had bad experiences with the business locally. At what point are you prepared to invest in companies that run businesses counter to your personal beliefs? How far removed do you have to be from those companies? For example, would you buy shares in a firearms company? What about buying shares in the bank that lends money to the firearms company?

Investors can have strong personal resistance to corporate names because of their line of business or due to investors' experience with a local representative. When is it worthy of having input into the decision making process?

This is a personal decision. If you don't want to own a particular investment for non-financial reasons, I challenge you to understand the scope of your approach. We all drive cars, contribute to landfills, waste water, consume natural gas, eat genetically modified grains and bank at the same banks that lend money to winemakers and army equipment manufacturers. We'd prefer to lift the carpet up and sweep this stuff under so we don't have to look at it.

What if you were to make a profit on some of these companies' share prices and use those profits to open a school in Africa, to adopt a highway or donate to the food bank in your local community? Beyond that, personal preferences can become a little problematic when they're intermingled in investment analysis.

From the opposite perspective, those same personal perceptions can lead you to buy a stock. I'm all for the pragmatic approach of investing in the shares of businesses that you use in your everyday life. There is some practicality in the notion that if you're using those goods and services, so are others. Unfortunately, it can be taken too far. When you choose a company based squarely on personal preferences rather than analysis, you can get into trouble.

One client, after returning from a trip to Arizona, noted that the Coach handbag store was much busier than other stores and that everyone on the streets was clutching a Coach bag. She wanted to buy shares of Coach based on this experience. More than likely she had a penchant for the product swaying her.

"After all, everyone is buying Coach handbags" is not analysis. That isn't to say that Coach isn't a good investment but make sure it is before you buy it.

The point is to invest based on facts. Take the profits back to Arizona and then buy a beautiful Coach handbag.

Nitty-Gritty

Top-down or **bottom-up investing** is only a perspective. My daughter's art class taped paper on the underside of the desk. When I picked her up after the class, she recounted that the teacher was named Michael and that he painted a church ceiling. Case in point.

Top-down investing is a macro approach, that primarily considers the overall market conditions where as **bottom-up investing** *is a micro approach, focused more on the specifics of individual security selection.*

Both directions qualify as analysis. A macroeconomic overview obviously begins at 30,000 feet. Technical and **quantitative analysis** starts at the nitty-gritty facts and works its way up. The process of investing often interlaces more than one directional view.

Quantitative analysis uses a strict regimen of signals and chart levels to identify **securities** to buy and sell. Computers make tracking and updating quantitative models useful. The practice is now honed to extreme levels where algorithms and other fast-paced processes are integrated into sophisticated, multifaceted models, but any sorting system may be classified as quantitative.

Fundamental analysis is the art of taking apart the financial statements of a company, reviewing its financial health and prospects, determining the effectiveness of management and ascertaining potential competitors in order to determine future value of the shares, from a qualitative perspective. If you believe the value to be appreciating in excess of the current trading value, it warrants an investment. The art comes from developing a thesis based on a pile of subjective inputs, any one of which may be misunderstood. There's more than one way to skin a cat, as they say, and **fundamental analysis** is as much opinion as anything. For every buyer of a security, there's a seller with the same information and inputs into the decision.

Think of **technical analysis** as a binary, graphical representation of share price movements. This method relies primarily on charting, predicting the direction of the price of a security based on **volumes**, historic price levels, relative price changes, direction and other market data. Technicians are not interested in management, global economic outlook or any other superlative qualities. Their only concern is the shape and momentum of price movements around them. Tools such as Bollinger Bands, Candlesticks, Relative Strength, Stochastic and **moving averages** measure price movements independent of any fundamental data. The popularity of **technical analysis** adds not only to its credibility but theoretically increases its predictive accuracy, the more the practice is adopted. If more investors subscribe to a certain technical process, the more it will play out the way it's expected as a self-fulfilling prophecy.

Most money managers employ an integrated approach, beginning with one strategy and mixing others in at various stages. It makes sense to set up a quantitative filter first in order to make your workload lighter. By eliminating the majority of stocks through a screen, you won't waste time performing **fundamental analysis** on companies that don't pass the initial litmus test. Also, it's interesting to see how certain sectors will crowd your screening results from time to time. Having a bunch of oil stocks or financials represent most of your top screening results is often an indication of a trend. This is useful information in formulating an opinion about what is transpiring in the market.

After **fundamental analysis**, using technical levels and readings can assist with timing decisions for the purchase or sale execution. Of course, pure techies would say that all you need is a chart and you are wasting your time with any other work.

The Trick to Selling

The decision to take home the puppy that's dancing on your heartstrings at the SPCA is much easier than giving one up. It becomes part of your family. You fall in love with it as the affection and unconditional attention sucks you so far into the abyss that you also laden your SUV with a new leash, squeaky chew toys and a bag of organic, grass-fed lamb puppy chow. Personify and adore a spotted beagle if a walk with a leash and a rumpled plastic bag in your hand every morning at 7 brings a smile to your face, but don't fall in love with a stock story. The euphoria of love blinds rational decisions in the latter every single time.

Beyond infatuation, the infallible optimism of human nature disengages our ability to define an exit strategy once the stick shift is in gear. Even the proletariat, with an IA's shingle out front, can find himself with no more will to sell a stock than the hobbyist investor, other than the marginal benefit of generating a commission.

There are clear and sound reasons to sell a stock. Here is a list of eight good ones outlining why and when to sell.

1. Business or economic fundamentals for the company falter.
2. The business sector is cyclically rotating out of favour. Commodities, trends, country biases and technologies all have a lifecycle. Take your piece and move on while the getting is still good and going higher. It's always better to leave money on the table than look back with regret.
3. Accounting, regulatory, significant management changes or other structural issues have come to light. Unfortunately, information about these changes zip through optic cable faster than you can watch a Vine video and pull the sell trigger. Regardless, sometimes taking a small loss now is worth avoiding a big one later.
4. The price of the stock has risen, increasing the total market value of the position beyond your intended allocation: take profit and reduce your exposure. On a regular basis sell enough shares to bring the size of the position back in line with your objectives. Quarterly is a reasonable frequency, but trim investment positions no less than annually.

5. You want to buy a competitor to a company that you already hold. If you own Anheuser-Busch (BUD), for example, and have a thirst-quenching desire to buy Molson Coors (TAP), you may want to count your cans before you get drunk. Keeping the concentration of a particular type of business is the kind of advice your mother would give you.
6. From a 30,000-foot view, you may wish to reduce exposure to an entire sector, regardless of the stocks you hold. Keep tabs on trends and macro decisions that you want directing your investment decisions.
7. When there are better uses for your invested capital, sell and use it for those and stop the argument tape-loop running in your head about why you bought the stock in the first place. Unwarranted justification is quicksand.
8. The golden rule: it's time to sell. Before you buy a stock, define when and under what conditions you will dispose of it. Before you buy it. Then sell.

When will you cut your losses? At what point do you plan to crystallize capital appreciation? Do you wish to withdraw your original capital after a particular event? What are the catalysts to reduce your exposure to this company? How do you weigh this investment against other opportunities and when does it become a motivation to move from this one to another? Is the sale of this position an all-or-nothing sale or some greyer quantity? And why did you buy it in the first place…has that changed?

In practice, it's a moving target, but if you can answer these questions before you invest, you'll be able to formulate an objective decision making process rather than an emotional one. Having an escape plan helps you avoid the well-trodden path of least resistance and sell what should be tossed out as swiftly as last night's oysters. One thing is for sure. Regardless of whether you're a lone wolf or an investment professional, having someone to bounce ideas off and poke holes in your theories, always increases your conviction.

When is a $20 Stock Too Expensive?

Every so often, clients ask what the price of a stock is. The question isn't to determine the number of shares to purchase given a certain amount of cash. It's not to determine the stock's value per share. It's nothing more than an arbitrary benchmark that they've determined to be part of their decision process. Some investors literally refuse to buy a stock over a certain price, regardless of the value of the slice of business that it represents. In fact, one investor elected to buy shares of Bank of Nova Scotia rather than shares of Bank of Montreal because the share price was $2.50 less, without considering which bank had better earnings prospect, cash, assets, etc.

Recall in the earlier discussion about holding onto or dumping dogs, we are hardwired to use cognitive shortcuts in our decision making. While we can make decisions quickly when we need to, this ability can wreak havoc on intended investment results and result in **anchoring**.

In 2010, shares of Apple Inc. were trading in the mid-$200 range. The arbitrary decision by owners to sell shares at $300, $400 or $500 over the ensuing 2 years became a joke around my office. Pundits discussed the likelihood of the shares advancing beyond these mileposts, which is completely irrational when you think of the investment in relative terms. The propensity of clients and professionals alike to place **stop-loss** orders at nice round numbers is more evidence of this issue. In great quantities, this can be problematic, especially in the age of electronic trading. With enough executions of buys or sells triggered at a specific price, the normal steady rise or decline that take place are dramatically overdone in an instant of electronic trading despite relative earnings and other sober thoughts.

> The propensity of clients and professionals alike to place **stop-loss** orders at nice round numbers is more evidence of this issue. In great quantities, this can be problematic, especially in the age of electronic trading.

Moreover, if you had arbitrarily decided that Apple Inc. was *too expensive* at $235 per share in 2010, you would have missed out on an almost 300% return over the following 2 years.

There is no way to ascertain the value of a stock on its dollar price alone. Despite some armchair investors' rants that paying less **cash per share** is a wiser investment, it's absolutely not true.

> "The stock market is filled with individuals who know the price of everything, but the value of nothing."
> —Philip A. Fisher, Common Stocks and Uncommon Profits and Other Writings

When considering the price of a stock, an astute analysis includes comparing the market value of the shares with the enterprise value per share: the price it's *trading at* and the price it's *worth*. The first is the current market price of the stock. The **market capitalization** of a company is the share price multiplied by the number of **shares outstanding**. The second is a subjective calculation made by dividing the assets and liabilities of the entire company by the number of **shares outstanding**. Once the hard value of the business is determined, some expansion multiple can be applied in order to value the expected growth. Alternatively, you may want to estimate the future income that the enterprise will generate and assign what that value is in today's dollars. If the calculated worth of a share of the company is lower than the price the share is trading at on the exchange, it's overvalued, and vice versa.

Companies will sometimes **split** their shares to make purchasing a portion of the company more inclusionary for those who have smaller amounts of money to invest. On a post two for one split, you would own twice as many shares, each worth roughly half of the value it had on a pre-split basis. Make no mistake, though. Conventional wisdom indicates that the prudent amount to pay per share be reflected in the relative earnings and growth per share.

The point I want to drive home is that the share price is almost insignificant when making an investment decision. The absolute price of a stock has little if anything to say about its **intrinsic value** or whether it's a good investment at all. The absolute amount that you spend on a share is only important when you compare it with the cash flow, book value, profitability and other **relative value** metrics.

Avoid the Temptation to Average Down

Sometimes stocks are cheap because they should be, because they're going to be cheaper still in the future. The **value trap** was coined to describe companies whose shares have traded at a low market price relative to their earnings (**P/E**), book value (**P/B**) or cash flow (**P/CF**), usually for an extended period of time. Investors looking for bargains are attracted to these companies by the sheer expectation that everything else being equal, higher multiples will prevail over time. By definition, either earnings will drop or the price will increase.

While that may be true in some cases, problems with a company may be systemic and unrecoverable. In extreme cases, share prices trading at low relative values is due to poor management, mature and declining product cycle or an offering that is being pushed out of the market by competition. In such a scenario, the price of these shares reflects the reality that the business is in decline with no change in sight.

Averaging down is a strategy formerly thought to be advantageous in lowering your cost base on an investment. When you hold a security whose value has dropped abruptly or ebbed away over time, buying more at a lower price reduces the average cost of what you paid for the investment. Think more carefully about this as a strategy. You hold an investment whose value has dropped for some reason. Then you decide to buy more of the investment that has already lost you money. You now own more of this investment than you wanted to in the first place at an average price that's higher than where the shares are trading currently.

*Rarely does **averaging down** make sense. A better reason for adding to a position is when you're increasing your allocation to a strategy, asset class, sector or company on purpose.*

Rarely does **averaging down** make sense. A better reason for adding to a position is when you're increasing your allocation to a strategy, asset class, sector or company on purpose. Otherwise, don't throw good money after bad. If you're tempted to average down, think instead about why the share price has dropped and consider selling your stake or holding it if you have a strong conviction. If you need to revisit the Unleashing the Dogs section in chapter 1, discussing the perils of falling in love with a stock, do so now.

Takeovers

Pricing a takeover value is similar to pricing the value of a company in general, except there usually has to be some kind of incentive to entice current shareholders to accept the deal. Often the incentive is monetary, but not always. A takeover offer typically has some **premium** attached, over and above the market value of the company. This is a balancing act for the buyers, as they don't want to price the deal so high there's no net benefit to their own shareholders.

Takeover offers can be made as an all-cash deal, receiving shares of the acquiring company, receiving new shares in a joint company of equals or some combination.

As soon as a takeover offer is announced, the share price of the stock being acquired will trade near the takeover price. The closer to the execution date and the likelihood that the deal is a slam-dunk, the closer the market price will trade to the offered price. If there is some question about regulatory or shareholder approval, the market price of the stock being acquired will reflect that risk of the deal not working out by trading below the offered price.

Similarly, if the offer puts the target company in play and there are other potential suitors, the market value of the stock may even peak above the offered price reflecting the market's anticipation of other offers, producing a bidding war. Buying the stock now, before the other offers are presented, may result in a tidy short-term profit. The risk, of course, is if there are no other offers or that even the original deal falls through. Then there will be a tidy short-term loss.

Commission Trading

Entering an order (instructing someone to buy or sell a stock) these days is as easy as completing fields in a computer-based form. Quantity. Currency. Buy or sell. Symbol. **Stop-loss** or **Stop-loss limit**. Order expiry date. Solicited or **unsolicited**. **Limit order** or market price.

Filling out the form isn't what you pay for. Well you do, but there's more to it than that. Knowing how to execute trades successfully, at what price and with what parameters, is the expertise at hand.

Back in my trading days as a broker, I thought it was reasonable to discount trades when they were **unsolicited**. I didn't ask clients to buy or sell a security or whether they had done a good deal of the legwork on identifying an idea for their own account. It made pragmatic sense. If I was the one who brought an investment opportunity to the table, I'd obviously insist on charging full freight. That sounded fair.

From time to time, clients ask how the commission structures work. Quite frankly, it's a calculation that has more variables than would make a simple answer apparent. Essentially, the greater the number of shares traded, the higher the price. The lower the share price, the higher the relative cost per share. The larger the total market value of the trade, the lower the average cost per share.

Most full-service investment firms have a minimum commission in the $125–$150 range, but that amount is increasing. If you're looking to trade a small market value, you may want to think twice about it. On a $1000 position, you're paying up to 30% in commissions for buying and selling. Ouch. Typically, the commissions on a single trade valued around $5000 per security starts making sense. Even then, you're still paying some pretty high fees, so think carefully about your conviction to buy in the first place.

Fee-Based Trading Limits

Fee-based accounts are set up so that your entire portfolio is subject to an average annual fee rather than paying a commission on each trade. Philosophically, I prefer this approach. The inherent conflict of interest with commissions is completely eliminated. Even perceived conflict. Since you pay fees whether or not you make a trade, you eliminate any question about the motivation for executing the transaction. Moreover, this structure puts you and your advisor on the same side of the desk. Both of you have a vested interest in the value of your portfolio increasing. You want the value to rise for the obvious reason, to pay more taxes! Your advisor also gets to pay more taxes since her compensation increases as the assets under management increases. (Sarcasm) Another benefit is that commissions charged on a taxable account are only deductible against capital gains while management fees may be deductible against any income you claim on your tax return.

Be aware that many fee-based accounts have a trading limit. The investment firm has an interest in capping your trading activities so that you aren't at liberty to **day-trade** positions or **churn** your own account. Investment firms pay a fee to execute each transaction so they need to keep that in check. Some limit each account to a set number, such as 30 trades per year. Other firms quote the amount of

Commissions charged on a taxable account are only deductible against capital gains while management fees are deductible against any income you claim on your tax return.

trading in terms of turnover. For example, you may be permitted to buy or sell up to 200% of your portfolio value. This is a very generous limit for most people. If you go over the documented trading limit, additional fees are levied against your account so you will want to keep tabs on that, especially as the year passes into final months.

A Cheer for Discount Brokerage

Discount brokerage accounts have made trading efficient. Most brokerages even offer an application for your smartphone to track stocks and enter orders. With this kind of slick ingenuity, pricing for no-advice trading has become quite attractive for do-it-yourselfers. Surprisingly, the popularity of these trading platforms hasn't catapulted to the stratosphere.

For those investors who want to take on the daily transactions of their own account, discount brokerage will save you hundreds of dollars. Even if you have most of your portfolio being managed by a professional, buying and selling the play-stuff cheaply can keep your personal interests and cocktail party stories alive without killing your entertainment budget. Discount brokerage is a good way to manage those one-offs that you have no one to blame but yourself. As a professional, I fervently support clients who want to buy Uncle Joe's submarine screen-door stock in a discount brokerage account. I don't even mind helping them understand the functionality of how to execute trades or open an account online. It only takes one failed stock position to blow up the returns on an otherwise well run portfolio, so I don't want anyone adding rogue positions and playing Wreck It Ralph with my work.

Even for people keen to make their own investment decisions, many still use a full-service brokerage to execute **unsolicited trades** for them. They may pay higher fees, but there's something to be said about having professional collaboration to make your conviction to pull the trigger that much stronger, conveniently building a scapegoat into the process. Having an IA agree or disagree with you before you buy or sell can be an integral part of an investor's process. For those with a high level of comfort and knowledge, discount brokerage still typically accounts for only part of an individual's trading and investment strategy.

Churning

Unwarranted, high turnover in a portfolio resulting in no real tax benefit or profit is sometimes driven by the expressed purpose of generating excess commission. Whether intentional or unintentional, churning benefits the trader at the expense of the investor.

Excessive trading is a grey area. A decent gauge pins the number of trades in your portfolio, especially those that you don't initiate, against the resulting profit (or tax benefit). Take a peek to see if the spreads on bonds and foreign exchange and the fees on trades, **new issues** and structured products, grossly outweigh your returns. If transactions are unnecessary or excessive and many of the commission-generating buys and sells are unprofitable, you may be subject to churning. While some claim it's unintentional, which may be the case, it's a difficult argument to win.

Keep in mind that some well-intentioned investments don't appreciate in value. That isn't what is being described here.

If you suspect that your account is subject to churning, have a conversation with your investment professional. It's a subjective area but if you suspect there is an issue, you can file a complaint with the management of the investment firm you deal with and ask them to review your account. If all else fails, contact the Ombudsman for Banking Services and Investments if you feel strongly that things have gone awry.

Realized and Unrealized Gains and Losses

The capital gains inclusion rate was lowered to 50% in recent years. For investors, this is a nice advantage for stock and even bond investors. Any security that appreciates in value from the Adjusted **Cost Base (ACB)** of the investment accumulates capital gain, which represents the growth in the value of the investment. You only need to include half of the value of your gain as income. Also, you can defer paying taxes on the gain by holding off selling the investment until some future date.

*If you have already paid taxes on **capital gains** in the last 3 years, you can offset the gains you claimed with your new **capital loss** and reclaim the tax dollars from Ottawa.*

Capital gains only need to be included in your tax return in the year that the investment is sold.

The ACB is generally the amount you invested plus any transaction costs or commissions paid. For example, if you buy a thousand shares at $27 each with a commission of $405, your ACB is $27,405. When you sell the shares at $32 with a commission of $420, you'll have a **capital gain** of $4175. The commissions you paid on both the buy and sale transactions are netted out of your profit before you calculate taxes.

Realized capital losses are just the opposite. The net value after commissions is negative.

Keep more money in your pocket by managing your taxable investment income. Postpone **capital gains** to the next tax year by selling them in January, crystallize gains in low income tax years or offset them with losses. If you have already paid taxes on **capital gains** in the last three years, you can essentially go back in time to offset those claims with new **capital losses** by filing an amendment to reclaim tax dollars paid to Ottawa. Alternatively, you can carry forward unused losses indefinitely and offset future gains.

A useful strategy is to calculate the **capital gains** you've realized near the end of the calendar year and sell other securities that are lower than what you purchased them to offset current realized gains and defer paying taxes. It's referred to as **tax loss selling**. You can repurchase the securities that you sell after 30 days, or you may decide to reinvest in a similar security instead. Buying the same securities within 30 days will nullify the **capital loss** claimed so count your days carefully. Remember that **capital gains** and losses only apply to non-registered accounts. Registered Retirement Savings Plans (RRSPs), Registered Retirement Income Funds (RRIFs), Registered Education Savings Plans (RESPs) and Tax Free Savings Accounts (TFSAs) are all sheltered from tax so gains and losses in those accounts do not apply.

Eligible Canadian Dividends

Another benefit of investing in stocks is the calculation advantage of dividends received from eligible Canadian corporations. In CRA's description of dividends as distributed profits by the companies that you own (invest in), you have to love its categories of eligible and "other than eligible" for the Canadian dividend tax credit. Someone must have dreamt that phrase up after an all night poker game that they "other than won". Feel free to interpret that as a catchall category for dividends that don't qualify for the tax credit. For eligible dividends, Canadian investors claim a lesser taxable value on Line 120 of their tax return than the amount of money they receive from their dividends. You can claim the dividend tax credit to reduce the amount of tax you have to pay on your federal and provincial tax schedules.

In most cases, this makes eligible Canadian dividend income advantageous over interest and **capital gains** on a straight taxation basis, except for the highest marginal tax brackets where **capital gains** are often the most tax sensitive of all other income.

Loving Volatility

If retail investors had their way, **volatility** would be spelled with four letters. Of course no investor wants to lose money on an investment, but that isn't the real issue. **Volatility** in the up direction is not a problem—it's only downward **volatility** that offers discourse.

Just this morning I was speaking to a client who is in the process of selling a large revenue generating property in British Columbia. The comment he made was that once he had **monetized** the property, his biggest concern was what to do with the cash. I have to repeat (for effect) that placing the funds in a new investment was ironically his biggest concern. I was keen to get to the bottom of this.

"Ideally," he went on, "I want to invest in something that will produce this level of income but that doesn't have any volatility."

It begged to be asked, "Why do you think that your real estate investment has no volatility?"

From the perspective of a person who trades daily in **capital markets**, finding the right qualities in an investment to fit the bill is pretty straightforward. The challenge is in matching the perception of **volatility** from a client's perspective.

Real estate is a long-term asset class. Historically, real estate is an **illiquid** investment despite the high demand during the last 30 years of dropping interest rates. The days of flipping condos with only a deposit invested and multiple offers on listing day only come during bubbles. Moreover, beyond the Multiple Listing Service (MLS) or www.craigslist.com there is no standardized live market for real estate. There are several methods for valuing real estate that appraisers rely on, including a technique evaluating **comparables** or similar properties, but with each property and building having unique qualities, the ultimate conclusion is entirely subjective. Ultimately, you will sell real estate if and when someone else wants to buy it and at a price they're willing to pay.

Real estate is a long-term asset class. Historically, real estate is an illiquid investment despite high demand during the last 30 years of dropping interest rates.

The point is with assets that are not valued regularly or listed on an exchange, you have no idea what the true value is until a transaction happens. If you were to receive a market value of your home every week, you would vomit at how volatile the price actually is.

*In layman's terms, the **beta** of a security can be thought of as the how closely it changes in line with changes in the overall market.*

In the same way that my client was focused on the income produced by real estate knowing that he intended to hold the property for a long time, he could apply that approach to investments priced in the **capital markets** by choosing something with relatively low **volatility** or low **beta** and collecting the dividends, interest or **return of capital** and not worry about the security price changes.

Conversely, don't get caught in the addiction to income at the expense of **volatility** by investing in overly volatile securities for the cash flow alone.

Inflation Risk

Recently a couple in their mid-fifties came into my office to transfer their accounts to my care. It wasn't surprising to hear they were still reeling emotionally from their losses of 2008 even years later. Due to the effects of the severe economic crisis, their retirement plans had to be deferred. This consequently amplified their sensitivity to market

volatility to the point that they were petrified to invest in anything with price fluctuations. The pendulum swings both ways. It was clear that the impact of this period of unusually profound **volatility** had undermined an otherwise prudent strategy.

The need for this couple to hold **equities** in their portfolio is the key to keeping up with inflation. When the economy expands and prices of goods increase, the value of businesses also increases. Although equities have a higher level of **volatility**, owning these in the correct quantity is what protects purchasing power over the long run.

If you're a conservative investor, holding a smaller amount of equities might suit your tolerance for **volatility**, but holding no equities whatsoever introduces a risk that you may not have thought about. Inflation risk.

Central bankers around the world have learned over various market cycles how to impact overall inflation levels by controlling the country's fiscal and monetary policies. Basically, they lower interest rates and increase spending in order to stimulate the economy and the opposite to slow down the pace of growth. The Bank of Canada has an objective to keep the inflation rate at a 2% annual pace. This is done to benefit the Canadian populous by maintaining consistency, gradually increasing the standard of living and protecting us from runaway inflation rates.

It was clear that the impact of this period of unusually profound volatility had undermined an otherwise prudent strategy.

While there's no guarantee that inflation won't spill over or the economy gets sucked down the drain, the Bank of Canada's objective is well footed on the lessons of the past. According to their historic data, interest rates peaked at 21.03% in August 1981, prohibiting many Canadians from borrowing money. Diametrically opposed to the inflationary 1980s, the extreme economic contraction of the Great Depression that lasted the entire decade of the 1930s was equally disastrous to Canadians' financial well-being.

From an investor's perspective, inflation cycles are important drivers to **asset allocation** decisions and the level of risk that convention indicates an investor take on. The amount that you place (allocate) in various asset classes can impact your overall performance. At both ends of the inflation cycle, it's advisable to rein in runaway asset classes that have significantly expanded in value. During times of stable inflation and economic growth, there are reasons to be less cautious.

Tulpenmanie

The first cultivated tulips were introduced in the Netherlands by a famous biologist from Vienna named Carolus Clusius in 1593. The bulb's popularity caught on quickly as much for medicinal developments as adorning gardens and ultimately found the pragmatic status as a trading product. As interest grew, botanists began producing hybrid species, further enhancing the appeal and demand of the flower, driving prices to ridiculous levels for a single bulb. Some accounts suggest that a house in the major trading city of Amsterdam was paid in exchange for some hybrid varietals. Not to be left out of the gargantuan profits that the rich traders were making, the enthusiasm for tulip bulbs spread to common men who were selling any assets they had to participate.

This added fuel and exacerbated pricing of the bulbs to unimaginable levels in the latter part of 1636 in a complete frenzy of buying. February 1637, traders paid over 10 times a craftsman's annual income for a single bulb. C.W. and A.J.K.D. (4 Oct. 2013) Economic History: *Was Tulipmania Irrational?* The Economist. Retrieved from http://www.economist.com/blogs/freeexchange/2013/10/economic-history.

It was all about unique varieties and accessibility to product. As with any commodity of extraordinary demand and price, the supply side finds a way to provide. Producers eventually jump in to flesh out the greedy demand. It doesn't take long when traders are left with excess product for prices to start dropping. The piercing sound of the tulip bubble popping and dramatic unwinding of the trade was swift and left many speculators behind penniless.

Some say in the heat of a bubble that the market determines the price of anything as what another is willing to pay. When the risk of loss is outpaced by the taunt of a huge gain, investors are lured into participating without contemplation of value. Where gambling is based on pure chance, **speculation** carries a false notion of calculated risk. We justify our participation by fooling ourselves into thinking that we have more than chance on our side.

If you do not determine the value of your investment before you put your money into it, you're speculating. If you buy shares of a company that does not earn a profit, you're speculating. If you buy an investment on a hunch, feeling or premonition; if your Ouija board gives you the ticker symbol; if your Uncle Joe tells you it's a good investment; if you feel peer pressure at a cocktail party, use the words, "Lottery Ticket" or utter the phrase, "I don't really care if it drops in value," you're speculating.

This is not an investment. If you must participate in this foolhardy approach, at least don't bet the entire farm. Maybe just a chicken or two. Or get out of your overalls and fly down to Las Vegas. Take in a show while you're there. I highly recommend Cascata if you're a golfer. It will cost less than what you'll lose on the tulip trade and is far more enjoyable.

Pink Sheets

Companies that do not qualify to be listed on a recognized exchange may be listed in the **Over-the-Counter (OTC)** market, also called the Pink Sheets. Companies are drawn to this environment because their principals do not wish to operate under the scrutiny of the exchange regulators. All I can say is, "Buyer beware." I've seen too many dastardly **reverse stock splits** with backdated **settlement** dates and other unsavoury, moustache-twirling manoeuvres that laid common investors across the train tracks. In one case, the investor was coached to sell his shares not realizing there was a reverse split (when 5 shares become 1, for example) already settled on the market. He ended up selling 5 times too many, leaving him in a **short position** on a company that had no **liquidity**. We were forced to call the promoters to cover the **short** position, ultimately costing the client $125,000 in losses.

If a company isn't listed on a regulated exchange, there's a reason. Either they don't qualify or they simply don't want to comply with the stringent regulations.

Basic Trading Orders

All or None – All shares must fill in order to have any filled.

Ask – The price offered to sell shares on the market. If you have a **market order** to buy shares, it will fill at the asking price.

Bid – The price offered to buy shares on the market. If you have a market order to sell shares, it will fill at the bid.

Limit – An order to buy or sell at a specific price.

Market Order – Offers to buy or sell shares at the current bid or ask.

Settlement – The date on which shares traded and the payment must be delivered. On common shares, that is the trade date plus 3 trading days. Mutual funds are T+3. Bonds are T+2. Money market is T+1.

Stop-Loss – An order to sell shares if the price drops to a specific price. It will then become a market order and fill at whatever bid is available. This type of order can be filled at *any* price.

Stop-Loss Limit – An order to sell shares if the price drops to a specific price but is limited to being filled at a specific floor price.

Chapter 3

Bonds, James Bond

> Miss Anders! I didn't recognize you with your clothes on.
> —James Bond, *The Man with the Golden Gun*

There is no coincidence that the notorious British Secret Service bad-boy became the analogy for every section of the original version of this chapter when I desperately ran it by my friends. I know that bonds are a technical topic that I tend to roll deeply in details, but my real objectives are readability and engagement. This may not be what Ian Fleming had in mind in 1953 when he wrote the first novel, but may I suggest that this chapter is paired nicely with a martini: shaken, not stirred.

At a recent Investment Club meeting, I handed out bits of this chapter to the group of professional women, each with a glass of wine in front of them. Legal, accounting, marketing, design: a wide range of talented gals. Despite my best attempts to keep the evening's topic on fixed income investing, the clacking of an 8mm movie reel spun with gunfire, poison-tipped shoes and glib sexist remarks were undeniably more colourful and far more interesting.

> *He ran his fingers through her flowing caramel-coloured hair, nibbling her lips, saying, "No. No names. No numbers. Just let me do this."*
>
> *She fell back on the boat deck cushions, moaning. "Yes, yes. Give me the fee-based bond purchase yields now! Now!"*
>   a.k.a. *Shades of Jane*

Money is the name of the game. The espionage equipment that businesses need to make profits has to come from a backer, if not a government agency. I'm trying to think of a clever way to say that before you can make money, you need money. It's tough to fight inertia and build financial momentum without **capital**, **leverage** or both. Businesses need money to run. Cash flow from operations can only exist by investing **capital** in the first place. As business owners are well aware, every business development or expansion needs more **capital** and if it isn't generated from operations (retained earnings) it needs to be sourced from banks, private investors or the **capital markets**.

> *"It is difficult to begin without borrowing, but perhaps it is the most generous course thus to permit your fellowmen to have an interest in your enterprise."*
> —Henry David Thoreau

Equate the **capital** that companies are trying to raise to the gadgetry that the Secret Intelligence Service, MI6, delivers. Without these endless, ingenious pieces of equipment, James certainly couldn't face villain after villain in combat. While he could simply go to Walmart (not in Canada!) to buy a LaserLyte Side Mount Laser for his Ruger for $94, having a watch that does the job and doubles as a lock pick is better! Instead of going to the bank and accepting the terms of its lending policies, companies can approach the **capital markets**, a.k.a. investors, and ask if they would be willing to lend them money instead. There would have to be some cool contraptions (**bond features**) attached, of course.

There is more than one way that a company can raise money in the markets. They could issue equity (shares) or they could issue debt (bonds). Borrowing by way of a bond issue increases the company's leverage. Surprisingly, the debt-financing route may be preferable since there is no dilution to current owners' equity in the company since no new shares are issued. Shareholders get more *bang!* for their invested buck since repayment of debt is capped at the interest rate while shareholders participate in the excess profitability of the company's growth.

Bonds do not trade on an exchange. Instead, the market is made among major investment banks.

Similarly, an investor may have strong motivation to participate in a company through its debt rather than its equity. For equity holders, the world is not enough. With bonds, by only lending money to the company instead of claiming a stake in the entire mission you limit your risk of *skyfall*. In the event of bankruptcy, bonds are safer than stock of the same company since bonds are paid out before the interests of common shareholders are recognized. In addition, bonds have a maturity date and fixed interest payments while shareholders are invested until they can find another buyer. For these perks, bondholders are part of the plan with almost no risk of being shot. The returns aren't as sexy as the equity players, generally limited to the interest paid and a refund of the invested **capital** at maturity.

Bonds are initially offered at 100 cents on the dollar, a.k.a. par. Bonds are always priced in terms of 100, so a $15,000 bond trading at a price of 89.7 is worth $13,455 or 89.7% of the **face value** or matured **principle** amount.

The **face value** is the amount that the principle of the bond is worth both when it's issued and also when it comes due at maturity. It represents the amount you are lending the company. It's also the amount the investor expects to receive at the end of the term.

Over the life of the bond, between the dates it was issued and it finally matures, bonds are traded between investors and banks. There is no listed market for bonds. Instead, major investment firms determine the market prices and trade bonds between investors and each other, based on several factors. The market values of bonds are directly related to the risk quality of the company that guarantees it, prevailing interest rates, and the term to maturity which creeps ever closer.

By investing in a bond with a $10,000 par or face value and an interest rate of 5%, you'd typically expect to receive two semi-annual payments of $250 until the maturity date. Let's say that your bond matures in five years, at which time you'll receive the initial $10,000 back. If you were born before the 1980s, you'll remember the days when Canada Savings Bonds were

*Be careful when comparing the returns of your bond portfolios with the **DEX** Bond Index. The index is made up of over 900 **issues** and it would be impractical for an individual to hold a comparable number of bonds.*

issued in paper form. Before computers, bonds were all printed on large sheets of paper with the biggest portion stating the principle, **par**

value or **face value**, with smaller cut-out **coupons** representing the periodic interest payments and the dates they were payable. Most of the terminology for bonds comes from the physical notes of years ago, even though today's computers track them and there are no physical copies produced anymore. We still call the semi-annual interest payments a coupon.

Wouldn't it be great to get your hands on a 12% bond from the early 1990s? The trouble is that as market interest rates change, the prices of existing bonds in the market also change. Going back to the example of a $10,000 five-year bond at 5%, assume that a year down the road, interest rates have dropped to 3%. Your 5% bond looks pretty attractive to other investors. In fact, they would be willing to pay you more than the **face value** for it. The additional amount they would be willing to pay for your bond is called a **premium**. It's the exact amount that would net the new investor a return of 3% (the prevailing rate) over the remaining four-year term of your bond. You get a little extra for selling the bond now, which makes up for the fact that you hold a desirable 5% bond and the new holder loses a little by paying extra for the **face value** of the bond. So, if you sold your bond at this point, not only would you have received your 2 $250 coupon payments for the first 12 months that you owned the bond plus your original $10,000, but you'd also gain the additional **premium** of $748.59.

Now assume that you decided not to sell your bond last year but now interest rates have jumped to 6% for bonds with 3 years left until maturity. You probably realize that no one wants your paltry 5% return anymore. If you needed to cash out, you would be forced to sell it at a **discount** below the **face value**. Essentially, you have to entice another investor to buy this bond from you and because current interest rates for other similar bonds are 6%, you'll have to **discount** the market price of the 5% bond. The sweetener that you have to offer is the difference that will make up the 1% shortfall in **coupon** payments for the time between the date you sell the bond and the maturity date.

When your bond is at a **premium** (above) or **discount** (below), the price will gradually revert to the **face value** as time marches toward the maturity date. It's interesting to note that when your bond is trading at a premium of $103 or $3 more per $100 of **face value**, the $3 is considered a **capital gain** if you were to sell it prior to maturity. As time passes however, the premium will erode and the price will drop from $103 to $100 guaranteed. The reason that the bond is trading at a premium in the first place is because it pays a coupon that recompenses the holder for the $3 loss over the remaining term. As the investor, you are happy to give up the $3 per $100 in order to receive higher semi-annual coupon payments for a net return equivalent to current market interest rates.

Featuring the Features

"I want a larger bond," she complained, her bee-stung lips pouting.

"Darling," he whispered, "I have an active bond portfolio that will nicely meet all your needs."

He pulled her glossy hair back and she screamed, "Give me transparency and give it to me now!"

"No," he growled. "I'm giving you my maximum commission and you are going to enjoy paying it!"

a.k.a. More Shades of Jane

Jane's vignette is more evidence that the educational component of the Women's Investment Club is taking hold in ways that I never imagined. Thankfully, bond terminology is not unlike golf where words can be fun to play with. It saves us from an otherwise brutal topic, as everyone who has read this chapter reminds me. At least the fixed income vocabulary becomes a little stickier with the metaphor.

Instead of borrowing within the rigid terms set out by a bank, companies that can issue bonds have a little latitude in creativity. Like asking for forgiveness rather than permission, corporate borrowers are in far greater control of the terms. The perks that they offer with bonds make their **issues** look more like an Aston Martin DB5 supplied by the Q branch than one you'd buy from a vanilla dealership. Issuers realize how these gadgets make bonds more attractive to investors and they can sometimes offer the perks in exchange for yield so the company can lower its interest costs. Sweeteners such as **retraction** or **conversion options** allow investors to either cash in their bond at certain dates prior to maturity or convert the bond into the company's shares, if it's to their advantage to do so.

The **retractable feature** is useful for investors who want to reduce their risk and lessen the sensitivity to rising interest rates. After all, he who pays the piper calls the tune. The bond investor instructs the company that issued the bond to pay back the investment and like a spring-loaded retractable cord, the bond is gone and the money is in your wallet ready for the next adventure. If interest rates rise, bondholders retract because they can cash in their investment on given dates at par and redeploy that **capital** at higher interest rates.

A **convertibility** clause can be a great hedge to inflation. Theoretically, when interest rates are rising, the economy is expanding. When interest rates rise, bond prices fall (recall the teeter-totter relationship between interest rates and bond prices). On the other hand, the likelihood increases that the stock of the company will rise with growing economic activity. A rising tide lifts all boats, except those with a hole in the hull, of course. Jumping into the right boat is the trick.

Convertible debentures are bonds with conversion options and no physical security. The best convertible bonds to buy are the ones issued by a company whose stock you'd be happy to own. The actual value of the conversion is only realized when the common shares rise above the conversion price attached to the bond. Additionally, without security, there is more risk in the event that the company goes bankrupt but if you are willing to buy the business through their equity, this is obviously not a risk you think is likely.

Colloquially called converts, acquiring these can be a great way to participate in the mission from the comfort of Ms. Moneypenny's swivelling office chair, behind her rotary tele. You aren't in the field like the stockholders are but you're paid a bonus based on their success. Initially, the conversion option is out-of-the-money, which means there is a gap for the stock price to rise before any participation in **capital** appreciation kicks in. So, with convertible bonds, you give up some of the early **capital** appreciation but in return you receive the steady interest payments. Also, in the event of bankruptcy, bondholders are paid back prior to common shareholders.

There are a few tricks with converts. Always read the terms of the **bond indenture**, the legally binding terms of the bond issue. The issuing company writes these rules of engagement and it's going to have some perks for itself, too. In some cases, the **debentures** may be paid back with shares instead of money, for example. Usually a company will have this option if their ability to repay the bond is dubious. How would you feel if you lent Jaws $5 and he paid you back in silver teeth? Silver is great but cash is better.

Another thing to be aware of with **convertible debentures**, especially if you're trading a large position, is that they can be difficult to buy or sell in large quantities and sometimes at all. Unlike regular bonds, converts are listed on a regulated stock exchange but each issue has a limited quantity. Some **issues** are very small and finding **volume** to buy or sell a specific one at the price you're looking for can be quite difficult, especially if the company is having sudden financial troubles. The already few bids (the price offered by other interested buyers) dry up leaving the last man standing in a ring of musical chairs.

Besides the sweeteners offered to investors, on the flip-side are the features that benefit the company. A **callable feature** allows the company can pay you back prior to the maturity date at its whim and fancy. In most cases, the company will state a date at which the call feature can be exercised and not before. For a company that is forced to issue debt at a high interest rate, call features can be a nice option to have. When prevailing rates fall to a more affordable level or if the company's credit rating improves, it may **call** in an older issue, to refinance the debt at lower rates. If you're enjoying those higher interest rates and suddenly get a knock at the door with a bag full of the money you invested and a thank you note, you're back to the drawing board for new investment options.

Worse is if the price of the bond suddenly drops on the risk of it being called. When it becomes likely that a bond may be called, the market price will reflect a value based on the **call date** and **call value** rather than the expected **matured value** and future coupon payments, since those likely won't happen. For **issues** in the market trading at a substantial premium over its **face value**, this can mean a sudden price drop in the market value of your investment.

Coupons and Residuals

Here is where I take out my black Sharpie, draw a big rectangle and write $100 as well as the issuer, maturity date and other details. Then, along the straight edge of a yellow school ruler, I add a row of 10 boxes appended to the right of the rectangle, assigning $2.50 and a date, six-months apart, to each.

In the good ol' days, investors used to clip off each coupon, literally with a pair of scissors, and take it to the bank for the $2.50 payment (in this example) as soon as it was due. Today, bonds are electronic and interest payments are deposited directing into investment accounts. But to really get the feel of how bonds are manipulated today, imagine the coarse green paper, the

*The longer the term to the maturity and the smaller the semi-annual coupon interest payments, the more sensitive a bond price will be to changes in prevailing interest rates (because it has a longer **duration**).*

thickness of pre-plastic money, and the smell of ink from the minter. Thread your thumb and middle finger through the plastic handles and spread the blades of the scissors apart to cut one of the interest payment **coupons** off and look at the payment amount and the date it is due.

You can sell piece of paper separately. It's worth what any investment is worth today if it promised to return $2.50 in 6 months, or 10 years, or whatever the payment date is.

Once all the **coupons** are stripped off the bond, like medals from a doping athlete, all you're left with is the **residual**. Referring to our original example, our $10,000 **face value** is also referred to as the residual once all of the 10 $250 semi-annual **coupons** have been cut off. It still matures in five years. Now that the holder of the **residual** doesn't have any interest **coupons** to cash in along the way, its market value is **discounted** in value, as well. The price of the **residual** on the market equals any investment that would result in a total return of $10,000 in five years' time. The amount by which it's **discounted** is the interest rate or return on the bond. For a five-year bond at 6%, the bond would be worth $7700 initially, gradually increasing in value to $10,000 at maturity. The amount of $2300 represents the total for which you could sell the 10 individual **coupons** of $250 each.

Interestingly, in the event of default, the stripped **coupons** are not backed by security. Only the **residual** may be depending on the terms of the bond since it's the principle of the loan that the company borrowed from investors and the **coupons** represent the interest payments. When a company is in default, it's the interest payments that don't get paid while the principle holds more rights over the value of the company, especially when it's backed by some kind of asset for security.

Chuck Your Bond Ladder Out the Window

Bond ladders were the fool-safe recommendation dispensed by almost everyone over the last 30-year bond rally. The idea was simple. Invest in bonds with staggered maturity dates. As each one matured, reinvest the funds in a new bond, rolling out the money for a longer term than the longest maturity date that you held. Usually, longer terms offer higher interest rates than shorter ones. The investor had a continuous string of bonds coming due each year. This provided liquidity if the money was needed for lifestyle expenses. More importantly, it provided additional stability during changing interest rate environments while garnering the best rates offered since they could lock up the new investment for longer terms, since other bonds were always coming due.

Many bond ladders were set up as relatively safe exposure to **volatility**. Technically, your average term to maturity and **duration** is shortened by holding bonds that are coming due in the near term, while still taking advantage of renewing the newly invested money at long-term interest rates. In fact, there is a high probability that at some point in the last 15 years, you were advised to split up your Guaranteed Investment Certificates (GICs) or bonds in this fashion. I'd put money on it.

It was considered a pretty brilliant strategy in its day. Interest rates were high and falling (falling interest means rising bond prices) and making money in the bond market during a 30-year rally is as tricky as flying a kite on a windy day. The bond ladder was a fantastic tweak to a good plan. When interest rates are near zero investors need more than a tweak. Short-term rates are well below the increases in the cost of living and longer-term rates are only marginally better, not to mention the effect of taxation on interest.

A better strategy going forward is **liability matching**.

Liability Matching

Liability matching is the art of funding future cash flow needs. Like any art, there are multiple strategies that will deliver the outcome, each with its own characteristics, risks and outlook. For our four scenarios, let's assume James has a cash delivery to make in five years from now, to save the day and win the girl, of course. For our illustration, none of the bond solutions will have coupon payments to complicate matters so in each of the cases the return will be the amount that the bond is **discounted** when it's originally purchased.

Scenario 1 – Invest in a five-year zero-coupon bond (a.k.a. **strip bond**) and hold it for five years.

Scenario 2 – Invest in a six-month zero-coupon bond and when it matures, invest the proceeds in a 6-month zero-coupon bond repeatedly for five years.

Scenario 3 – Invest in a two-year zero-coupon bond and when it matures, reinvest it in a three-year zero-coupon bond.

Scenario 4 – Invest in a 30-year zero-coupon bond and sell it in five years.

In each of the scenarios, the five-year cash flow funding objective is achieved from various investment outlooks and levels of risk.

Scenario 1 represents the lowest level of risk. Once the **strip bond** is put into place, there is nothing to do except wait for the maturity date in five years when the money is needed. The total return is established at the onset and any changes in the market pricing are irrelevant since the bond will not be traded and no new bonds are introduced throughout the term.

Conversely, Scenario 4 is the most risky due to the fact that the bond does not mature when the funds are required and the return on the investment is entirely at the whim of the market price when James needs to deliver the package of bundled hundreds. If interest rates rise over the period, the bond will likely be worth less than the original investment.

The two scenarios in between, offer an opportunity to split the risks among several or a couple of maturities. In a rising interest rate environment, the 6-month rollover is the best way to manage the portfolio, since your returns gradually increases rather than locking into lower rates for the entire five years today.

If James smashes his Lotus Esprit in a quick escape through narrow streets, a conveniently abandoned BMW R1200 C Cruiser is always close at hand. We aspire to movie magic where money is never an issue. However, if you aren't sure when you will need to replace your Lotus, then Scenario 2 is the least risky because the funds become available to spend every six-months.

Strip-Tease

Each piece of a bond, the **coupons** with various payment dates and the residual principle payable at the final maturity date, can be sold separately. When a bond is in its complete form, the investor would expect to invest the **face value**, receive interest payments every 6 months and have her **principle** amount paid back at maturity. What would it be worth today to receive no semi-annual interest payments but only the $10,000 **face value** in five years if current interest rates were 5%? You'd be willing to invest an amount less than $10,000 so that the future $10,000 that you receive represents a 5% return over those five years. Instead of investing $10,000 and receiving $250 payments every six-months on a 5% bond, you invest $7792.05 and receive $10,000 in five years. Both are 5% investments over five years.

Running with the example, the five-year bond with semi-annual interest payments can be separated into 10 coupon interest payments of $250 each payable every six-months and the $10,000 **principle** payable in five years. The first $250 coupon comes due in 6 months, the second in 12, the third in 18 months, and so on. Imagine that each of these pieces of paper is sold individually. The first coupon with the nearest maturity will be **discounted** and sold at a value representing a 5% investment return over 6 months while the last $250 coupon payable in five years is a much smaller initial investment to equal the return of 5% interest for a much longer period of time. As the investor, you would pay much more for the coupon being paid in six-months than the one in five years because it's much closer to the maturity date. The first coupon maturing in six-months is worth $243.90 today while the final coupon is priced at $195.88.

Interestingly for the mathematicians in the crowd (others feel free to gloss over this part), when you add up the present values of all of the **discounted coupons** and the **discounted** value of the **residual** principle, the total sum will equal $10,000, the same as the **face value** of the bond! The present values always add up to the total **face value** of the bond when the interest rate on the bond is the same as the prevailing interest rate by which the bond is being **discounted**.

You cannot strip a bond yourself but you can invest in a bond that has already been stripped by a financial institution. **Strip bonds** are designed for situations where you don't want the hassle of reinvesting the small amounts paid out in interest every 6 months or when you want to have a certain sum of money come due at a particular date in the future.

Strip bonds (called that because the components of the bond have been stripped apart and have none or *zero* coupons) can also be useful for liability matching. By matching the maturity date of the bond, you have the exact amount of money coming due when you need it, leaving your other investments available for strategies that may fluctuate with market cycles. You don't have to worry about selling those longer-term investments if the market prices drop because you have the cash you need from the maturing **strip bond**.

Keep in mind that with **strip bonds**, you must pay the taxes on the interest every year, even though you do not receive any cash payments from the bond. Therefore, these investments are best suited for a tax-sheltered account such as an RRSP, RRIF or TFSA. They're also ideal for an RRSP or TFSA because there are no coupon payments or cash flow to reinvest.

Real Return Bonds

For some time now, investors have been faced with a difficult situation. While bonds appreciate in value as interest rates drop, when facing historically low interest rates near zero, the likelihood of rates rising is far greater than them falling. For conservative investors, there are few places to hide from rising rates to protect your **capital**. One way is to stick with near-term maturities and short-duration bonds. Another is to consider **Real Return Bonds (RRB)**.

The RRB is different from all other fixed income products. The semi-annual interest payments and the **capital** of this type of bond tracks the Canadian Consumer Price Index (CPI). This makes the bond effective in maintaining purchasing power as inflation rises. As the price of goods and services in Canada increases, so does the value of your RRB.

In Canada, these notes are currently only issued by the Federal government and the province of Quebec.

Dangers of Low Interest Rates

During times of profoundly low interest rates, bonds offer pathetic returns. Factor in taxation and inflation and in most cases you've guaranteed yourself a negative net return. Your ability to purchase goods in the future diminishes substantially eroding your long-term purchasing power significantly. Layer in the effect of buying government debt versus corporate debt and the issues exacerbate. What used to be a safe investment category is fraught with pitfalls as even government-backed bonds face downgrades and possible bankruptcies.

> *"Given the volatility of markets and the high level of central bank stimulus (artificial demand) in the system, it is very difficult to construct an investment portfolio that you can have confidence in for more than a few months. Nevertheless, there are a few things that should hold up regardless of what the global economy and financial markets do. The first is quality: AAA/AA corporate bonds of multinational corporations will hold up as corporate balance sheets are in the best shape in decades. Stocks of high quality, consistent dividend payment companies will also weather volatility better than higher **beta** lower quality companies. The second is insurance or hedges: a modest exposure to precious metals will provide protection in the event that government debt problems resurface. Also, **short** positions in U.S. government bonds, and major equity indices, perhaps through inverse **ETFs**, will protect your **capital** when interest rates rise and/or equity markets suddenly move down."*
>
> —Barry Allan, Founder,
> Marret Asset Management

A portfolio consisting exclusively of bonds is more risky than a portfolio that holds a small equity weighting as well as bonds, according to Markowitz, a Nobel laureate in economics.

To say that government agents are overextended is an understatement. Several rating agencies have downgraded many of them, including the United States government. After the liquidity crisis across 2006 to 2008, corporations and businesses have strengthened their balance sheets and reduced their levels of leverage. Still in 2013, there are four corporations in the U.S.

that still retain a AAA rating—higher than the U.S. government—that yield a higher dividend than the 10-year government bond.

The name of the game is purchasing power. Not only do bonds decrease in value when interest rates rise, but the paltry returns of the government issued bonds, bank issued GICs and "safe" investments are, in some cases, ensure a loss on your money after taxes and inflation are accounted for. A guaranteed loss is far from safe.

When discussing diversification, it has been understood that bonds behave differently in markets than equities and other investments. Load on their other attributes of finite maturity dates and dependable coupon payments every six-months, and the attraction to them as an asset class is warranted. In former times, the risks associated with investing in bonds were priced into the interest rates offered. The higher the risk, the higher the interest rate offered (return).

In the late 1980s, interest bearing investments including bonds, mortgages, money market funds, bank deposits and guaranteed investment certificates, offered double-digit nominal returns. Now the tide has changed. With interest rates compressed to low single digits, income taxes reaping their fair share and inflation devouring the rest, the only real opportunity to afford the rising costs of goods and services is if interest rates fall. Obviously, an unlikely scenario when they are close to zero already. There's nowhere for interest rates to fall anymore and the cycle has climaxed.

The **beta** (sensitivity to the stock market) of bonds may be zero but at this juncture, their risk is just as great as stocks, if not arguably greater.

Thanks to the highest level of taxation applied to interest payments money invested in bonds that pay very low rates of return are difficult to justify. Even though bond investors receive interest and **principle** repayments on schedule their ability to buy a loaf of bread is devoured by the effects of inflation and tax with no consideration for the risk of rising rates clawing back **capital** as well. That makes for a crumby investment. (I realize that was a really bad pun, but I couldn't resist. I tried removing it several times but here it is in print.)

Current interest rates fall short of compensating investors against the risks they're accepting. If the erosion value wasn't bad enough, layer on credit risk, issuer risk and other traditional problems that haven't even been considered yet and it becomes very difficult to rationalize the interest rates being paid to investors to stick it out. If you were a gambler, you wouldn't lay three chips on the table to get one back, would you?

> "Owning fixed income now is akin to owning Tech stocks in the late 1990s and mortgage securities in the late 2000s. Yes! It is that bad. The bond market is crowded with buyers who are accustomed to consistent returns and low risk. Many are misled into thinking bonds are safe, simply because they will more than likely repay their **principle** and interest on time. However, when rates rise, and the multitudes of risk-averse investors crowded into high quality bonds all make for the exits it is going to be ugly. Interest rate, liquidity and basis risks will all come home to roost at the same time.
>
> The best case for bond investors is a continued low rate environment, caused by deterioration in the economy and worsening credit conditions. This is still not good, as this means more government money printing, higher inflation and substantial negative real returns. From any perspective fixed income securities (especially high credit quality and government bonds) are a highly over-priced, risky asset class."
>
> —Craig Jacobson, Portfolio Manager, Roads Capital LLC

Secrets of Senior Secured Loan Funds

The insatiable appetite for high cash flow investments has driven a variety of products to the market of late. One of these products adopted in Canada, already representing an over $600 billion market in the U.S., is the **Senior Secured Loan Fund**. Despite the misleading name, these investments individually are of low quality and as the **ABCP** fiasco of 2006 so acutely illustrated, large diversified pool of poor quality investments sewn together with a magic wand do not transform into good quality investments. Combining high-risk assets does little to mitigate folly when markets become illiquid and volatile.

This **private debt** financing extended by banks to medium and large corporations is referred to by a variety of terms including leveraged loans, bank loans, high yield loans, syndicated loans or sub-investment grade bank debt. Essentially, they represent speculative debt rated below investment grade and are partially or fully **secured** by receivables, inventory or subsidiary stock. Since the loans are private, there are fewer regulatory disclosures required, which is steeped in lack of transparency.

Private debt refers to fixed income investments issued by a corporation that are issued to and traded by private parties.

The interest on these loans typically floats at a rate over the London Interbank Offered Rate (LIBOR) therefore, as interest rates rise, so do the obligation payments of the companies who borrowed the funds. If interest rates rise enough, the debt costs may become too difficult to bear leading to increased probability of default on the loans.

As an investor, you should be aware of the risks of this type of fixed income investment as a unique part of the market. Despite the low historical variations in this asset class, the risks are lurking. During times of high **volatility**, these loans will be subject to extreme price and liquidity risk. In the 2008 financial crisis, this market lost a third of its value and became difficult to sell at all. Also of note is the pooled funds available in Canada often use leverage to enhance distributions, accentuating the risks.

Timing the interest rate market with these investments is also crucial. During falling interest rates, these loans will perform poorly against safer fixed income vehicles due to the variable interest rates. If timed properly, an investor could outpace other vehicles, but if the interest rates move against you, you could find these investments underperforming against other safer investments.

If you are interested in the **Senior Secured Loan** market for its high yields, be aware of the potential pitfalls and nuances that this unique group of securities offers, before you wade in.

Pricing

Except for **convertible debentures**, bonds do not trade on an exchange like stocks do. Instead, major financial institutions make a market for them by buying and selling between investors and themselves. Banks and brokerages carry an inventory of several bond **issues** and are willing to make a market for buying and selling most bonds during the entire term of a bond issue. As an investor, this makes investing in bonds much more liquid or easy to manage.

In order for a trade to take place, both the buyer and seller must agree on the price. There are a number of factors taken into account to determine the price to trade each bond, including who the bond is issued by, the coupon interest rate that is paid, current market interest rates, when the bond comes due and if the bond has any extra features.

The Issuer

Companies are not the only entities that issue bonds. Municipal, provincial and federal governments all issue bonds for a variety of funding needs. Keep in mind that the guarantees of a bond, the interest payments and repayment of the **principle** are only as good as the one guaranteeing it.

Maturity

The longer the term to maturity, the more risk there is in a bond because more elements can change. This is also why long-term interest rates are more volatile than shorter periods and is part of what makes up a bond's duration. Duration is the sensitivity a bond has to changes in interest rates in the market. Since the coupon interest paid on a bond is fixed, changes in the market interest rates make investors think differently about a bond with a higher or lower rate than the market offers. This drives the bond price higher (when in demand) or lower (when no one wants the bond).

Features

Features are either for the benefit of the investor or for the bond issuer. Some features, like **callable features**, allow the issuer flexibility with financing options. For example, if a company borrows money by way of a bond issue when interest rates are high, having the ability to **call** the bond prior to the regular maturity date and reissue a new bond at a lower rate can be a cost saving advantage for the company. This option works against the bondholder who naturally prefers the higher interest investment. Other features, such as conversion or retraction options, are a sweetener to attract investors or to allow the issuer to offer a lower rate of interest in exchange for these enhancements: A win-win scenario for both investor and issuer.

Interest Rates

Prevailing rates of interest are a key factor in determining your investment value. As pointed out previously, when interest rates drop, an existing bond carrying a higher coupon is in demand driving its price higher. The reverse is also true.

Fees

If you have an account where commissions are charged on your stock trades, you are probably being charged a commission on buying and selling bonds, as well. Generally, you do not see a commission on a bond trade, even on your trade confirmation slip, but you can be assured that it's worked into the price of the bond. In a **fee-based account**, you are able to obtain bonds without trading costs by instead, paying an overall management fee on your entire account. It's a much more transparent way to observe the costs involved.

Let me show you an example of the difference between bonds purchased in a **commission-based account** (where each trade in the account generated a transaction fee) and a **fee-based account** (where a management fee is charged each month according to the total value of the account, so no commission on the bond trade).

Example: Sherrit International Corporation

Purchase Date: March 14, 2012
Face Value: $10,000
Coupon: 8%
Maturity: 15 November 2018
Rating: BBB

Commission-Based Bond Purchase Price: $110
Yield to Maturity: 6.144%

Fee-Based Bond Purchase Price: $108.75
Yield to Maturity: 6.364%

Notice that the **commission-based** bond purchase price is more expensive and the yield is lower than for the fee-based account. These are both a function of the fees being integrated into the commission purchase where the fees are charged separately each month on the account rather than on the transaction.

In today's market, bond commissions are not disclosed, leaving room for larger fees to be charged than you realize. Credible IAs will price your bonds fairly but there is a real temptation to bury fees in bond prices. This is especially true when interest rates are high as there is more room to move the period around. In a lower interest rate environment, there is margin to play with pricing.

When investing small amounts in bonds, you can imagine the implications to the price of the bond if you're paying a minimum commission of $150 per bond. The $150 dollars of commission is 1.5% of a $1000 bond but only 0.75% of a $3000 bond. In some cases where minimum commissions are charged, it may become prohibitive to invest small amounts due to the proportionately higher level of commissions.

If you plan on holding bonds until they mature or rarely trade bonds, you're better off to stay with a commission structure, as your overall fees will likely be lower. If you have an active bond portfolio, the fee-based approach may be better. The best way to determine the ideal fee structure is to look at the trades in your bond portfolio over the past few years and evaluate the commissions charged in relation to what a management fee would be over the same period.

Additionally, management fees may be deducted against any income reported on your tax return, whereas commissions on bond trades are embedded in your return by increasing the **ACB** of your bond (the initial bond price).

Luckily, the Investment Industry Regulatory Organization of Canada (IIROC) will enforce fee disclosure on bonds, mutual funds and other investments where fees are buried. Like Zerilli's admissions, the next few years will bring disclosure…and we may finally find Hoffa's body after all these years.

Tax Tips

Tax law changes all the time. The tax act is thick and deep and I'm not an accountant. Nevertheless, as a **PM**, I can speak to generalities that benefit investors in general.

Tip #1: One of the tactics that most investors miss is an easy way to convert what could be interest to a **capital gain**, reducing your tax implications by about half. If you own bonds in a taxable account (not a tax sheltered account such as an RRSP, RRIF or TFSA) it makes sense to sell them before the maturity date if the market value of the bonds (what they're trading at) is higher than the price you paid for them. For example, if you purchase a bond with the **face value** of $10,000 for 89 cents on the dollar (invest $8900), sell the bond before the maturity date. The bond price will be the **face value** at maturity, which in this case is $10,000, and the difference between what you paid for the bond and the mature value is considered interest income. Interest income is fully taxable at your marginal tax rate. If you trade the bond before the maturity date, the price difference is a **capital gain**, only 50% of which is included in your income for tax calculations.

Tread with caution. This is a strategy that you have to ensure is clearly a trading strategy and not simply tax avoidance. If you sell the bond the day before maturity, you will likely have to treat the gain as interest.

Tip #2: Another tax issue also associated with the market price of a bond happens when purchasing a bond at a **premium** (some amount over the **face value** of the bond) in a taxable account.

Premiums are the market's way of saying that your coupon interest is higher than current bond yields. Bonds that carry higher interest **coupons** have a higher tax burden because the **coupons** paid each year are treated as interest income.

When you sell a bond that continues to drop closer to par value as the maturity date draws nearer, the difference between your original investment and the price you sell it for is a **capital loss**. Since **capital losses** can only offset **capital gains**, these bonds carried in taxable accounts have punitive consequences because the full coupon payment is taxable at the highest rates, while the net return on your investment is a smaller amount.

One way to deal with this is by buying **principle adjusted rate securities** (PARS) or **coupon adjusted rate securities** (CARS). Investment firms manufacture these by throwing existing bonds into a high-speed food processor and baking them for 25 minutes. Actually, these are brilliant solutions for investors since they are bits and pieces of the original bond, reconstituted to form a new bond issued at a par value. Eliminating the **premium**, eliminates the tax issue.

If you are working with an investment professional and the bond that you are considering buying is large enough, you can request the firm to do some slicing and dicing for you too.

Tip #3: When you invest in **strip bonds** they're purchased at a deep **discount** to the **matured value** but offer no coupon payments along the way. Your reward is the difference between what you pay for the bond and the value at which it matures. With this kind of bond, despite the fact that you don't receive any cash payments, CRA still wants its dues. Taxpayers must calculate the amount that the bond increases in value each year and declare it as interest, paying taxes on the change in value. This is considered punitive since you pay tax but you don't have any cash in your hands. As mentioned earlier, **strip bonds** are best held in a tax-sheltered account such as a TFSA, RRSP or RRIF.

Risks

Investments with guarantees ironically carry risks. This is by no means an exhaustive list of potential issues, but some common pitfalls of which to be aware.

Yield–Price Seesaw

Interest rates go up, bond prices go down. Interest rates go down, bond prices go up. That's the risk. The value of your investment will drop as interest rates rise and if the level of interest rates is near zero, they ain't gettin' much lower.

If you plan to hold the bond until maturity, the value of your investment will be 100 cents on the dollar despite rising or falling rates. Even if you don't plan to sell your bonds prior to the due date, your investment firm will value the price of the bond at or near the price where it was recently traded in their systems. This is called marking it to the market (mark-to-market) which is nothing more than giving you an indication of what you may be able to sell the bond at on the date your statement was printed. Don't worry about changes in the bond price if you have no intention of selling it mid-term but be aware that statements will reflect the market value of your bonds and report a depressed or inflated value for your overall portfolio.

Downgraded

There are several rating agencies in North America and worldwide that rate the credit quality of government and corporate bond issuers as well as other securities. Ranging from the safest levels of AAA, AA, A and BBB for investment grade and BB and below for high yield bonds, credit rating agencies including Standard and Poor's (S&P), Dominion Bond Rating Services (DBRS), Moody's and Fitch attempt to maintain a standard for assessing the solvency and safety of monies lent to various parties. The credit rating of the company indicates the risks associated with default and bankruptcy if prevailing circumstances are unchanged. New information on a company specifically, or the economy in general, can cause any of the rating agencies to re-evaluate the score of the debt of a company. In addition, different **issues** of the same company or government can have different ratings due to the risks of a company refunding near-term maturities over longer term ones.

The pricing of bonds is determined by a number of inputs, including the credit quality of the company and the issue. Due to this, a change downward in the company's credit score will obviously have negative implications on the price of its bonds in the market as new investors will demand higher yields for those riskier **issues**. The converse is also true.

Credit Risk

Ever miss a loan payment? Default risk is the chance that the borrower will not be able to meet payments due. With an investment in bonds, you're the lender.

The credit risk of a bond refers to the possibility of the issuing company not being able to meet interest payments or declaring bankruptcy and not repaying the bond at maturity. Bonds with security are ranked higher than bonds without. Bonds with longer terms in a troubled company would be ranked lower than those with shorter terms and a higher likelihood of the obligation being met. And so on.

As grading goes, most of the rating agencies use the format of BB, B, CCC, CC and C for high-yield speculative **issues** with BB being the first rung under investment grade and C just above the rank of default. As a group they're literally called **junk bonds,** yet despite the inflammatory term, these investments are not trash. Actually, these may be suitable (depending on your investment stance) to invest in for higher interest rates or for **speculation**. If you're happy to own a company's common shares it may be of interest to invest in its bonds, even if they have junk status. Remember that the bonds rank higher than the common shares of the same issuer in the event of default or bankruptcy, especially if they're backed by collateral. They aren't safer than investment grade bonds, just better than the equity of the same issuer. If you don't want the higher level of risk though, stick with investment grade rankings.

The only rating agency that reports credit ratings differently is Moody's, which uses the notations Aaa, Aa, A, Baa, Ba, etc.

Bankruptcy Risk

Distressed-bond managers make a practice out of buying the debt of companies at risk of declaring bankruptcy, for pennies on the dollar. They specialize in evaluating a company's assets and capital structure to determine whether investing in the bonds of a company at risk of bankruptcy would result in a profit. They must be willing to wait out the

Bonds are safer than stocks from the same company.
In the event of bankruptcy, bondholders are paid-out after bank loans and before equity stakeholders.

arduously long turnaround time through the bankruptcy process and in some cases, they're required to take control of the company during and once they emerge from bankruptcy protection. Often, the bondholders become the new equity stakeholders after bankruptcy and the value is then realized once the company is re-established with newly issued common shares. Patience is not only a virtue but a profitable venture.

The risk of bankruptcy is a process that starts with a company taking on too much debt. Living beyond our means isn't reserved for college students. Sudden changes in the market can wreak havoc on the cash flow of a company right when its principals weren't expecting it. Also, changes in the availability of credit in general (as we witnessed over the financial crisis of 2008 and 2009) or for a certain business specifically could halt a company dead in its tracks. When a corporation can't meet interest payments, renew its line of credit or reissue a bond, it's forced to sell assets. Usually, it's the corporation's best assets that are easiest to sell and the ones that it can't afford to sell!

Credit rating agencies take action by downgrading the corporation's debt rating. White knight lenders swoop in on their stallions insisting on collateral security and demanding higher interest rates to compensate for the risk. The road to bankruptcy is usually along low rolling hills, but given the right conditions, it may be a quick step down a deep crevasse.

Both bond and stock prices of a company reflect the bankruptcy risk of a company, usually in anticipation. Overzealous sellers will capitulate at ridiculous values providing opportunities for **distressed-bond investors** and other speculators, and so the cycle continues. If I had a nickel for every time the market overreacted, I'd write an algorithm to match and call the strategy: The Zealot **Hedge Fund**.

There are real opportunities to make interesting returns in the distressed market based on **fundamental analysis**. Analyzing the assets of a company and managing a company through a bankruptcy may offer great returns. The turnaround on these investments is long and the risks are quite high even during normal market conditions driven by supply and demand. Recently, however, there have been risks that even distressed-investment managers could not have predicted, where governments stepped in, acquired the equity of a public company and left bondholders out in the cold.

Chapter 4

Alternative Investments: The New Frontier

If you want a guarantee, buy a toaster.
—Clint Eastwood

Hedge Funds

A hedge is a row of closely planted shrubs as a barrier to wind, predators and other risks. An investment hedge is meant to protect your money from **volatility**, especially the downside type (no one minds upward volatility).

The label comes from the axiom "hedging your bets," implying that you can limit losses, hinting at strategies beyond traditional diversification. In practice, however, the term 'hedge fund' is grossly inadequate for describing the myriad of investment strategies that fall into this catchall category. Today, most hedge funds are trying to distance themselves from the overused title and re-categorize as **Alternative Asset Classes**. At least this nomenclature implies that you're investing in something different—unconventional or a substitution—but it's still too broad to reveal much about what you're investing in specifically.

More recently, one company has adopted the namesake of authentic hedge funds. Picton Mahoney's idea is moving in the right direction by matching their wording with clear objectives to offer a true hedge to traditional asset classes.

> *"Authentic hedge funds are all about lower volatility, low correlations and more consistent returns."*
> —David Picton, President and Portfolio Manager
> Picton Mahoney Asset Management

Although most **alternative strategies** invest in traditional assets such as bonds and stocks, the way that they manage those investments and their execution sets them apart. These strategies may be based on algorithms or fast-moving computer trading, or the manager may simply specialize in finding broken-down golf carts and turning them into hovercrafts to float over the greens and water hazards. In any case, they're offered to investors differently than mutual funds and other pooled investments, under strict regulatory guidelines.

Hedge fund strategies dreamt up by investment opportunists veer sharply from the conventions of tradition. Their entire *raison d'être* is to profit from inconsistencies in the **capital markets** wherever they lurk or to mitigate risks in innovative ways. In an undefined world, adjectives such as no-rules, opportunistic and other flagrancies are too dangerous from a marketing perspective and too indigestible for the general public. The "just trust me" tagline doesn't naturally instil confidence. In its evolution, however, this industry of resourceful managers has migrated into several groups defined by strategies that have become repeatable and in some cases, almost standardized. With all of these strategies forming natural groupings, a more descriptive approach would be offer these unconventional investments in terms of their general approaches. Unfortunately, most hedge fund managers feel the need to fiercely guarding their uniqueness and would rather blush under the broad umbrella of hedge fund or alternative investment.

Types of Funds

The four most common approaches are **market neutral**, **event driven**, **macro** (or top down) and **relative value** strategies.

Market Neutral

A hedge fund chameleon I met during a conference in Scotland used to send me emails whenever the stock market dropped significantly. "I sure am glad that I'm not long the market and all of my assets are in **managed futures**," she'd playfully jeer. She wasn't short the market profiting from the downdraft in prices but invested in a totally different strategy that doesn't care much about which direction the market is going. Managed futures are a trend-following strategy that can make a profit in either rising or falling markets. The truth was, however, she reluctantly admitted to owning two stocks in one of her accounts. Blackberry Ltd. (BB), the Canadian smartphone maker formerly known as Research In Motion, and its U.S. rival, Apple Inc. (AAPL) that makes iPhones, iPads and other portable electronics.

I suppose you could say that she was hedging her bets in the sense that **diversifying** between handheld device makers is a way to mitigate risk in that sector. After all, BB's share price dropped from a peak of over $137.41 Canadian in May, 2008, to a low of $6.25 in September, 2012, while concurrently AAPL rose from $174.96 U.S. to $700.09.

Unfortunately, the trouble with this reasoning is that long investors, who buy stocks for a profit, are hoping that both stocks will appreciate. A better way to diversify is being long and short in the market at the same time, but make sure you're long AAPL and short BB in this case. The opposite would make you cry.

On September 23, 2013, BB signed a provisional agreement to be bought by a consortium led by Fairfax Financial Holdings Ltd. (FFH) for $9 per share. Subsequently, BB began flogging slices of its business to a variety of suitors to extract a maximum value for shareholders. At the time of writing this book BB traded in the $8 range. Meanwhile, AAPL's share price dropped to the $400-$500 range. During this period, you would have wanted to change the stock you were long and which one you were short.

There are several ways to neutralize your portfolio against a stock market decline. Adding a short index position to offset drops in the stock market, buying an index **put option** that allows you to sell the index at a predetermined price and holding risk-free assets (cash) are

3 executable ways to counteract market declines with slightly different outcomes. A brief look at the different results you can expect from each will point you to the best way to produce a variety of desired outcomes and avoid a few unintentional snags.

Long and short investors have opposing prospects. The first wants the share price to rise and the second, to fall. Investing in **low correlated** assets is true diversification. When the assets behave differently, their relationship to each other is opposing, resulting an overall stabilizing effect. In and of itself, a short position has unlimited losses, since the price of the stock or index can continue to rise indefinitely but when added to a traditional portfolio of beloved stocks, a short position can have a nullifying effect on **volatility** of your other investments. If the market continues to rise, however, the short position will simply drag on your **capital gains** since it's only profitable in the event that the position or market declines in value.

*The inverse relationship that the short index, **put option** and cash have to the group of stocks that you own offsets some or all of the losses that you would have otherwise sustained.*

A **put option** on the other hand can be used to neutralize a portfolio in a different way. This is a contract that you can buy (or sell) where the holder of the contract retains the option to sell a certain stock or index at a certain price by (or at) a certain date. If you buy a **put option** on the **S&P/TSX stock market index** that expires 6 months from now, for example, that guarantees you the ability to sell the index at today's value (**strike price**). You will profit on the difference between the price you can sell the position at on the contract and the actual value of the index, assuming the stock market dropped below the **strike price** on the option agreement. This profit offsets the losses on your stock portfolio, which would have also declined in market value. **Put options** are standardized and listed on the stock exchange. They can be purchased and sold for a small fee (**premium**) with a variety of expiries and execution prices. If you purchase a **put option** to protect your portfolio and the market doesn't drop, your losses are limited to the amount you spent to buy the option. Repeating this strategy regularly can be expensive, however, eroding the returns on your portfolio by spending profits to buy **put options**.

The most conservative hedge is holding cash in your portfolio. Cash is cash. It doesn't have any **volatility**. The flipside though, is that it makes little in the way of returns at current interest rates. You trade profit for safety. It isn't difficult to see that cash would drag your overall portfolio returns as an extremely costly hedge, so you wouldn't likely hold high levels of cash for long.

When one zigs the other zags. This counter-behaviour provides diversification and counteracts market movements. But like all good things, it falls short of perfect. The first cost is the **premium** that the investor has to pay to buy a **put option**. This cost is not recoverable when the option expires. Secondly, cash is a drag on portfolio performance since the best-case scenario is that you preserve the value of your money if the market drops but your returns will be exceedingly modest. Shorting doesn't make any money at all unless the market drops. In fact, the losses on a short can be substantial if the market rises.

The real profit on any hedge is made if the worst-case scenario unfolds. Counterintuitive but true nevertheless. Finally, consider that using part of your money to invest in this strategy means that you can't do something else with it. There is an opportunity cost compared with what you could have invested in. If you don't invest cash, the value doesn't increase (or decrease). Moreover, interest and dividends are not paid on it, either.

Professionally managed equity market neutral portfolios are one of the most common hedge fund strategies. The manager will be long the stocks that he likes and short the ones that he doesn't. This is a real test of skill and analysis as the profit comes from the spread in the performance between the long and short stock or ideally if the stocks move in opposite directions.

A specific type of market neutral is called pair trading. In this strategy, not only is the portfolio long and short but also it's long and short two similar companies, either in the same industry or market. For example, buying Toronto Dominion Bank (TD) and shorting Bank of Montreal (BMO) is a pair trade. They are two Canadian Schedule A banks, each with different management and business profiles but within the Canadian marketplace in the same industry. In this case, if TD performs better than BMO, the portfolio will net a profit regardless of the overall market moves up or down by negating the volatility of the market in general and the banking sector specifically. The profit from the pair trade is limited to the marginal difference in the opposing performance of the two companies, substantially less than if you were to purchase both companies outright during a rising market. To equalize this, the **market neutral manager** will often take on leverage to increase the marginal returns of the strategy. While **leverage** generally increases risk, the manager justifies the introduction of **leverage** because he has taken out the market risk (referred to as the **beta**) by holding both long and short market positions.

*The more **leverage** in the portfolio, the more important a manager's abilities become. As **leverage** increases, so do **volatility** and the variance of possible returns you accept. **Leverage** always increases your risk.*

Baseball is one of those sports built on strategy, statistics, hotdogs and keg-beer with long strings of time between spurts of action. Being slightly ADHD, it helps to have a little skin in the game to keep things lively. I always favour the home team despite the odds, just because I like to belong to the native crowd. When you're in the 'hood you don't want to ruffle too many feathers and the conversations with the volunteer ushers that meander through the glory days of summer, are always pro-home team.

Last year, I was in Chicago with a gaggle of CFA® charterholders with a free Sunday afternoon. We piled onto the subway and headed down to Wrigley Field to see the Cubbies face the Braves. The odds were 7 to 1 for the away team but my rule is impervious. I placed a series of $5 bets with several of my colleagues, taking the other side of whatever their choice was, but finally ending $5 net long on the Cubs. In total, I had $15 for Atlanta and $20 for Chicago. You might be wondering why I didn't just bet one $5 lot on the home team and leave it at that. Well, imagine the fun of being able to text winning taunts to three different people when the Braves were up and a whole different group when the Cubs pulled ahead.

I probably could have had just about as much fun being net neutral on the outcome of the game but when the home team wins, especially as the underdog, legitimately participating in the stadium fever is worth the risk. This isn't an ideal example of market neutral, only because there were just two possible outcomes. It was too perfectly neutral so not very interesting. I could have gone home if it wasn't for the extra $5 for the Cubs, the ice-cold draft and the smell of summer in Wrigley Field.

It would have been much more interesting if there were multiple teams or investment options offset by a basket of the alternatives or if I had borrowed the $5 from a friend to place the bet. Then playing the options on a variety of outcomes becomes much more interesting.

Similarly, many true equity market-neutral strategies find the marginal return too small to justify the work so they typically employ **leverage**. By borrowing extra funds against the value of the portfolio of investments or by using derivatives (including options), the manager multiplies the exposure to the market. This way she can amplify the small returns. There is an upward bias to markets over long periods of time due to business growth (the eternal optimist!) so, in general, holding more long securities than short ones usually makes sense.

Although I was net-long on the Chicago Cubs, I didn't have a real short position to generate additional cash to invest (because I didn't sell anything) so I could only place as many bets as my wallet could satisfy.

The odds were 7 to 1 for the away team but my rule is impervious. I placed a series of $5 bets with several of my colleagues, taking the other side of whatever their choice was, but finally ending $5 net long on the Cubs. In total, I had $15 for Atlanta and $20 for Chicago.

Selling a stock or index puts cash in your hands, even if you didn't own the position before you sold it. In shorting, the investor borrows the stock and sells it hoping it will drop before they have to buy it back. The money from the sale can either be held in cash or invested in other securities. For example, with a $100,000 stock portfolio, the manager may decide to sell short the broad index for 50% of the value of the portfolio. This gives her $50,000 additional money for a total of $150,000 to buy the selected stocks she likes. The 150% long and 50% short portfolio is commonly referred to as a 150/50 portfolio. For a more upwardly biased approach, she could hold even fewer short positions. For example, a 120/20 is more bullish with higher expectations that the market, in general, will appreciate in value. A 200/100 is more bearish and a 100/100 with the cash from the short sale of the stocks held in money market is entirely neutral. The more **leverage** in the portfolio, the more important the risk of the manager's abilities becomes and the more potential **volatility** and variance of possible returns you accept. **Leverage** always increases your risk.

Event Driven

Whenever an abrupt event occurs to a publicly traded company there are brief opportunities to capitalize on the ensuing price fluctuations as the market digests the information and rationalizes the prices of traded securities. You have to be quick and accurate to realize this value. Anticipated events rarely offer profits as investors incrementally bid up the prices on securities, as they understand their worth in a slow and methodical way. Unanticipated events occur due to swift changes in market conditions or regulations; management initiated transactions, including mergers and acquisitions; or forces put on a public company by outside sources.

The most visible hedge funds are **activist managers** due to their vociferous approach to extricating returns from the market. If you hear the business news announce that some hedge fund guy has purchased a minority or majority interest in a company, it's likely because he intends to exert pressure on the management or board of directors to make changes. His strategy is to buy the shares of a company at the current, sombre market price, step in, fix the problem to unlock the value of the enterprise driving the stock price up. Once the fund manager acquires enough interest in the company it effects change by forcing issues to a shareholder vote. The fund manager might use a more congenial approach, suggesting recommendations, but sometimes force is the only way to alter well-entrenched ideals of current management. At times, the pieces of a company are worth more than the whole. In those cases, the strategy to unearth profit is to break the company up to sell off the bits, one at a time.

Not all attempts are successful. In 2013, for example, Jana Partners was shut out in its attempt to install several directors on the board of Agrium Inc. (AGU) and push forward their agenda. In that case, the shareholders voted resoundingly against the proposal.

*When a profitable opportunity to buy and sell a similar investment on different markets, at different prices exists, it's called **arbitrage**.*

Arbitrage, another event-driven strategy, is the execution of two simultaneous trades to profit on small price discrepancies in the market. Usually, **arbitrage** trades are executed in huge quantities in order to be worthwhile. Imagine that public company ABC offers to purchase public company XYZ for $35 per share. Assuming there are no regulatory issues, the shareholders all approve the combined company and all of the moons and stars align throughout the galaxy, the shares will trade at the acquisition price. That's the fixed future price of the shares, after all. To buy or sell the shares above or below that price doesn't make sense.

Looking back at the $9 per share offer for Blackberry Ltd. by the group headed up by FFH in September 2013, BB shares were trading in the low $8 range for several weeks. This market price was an argument between those who thought that the FFH offer would go through and those who didn't. The nay-sayers believed the value was something less than $9 so they were sellers of the stock. Either way, neither party felt the shares were worth $8 but that is the price it stayed at for some time due to the push-pull of the sellers against the buyers. Either get long or get short 'cause eight bucks was not an accurate price for that stock. It was just the midpoint of the tug-of-war.

Generally, an offer to purchase the company must come in above the current market price. Shareholders aren't interested in selling to a takeover for $35 if the shares trade on the market at $42! Let's assume that ABC is trading at $28 dollars, so the acquisition price offered is at a **premium** of 25%. Everyone sees the opportunity to make $7 per share and rushes to buy the shares at any price below the $35 offer. This increased buying interest drives the price of the shares up until the **arbitrage** no longer exists.

Similarly, if XYZ offers shares instead of cash, the total value of the shares offered is higher than the market price of ABC prior to the takeover offer. Assume that XYZ is offering 1.5 shares of XYZ for every ABC share and XYZ is trading at $29. To execute a perfect **arbitrage**, you would buy 200 ABC at $35 and sell short 300 XYZ at $29. The short sale gives you $8700 minus the $7000 to buy the shares of the acquisition company for a net profit of $1700. You have no interest in the combined company once the dust settles and you have completed your first **merger arbitrage**.

Other types of arbitrage may not be perfectly offset, yet close enough to be neutral. For example, in capital structure arbitrage, the investor may buy the bonds of a company and short the common shares of the same company for the expressed purpose to take the risk of the company out of the equation. In the extreme case of default or bankruptcy, the common shares drop dramatically or eventually become worthless, on which the short investor makes a profit. That profit offsets the loss on the bonds, which drop in value, as well. The difference between owning a bond and a stock on the same company is the bond ranks higher in terms of safety and the order of being paid out. Recall that common shareholders are the owners of the company while bondholders are the lenders to the company with certain guarantees and sometimes assignment to collateral. If the bonds offer a better expected return for their lower risk level than the common shares, a capital structure arbitrage investor would buy one and short the other to make a profit when the pricing reverts to normal. In this example, the same company issues both of the positions so the investor is long and short different parts of the company's **capital** sources.

These are typically long-term strategies since bankruptcy can be a lengthy process. There are usually hundreds of irons in the fire at any given time because of the long time horizon required. Investors need to be patient with this strategy but when it finally pays off, the spoils can be handsome and those profits more than offset those situations that flounder.

Other examples of event driven strategies include **distressed investments** and **special situations**. When a company files for bankruptcy protection, event-driven managers assess the value of the business assets and compare that with the price of the company's bonds. In bankruptcy, the bondholders often end up owning the company, or what's left of it, once it emerges. These are typically long-term strategies since bankruptcy can be a lengthy process. There are usually dozens of irons in the fire at any given time because of the long time horizon required. Investors need to be patient with this strategy, but when it finally pays off, the spoils can be handsome and the profits more than offset those situations that flounder in a portfolio.

Macro

Imagine yourself on a satellite where you could hear the chatter of the entire world from the vantage of a celestial orbit. Delving into areas of interest from that top-down perspective is steeped in broad economic and political opinion. Macro strategies start from a thesis developed from 200 kilometres up and the investments are broad and directional in nature.

Macro investments are expected to profit excessively over the general market as a result of the investment calls made. Active traders in specific business sectors including commodities, agriculture and currencies are all macro-minded. Their approach is typically systematic and thematic in nature and it's the manager's overview that drives the trading strategies.

Relative Value Meets Tim

There were 3 of us at the Tim Hortons during the Rrroll Up the Rim to Win contest reaching across the register for our medium Double-Doubles. By the time we found a table I had already offered my colleague a quarter for his option to win one of the in-store prizes hidden beneath the waxy paper rim of the cup. With a one in six chance to garner a prize, the coveted cup was not going to sell for nothing. The price would have to be some amount less than the value of the 210-calorie cup of hot milky beverage because I could simply buy another cup for just over a buck and a half to have another chance and a second drink. We settled at 50 cents in trade for the chance to be a one in six winner, but not without hard negotiations on both sides. After our creamy elixirs were drained, I rolled up both of my paper cup rims excitedly revealing the anticipated spoils.

My colleague was happy to give up his option to potentially win for 50 cents, ostensibly reducing the cost of his coffee by just shy of a third of the price. That's a great deal no matter how you look at it! To me, a one in six chance was worth the 50 cents I shelled out for it or maybe the game itself was what I found worth the exercise. For a transaction to truly be fair, both parties have to feel that the other got the best deal.

In any investment, all of the components can be pulled apart in order to determine the value of each piece. In this case, the one in six chance to win was worth 50 cents in the marketplace of three 40-somethings sitting on swivel chairs around a bolted-down table in a cold Canadian suburb. Tim Hortons assigned some monetary value to the game that must have been higher than the $60 million in prizes being doled out, otherwise the business idea would lose money. The company was likely counting on increased coffee and food sales because of the game and the resulting additional profits to offset the cost of the actual prizes awarded. Otherwise, there'd be no point.

So, what if there was an active Tim Hortons Cup Rim Exchange (THCRE) where people could sell their unspoiled cups at a price of $0.50? Would the value of a cup of coffee eventually be only a dollar instead of a dollar and a half after the cups reverted to the regular brown paper version without the game? Before the THCRE, folks happily paid a $1.67 (with tax) for their Double-Doubles. Once the value of the option is determined, they may very well demand a lower price for the coffee.

Relative value is a judgment call on what something is worth within the context of other assets, markets or some other goal post, in an effort to taking advantage of mis-priced securities. For example, within the **capital structure** of a company or related companies, there may be bonds, **convertible debentures**, preferred shares and common shares. Each issue is traded separately on the listed exchange or **OTC** market, as in the case of bonds. A **relative value manager** will look for **arbitrage** opportunities between these **issues** and short the one that is too expensive compared with the one that is undervalued and capture the margin between them. This can be quite interesting in the case of **convertible debentures**, for example. They're like bonds in that they pay interest, have a fixed maturity and rank higher than common shares in the event of bankruptcy but they also carry an option to convert to common shares of the company at a predetermined price before the bond term ends. If the common shares are trading at a price higher than the **conversion option** price, the bond is more valuable by at least this difference. Since the debenture holder can convert the bond into common shares and make an extra profit, that value is reflected in the debenture's price so there is no need to actually convert the bond to realize this value.

To make this illustration work, picture the bond as separate from the option to convert to common shares. The conversion option is similar to the Timmies Cup. The relative value manager separately considers value of the bond from the value of the option to convert to the common shares. If you take out the share price and the risk of the company from the equation by shorting the common shares and removing other noise mathematically by pricing **volatility** and time to maturity, your remaining value should equal the bond. (Don't worry, there's an example coming). If it doesn't, there is an **arbitrage** opportunity to capture the marginal difference.

If a Double-Double costs $1.67 and we determined that the paper cup can be traded for $0.50 and the creamy, caramel-coloured coffee inside only costs $0.75, you could short the Double-Double on our fabricated THCRE for $1.67 minus the $0.12 trading costs. Then you you're your was to your nearest Tim Hortons coffee shop and buy the coffee and the cup separately over the counter for a total cost of $1.25. You then replace the borrowed Double-Double to flatten your position (offset the long and short) in coffee and keep the $0.30 difference. This results in an 18% gain on two equal investments trading at different prices on two different markets. That's relative value **arbitrage**!

If you've ever comparison-shopped for an investment condo, you've been a relative value investor. You are a relative value investor by evaluating the price, size, renovation costs, financing rates, strata fees, maintenance and potential rental income among multiple properties. Heck, if you've ever bought a home, you did exactly the same thing but without consideration for income, rather, possible resale value. Whether evaluating the benefits of owning one bond over another or one piece of real estate over another, relative value once again is a judgment of comparing two or more investment options. By evaluating the characteristics of an investment compared with its price, a relative value analyst determines the benefits of one investment over another, in order to make excessive profits.

Multi-Strategy

In a world of non-traditional, low-correlated investment portfolios, it makes sense to create the ultimate, low **volatility** portfolio with a combination of these widely varied strategies. A flood of multi-strategy funds came to market for just that reason only to languish on the sidelines due to their inherent fees upon fees upon fees. The singular strategies each bore their own administration and performance fees (see the 2 and 20 section below) but the agencies that combined these mandates in one offering also charged a layer of administration and in some cases, performance fees as well. The low **beta** and low **volatility** objectives were accomplished but the theoretical benefits were raped by the costs and the low correlation among investments produced mediocre returns.

Today, multi-strategies rarely take additional performance fees over the singular offerings and some have rationalized fees to be much smaller as competitors made their mark and diluted the interest of these creatures. **ETFs** that map the performance of various hedge fund strategies became a decent replacement and investors' tolerance for layers of hidden fees and low transparency weeded many of these original cowboys out of popular circulation. Nevertheless, as an investor considering a multi-strategy approach, do the deep dive into the approach and fees alike, to ensure that you're getting what you want. A good way to evaluate these funds is to see what transparency is offered and to measure the **volatility** during various market cycles and events, including the monthly returns reported to watch how it behaves in real life. The main reason these portfolios exist is to provide a low **volatility** solution so consider that in evaluating whether this option is what you're looking for.

> "The Fund of Funds (FOF) business has been in a tough spot for years. There has been a belief that FOFs are a fee on fee structure. While that is true in some instances, it cannot be said of them all. Regardless, it's too late to counter investors' perceptions. I actually don't think that is the number one issue. If performance were great, people would overlook an expensive price tag and see the benefits of owning it. The main issues facing FOFs is that isolated cases of fraud within this arena have tainted the perception of these strategies, coupled with the fact that other products have produced better returns.
>
> Performance has not lived up to the expectations behind the theory. That is not to say that performance has been dreadful, however, the investor looks at the entire universe of options. While FOFs have made some money, many investments have made more!
>
> Most notable are quality, single manager hedge funds. Many of these individual strategies have done well and are straightforward to understand.
>
> Are FOF's useful? Yes, for the right person they sure are, however, there are not enough 'right people' to make the FOF industry grow in a meaningful way, going forward."
>
> —Nigel Stewart, Managing Director, Sales
> Arrow Capital Management Inc.

Alpha and Absolute Returns

Alpha (α) is the indication that the manager matters. The latitude to invest beyond standards in the alternative strategy arena is as far reaching as the imagination of those endowed with the task. These creative executioners' mission is to produce **alpha**. Some managers seek to reduce **volatility** by creating a hedge. Others endeavour to produce **absolute returns**. Regardless of the underlying objective, they all strive to produce **alpha**. Each of them has the goal to prove that the management and strategy matter.

The first letter of the Greek alphabet is widely used to denote a variety of factors in physics, chemistry and mathematics, but the notation applies to investing as a statistical reference in proving a null or alternative hypothesis. Basically, in a set of random return outcomes, does this investment produce higher absolute returns or substantially more stable returns than the market? Alpha denotes that the outperformance is statistically significant, attributed to the manager's ability rather than by accident.

Recall that shorting an investment is when you borrow it, sell it and hope that it drops in price. The profit comes from buying the investment back at a cheaper price in order to return it to the lender. The opposite, buying an investment and hoping that it rises in value is called being **long**.

Why stop at just mattering? The breadth of available strategies, including being **short** in the market, makes it possible for these managers to make a profit regardless of what is happening in the **capital markets**. Recall that shorting an investment is when you borrow it, sell it and hope that it drops in price. The profit comes from buying the investment back at a cheaper price in order to return it to the lender. The opposite, buying an investment and hoping that it rises in value, is called being **long**.

By being short, a manager can make money when the market drops. On a broader scale, a manager can be short an entire stock market by selling short either an **ETF** representing the market or the collection of actual individual stocks that make up the market. You'd do this in order to protect a portfolio or single stock against a drop in the market. It could also be set up in anticipation of a stock market drop to simply make a profit. When the stock market declines 10%, the short investor can make 10%, assuming no transaction costs.

Managers of these strategies never position the portfolio entirely long or short a market, at least not for any length of time, so their returns don't entirely reflect the direction and depth of a change in the market. In the case of a **long-short hedge fund** strategy that holds traditional investments together with short investments, the manager plays both directions of the market at the same time. Obviously, expecting both a rising and a falling market at the same time is counterintuitive, but if you're long and short the right things, you can make a marginal profit based on the quality of the decisions. Pick the good stocks to own and the crappy ones to short. Another way to think of it is to have short positions in place to limit potential losses on the long holdings that you want to grow over time.

Assume you have a handful of specific stocks that you believe will offer excellent returns over the long haul but in the next few months you are anticipating that the stock market will drop in value. You could sell those stocks and buy them back again lower, assuming that they are among the stocks expected to drop among the **aggregate market**. Unfortunately, if you've held them for any length of time, you may be crystallizing a **capital gain** on which you will have to pay taxes. As an alternative, you can short the broad market (with an ETF) while still holding the stocks that you love. I mean *like*, not love. When the market drops, you offset your losses with the short position profits and you don't have to sell the long stock positions that you want to maintain going forward. Presto. You've created a hedge and mitigated the impact of the negative returns of a market drop on your overall portfolio.

This avant-garde investment space has attracted some of the most clever and innovative money managers. The talent. This is also why most of these portfolios are only offered through an **offering memorandum (OM)** to sophisticated investors and why the fees commanded are much higher, primarily driven by the returns of the fund rather than a flat administration and management fee.

It's the ability to produce **alpha returns** and **absolute returns**—not an easy task—that attracts talented and innovative managers to the hedge fund world, as much as the fees do. Traditional long-only mutual fund managers ride the market tides. When the stock prices go up, most of the boats float. When the markets drop, it's accepted that a good **long-only manager** loses less than the market, a strangely worthy pursuit. Those who dare to accept the challenge of earning profitable returns in both up and down markets, demand higher fees.

As with anything having these kinds of expectations, they live and die by the sword. After meeting some of these folks, you'd venture to say that it's the brain challenge as well as the higher fees that attract this clever group of money scientists. If you always produce positive results regardless of market conditions, investors would be tripping over themselves to pay whatever deserved fees were requested. If the results don't warrant the fees, investors wouldn't pay a penny, rounded to a nickel if you're using cash. Investors can lose money all by themselves with no fees, after all. If the market won't bear the higher fees, no one could charge them.

When Low Correlation Means Underperformance

The pitch of a hedge fund invariably stands on the offer to reduce overall **volatility** of a traditional investment portfolio. Mathematically, combining investments that behave differently in various market conditions results in lower total stability. That stands to reason. If some investments are down while others are up, you'll feel less capricious about them in general. If your feet are in the oven and your head is in the fridge, on average you're about right. By the same token, your net return is reduced compared with investing in only those holdings that go up, if only you knew in advance which ones those were.

This happens in real life when a hedge fund strategy no longer works. After time, some strategies are no longer profitable because markets change or there are too many people trying to execute the same trades. Certain market conditions can render strategies useless.

Markowitz's ground breaking theory aside, where mathematical calculations are used to maximum utility of returns for the amount of **volatility**, adding **low correlated** assets makes sense as long as it isn't too much of a drag on a successful performance. It's all fine and dandy to reduce the nausea of the ups and downs but if the performance of that additional investment doesn't add to the bottom line, the reduction in **volatility** is a moot point.

This happens in real life when a hedge fund strategy no longer works or doesn't work for long periods. After time, some strategies are no longer profitable because markets change or there are too many people trying to execute the same trades. Certain market conditions can render strategies useless. For example, a trend-following strategy will lose money at the point when the direction of the trend peaks and reverses. As the name implies, this strategy is profitable by following trends. If the market consistently flows in one direction, it makes money. Whether the direction is up or down is immaterial. This is called **serial autocorrelation** for those of you wanting a new word to impress the Wednesday morning running group.

The trend is your friend, to borrow an axiom. In a market of high **volatility** where trends are not present for long and reversals happen quickly and often, it's tough to be profitable with this strategy. I'm not intentionally picking on trend following because in practice, these strategies follow multiple markets in order to diversify their portfolio. If one market continually faces directional changes, the others may be enjoying long trends of profitability, offsetting the losses of those with reversals.

Nevertheless, all hedge funds need to stay current in their strategy to remain effective. In the event that a strategy is no longer profitable, it's obvious that adding it to a portfolio is pointless. If my other investments are profitable, adding something that loses money may lower **volatility** but at too costly a price.

Buy and hold forever isn't advisable with hedge funds any more than any other investment. Understand how these instruments work, why there are **drawdowns** (high to low drops) and whether the strategy makes sense in current conditions. And don't be afraid to pull the pin.

Offering Memorandum and Accredited Investors

Most alternative strategies are still sold through an offering memorandum (OM) and available only to accredited investors because of the strategies' sophistication. Generally speaking, accredited investors are either registered industry professionals; a person or a couple with assets of more than $1 million; someone whose income is over $200,000 or over $300,000 when combined with that of a spouse; or some other corporate or trust entities managed by accredited individuals. Some provinces make exceptions to the accredited investor restrictions. In British Columbia, anyone can participate in OM investments if they invest $150,000 or if they sign a risk disclosure document. The rationale for allowing investors who commit $150,000 to be exempt from the **accredited investor** restriction is beyond me. I've never understood how those with less than $1 million in assets who commit a decent size cheque to a so-called risky strategy are fine but if you put less in, you're required to sign a waiver. The logic escapes me, but it's the case, nevertheless.

Given that alternative strategies are sophisticated investment pools and carry a wide variety of risks, taking pause is a great idea but it falls short of understanding what you are investing in. Granted that many strategies are beyond most investors, at least your advisor should understand what you are investing in.

Risk disclosures are an interesting beast complete with fur and teeth. First of all, they're exclamatory. Investors who sign them acknowledge they can lose all of their investment. Given that alternative strategies are sophisticated investment pools and carry a wide variety of risks, taking pause is a great idea but it falls short of understanding what you're investing in. Granted that many strategies are beyond most investors, at least your advisor should understand what you're investing in. Perhaps a better route would be for the investment professional to demonstrate an understanding of the strategy, or for the investment firm that he works under to vet the strategy and insist on an accreditation to offer hedge funds. In place of this education and accreditation, the risk disclaimer removes fault to a certain extent, like proclaiming to be over-served at the local tavern.

Beyond the risk disclosures, the documentation is heavy. Paper applications need to be approved internally by the investment firm and sent off to the hedge fund company prior to your investment into the fund. Due to these rigours, alternative strategy providers have been trying to find ways to package their investment pools and offer them under a prospectus format, with the same guidelines as mutual funds. These have much less paperwork but more importantly, the audience to whom the investment can be marketed

*A **prospectus** is a standardized legal document given to every investor providing details about the investment. This is applicable to mutual fund and other similar investments.*

is enhanced in multiples. The greater the number of investors, the more money there is to manage and the more fees there are to charge. A few hedge funds are now offered in Canada this way even though they still represent as sophisticated of trading strategies as their OM counterparts.

Drawdowns

The first time I heard the term drawdown, an alternative strategies sales team used it as a kinder, gentler way to describe a loss. It's funny. When you buy a new car, you suddenly see that model everywhere. Drawdown descriptions began popping up in conversations about other alternative strategies, **new issues**, structured products and even mutual funds.

I like how it sounds, as if it was a necessary, predictable and temporary change in market price. It was introduced as a springboard to sell the timeliness of adding Tupperware-fresh money to an investment that had dropped in value. As the fund price per unit was lower, it was argued that one could take advantage of purchasing more units with less cash. They presented the idea less colloquially, of course, but I hope you see the irony regardless.

A drawdown is a peak-to-trough drop in value of the fund. On a graph, measure the change in value from the highest point of the fund to the lowest in a single direction. The drawdown is the loss in the **net asset value (NAV)** and the value of your investment. Although there are reasons that you may want to add to this portfolio, do not do so based on the sole fact that the unit price is lower. If you're applying **tactical asset allocation**, where you systematically rebalance your portfolio into the variety of investments within your account, go ahead, but only after you assess the reasons for the drop. When it comes to alternative strategies, drawdowns are not the intuitive traditional investment in business and economies, debt or other assets. They aren't supplied with tangible value but focus on a trading strategy and an investment in a pattern of executions. If that strategy has dropped significantly, especially if this is not characteristic of the way the portfolio has behaved in the past, this would be a good time to call your investment professional or the company running the fund to find out what's developing.

A Crowded Trade

With the increased popularity of some strategies, especially successful ones, they can become less effective and even rendering the profitability completely out of them. The more people executing the same methods, the fewer the opportunities and the quicker you have to be. Managers call this a crowded trade like the clearance table at the Coach outlet store. The low-hanging fruit is picked first and the strategy must be modified to identify new opportunities before everyone else does.

by Sofia Sol Strozberg

In **arbitrage**, the margin of profit is conventionally small, the trades are huge in order to extend the small profit and the moment the trade is executed, it doesn't exist anymore. The low priced security is driven up to fair value by the **volume** of purchases and the higher priced security is driven down to fair value by the **volume** of sales or short sales. On top of that, the opportunities disappear as fast as a bucket of Halloween candy in the office lunchroom. With the speed that Internet-information and computer-driven trading strategies fly, chances to identify mispriced securities that haven't been caught by some other bright mind are tougher and tougher.

For managers who have built a reputation on one strategy or another, returns can diminish over time as the fields of their intellectual property are picked. Style shift is inevitable, as taking more risks and moving into new areas to prosper become the next best option. As an investor, it's difficult to ascertain whether a strategy is no longer working or whether it's just a temporary period of underperformance. It isn't in anyone's best interest to capitulate after a short period of underperformance, but common sense prevails. In the same way that **averaging down** is a temptation to avoid, think twice about throwing good money after bad on outlived strategies, an evolution that can be decades or years.

Consider the entire marketplace and the relative value of a strategy going forward. If there are other opportunities that fit your investment objectives better, don't be afraid to veer in a new direction and speak with your portfolio decisions. There are fads in investments as much as there are in fashion but at the end of an investment fad, you stand to lose much more than the cost of a frilly shirt at the back of your closet.

NAV and Rebalancing

One of the benefits that hedge funds introduced to the retail market is the adoption of monthly performance reporting that the investors' demand from these otherwise low transparency investment pools. Since the specifics of each hedge fund strategy is well-guarded, if not entirely secretive, watching how a strategy performs on a monthly basis lends credibility to the manager and his success in real markets. Transparency is a hallmark oxymoron in relation to hedge funds, except when it comes to the monthly return calculations.

The NAV is calculated by valuing the cash and investments held in the fund minus administration and performance fees and dividing the total by the number of units in the fund, not unlike other pooled investments, including mutual funds. The calculation of the assets in some of these alternative strategies is difficult. The investments in which the manager partakes may be extremely illiquid having no market to buy or sell the asset until the maturity date. Real estate in Third World countries or rights to water or land may be difficult to value if they're not regularly traded. The only way to value certain investments is to have a buyer for them. For this and other reasons, many hedge funds restrict investors to limited dates on which the NAV is calculated and the investors are allowed to withdraw their capital.

> *"My advice regarding hedge funds is to pay a little more attention to them and trim them regularly to ensure they stay healthy."*
>
> —Ron Hull, Deputy Fire Chief

Although meant to be a pun, Ron's statement is ironically correct when it comes to hedge funds. It's difficult, however, given the **liquidity** restrictions imposed by many hedge funds, but they are investment pools that you need to keep a close eye on, trimming those that have enjoyed a significant upswing and tactically adding to good strategies when warranted. When the NAV is calculated infrequently, this may be difficult. In extreme cases, some funds may only be sold at a future date; two to five years down the road. Most hedge funds offer an opportunity to withdraw funds every month or every three months. Some value their funds for withdrawals weekly and some even offer daily liquidity. Confirm with the investment provider before placing your funds with them.

2 and 20

The argument that hedge fund managers make for charging two levels of fees is that if you want to attract the brightest minds in the investment business to manage sophisticated strategies, you need to pay them well. While we probably all agree that some of these strategies are complicated as much as they're cleverly devised, the managers who develop and execute them may or may not be deserving of the huge fees that are charged. There are a couple of things to be aware of. Firstly, similar to mutual funds, hedge funds typically charge a management and administration fee of around 2% of the NAV of the fund. Also, there are other costs associated with various strategies that are not included in that figure. For example, if there are forward contracts or swaps used in the strategy, that can cost another 35-50 basis points. Other trading costs may also be omitted from the management expenses. If there is currency hedging, a strategy using derivatives to neutralize the effect currency exchange rates have on the investment, more costs pile up. These fees are also true of mutual funds and investment pools that employ these techniques.

This is a double-edged sword though, as a natural conflict occurs. If the manager is rewarded by higher returns, he may end up taking larger and larger risks in order to produce these returns. Not to say that this is always an issue, but left unchecked, investors should be made aware of the potential issue.

In addition to these come performance fees. This is the juice that the manager squeezes off of the top of the performance before you get your returns. If you have heard the term "2 and 20," this fund is charging at least 2% in management fees (which may or may not include other aforementioned costs) plus 20% of the increase in the performance of the portfolio. To be fair, this is an excellent motivator for the manager to produce higher returns. As an investor, you and the manager are similarly motivated to make the size of the portfolio increase. That means you both want good returns to innately increase the value of the investments he already manages through profitability and to attract new investors. You care more about the former.

Theoretically, however, in the spirit of full disclosure, a natural conflict could occur with performance-based compensation. If a manager is rewarded by higher returns, they may be tempted to take larger risks in order to produce these returns.

High-Water Mark

As motivating as it can be to garner higher fees for increasing the value of a portfolio, the safety net that many hedge funds institute can cause the exact opposite effect in the event of a significant drop in the value of a portfolio.

When the sea rises and the tide shifts inland with the moon, the last wave at the highest level washes across the beach leaving a handprint behind. The last wave marks the highest level at which the water has hung onto the rocks. The high-water mark on an investment portfolio indicates the highest level that the NAV has been for calculation of the performance fee paid to the fund manager. On the 2 and 20 example, 2% represents the administration fees and 20% is the performance fees. In this case, the manager keeps 20% of the rise in value of the portfolio, which then marks the highest level that the portfolio rose due to returns and on which, the manager was paid. A fund that starts at $10/unit and rises to $17/unit pays the manager $1.40 or 20% of the growth. Going forward, the fund has to usurp the $17 value before the 20% fee is calculated since the manager was already paid on the growth up to $17.

That is all well and good, unless something catastrophic happens as we experienced in the 2008 great recession. Imagine that this same fund dropped to a value of $6/unit. The manager has to increase the value of the portfolio by over 183% before she will receive any further performance bonus cheques. Understanding human nature, you can appreciate that her enthusiasm has fallen off the truck and opportunities to manage a different portfolio or to close this portfolio and start over are tempting. In some cases, funds in this situation end up lowering their high-water mark, opting to keep the fund alive.

This is a tricky balance of integrity against pragmatism in a marketplace of stiff competition. You'd feel duped if the high-water mark was dropped, but by the same token, the business reasons are understandable. Regardless, investors always have the option of voting with their investment dollars.

A Unique Case of Fees

In one case, I began investigating a uniquely promising portfolio offering a true hedge to extreme events. It was intriguing in particular because most strategies attempting to hedge a complete portfolio are too expensive to implement, otherwise, everyone would do it. It's a brilliant strategy. When catastrophe strikes, this particular two-tailed strategy pays off handsomely. It protects you by making huge gains when your traditional asset classes drop and injects those profits into your account when you most need it: when investments are cheap. You don't necessarily need to understand how this works but for those who are interested, the structure is to buy near-the-money **put options**, which lock in the value at which you may sell the index. If the index drops significantly, the put is in the money by the amount of your portfolio loss. Your initial investment and the option writing that the strategy executes mostly pay for the costs to buy the rolling **put options**.

The problem is, if no catastrophe happens and markets are calm, the **put options** expire worthless and new ones need to be purchased. Eventually, you have to invest more money as the costs to buy the puts erode your entire investment.

The total strategy can be executed using about 5% of your total investment account, so practically speaking you'll likely lose your 5% over the ensuing years as a trade-off for protecting your entire portfolio, if nothing tragic happens. Suitably impressed by the strategy, I started asking some detailed questions including how the fee structure works. I was told the fees cost 2.65% with a 20% performance fee.

Okay, that sounded conventional for such a unique strategy. Then I thought about it for a moment and needed more clarification. I began to deduce that since you only need about 30% of the **notional value** (the total amount of exposure to the investment) of your portfolio due to the natural **leverage** of options (one option represents 100 shares and the **premium** cost only a few dollars when the amount that it represents could actually be thousands of dollars), your investment in the strategy was only about 3–5% of the value of your whole portfolio. I asked the company if the fees were based on the funds they were managing or on the notional amount that they represented. The second option was the correct answer, which made the fees approximately 17% of the amount handed over to them. Ouch. Those fees may be justified as the portfolio protects your entire account, but it's still a tough pill to swallow. The point is to dive deep into the caverns of any strategy. I'm not saying that exorbitant fees are unjustified, just that you should know what you have and what it's costing you.

Tax

Since hedge funds have quite different mandates, dealing with taxes can be unique to each strategy and each manager. The investment is managed as a pool so it's allowed to offset gains and losses prior to them hitting an investor's tax return. Also, some managers convert income into **capital gains** and **return of capital** by using swaps, a strategy that may no longer be available after the changes to the federal budget first announced in 2013. To oversimplify the term swap, the fund manager agrees with another party to swap the returns produced on the portfolio, with more favourably taxed income from a basket of other securities.

Overall, most hedge funds are managed on a NAV **per share** basis. When the price of these units increases in value from your purchase price, you'll have a **capital gain** when you sell the units.

Liquidity Risk

When markets are robust with many participants exchanging securities at current market prices, the world is very liquid. Buying and selling assets under these conditions are relatively easy. It flows, hence the term 'liquid'. Liquidity risk comes when you want to sell something but you can't because there are no buyers. Further, when everyone else is selling what you have, the price is driven down and you may be forced to take a loss due to liquidity conditions.

On the other side, real estate investors have enjoyed unconventionally high liquidity due to unprecedented demand recently in Canada. Flipping properties like pancakes became a short-term phenomenon. At the peak, investors literally stood in early morning lineups to drop multiple deposits for the right to buy condos still in development. They never expected to complete the contract, rather to sell the contract at a higher value before the condo was delivered.

Real estate is a long-term asset, despite recent memory. The ability to sell real property quickly is good fortune but should not be expected. Each property is unique and generally attracts a specific audience. In other words, there may be a buyer for everything but with the unique specificities of real estate, you have to find that person first.

> "Cash is cash: cash doesn't mean some illiquid money market product (don't chase yield) or some funky Latin American short-term whatchamacallit. Safety and liquidity—cash deposits, CSBs, Canada T-Bills. For example, and speaking from personal experience, if you

are doing a home renovation, have a budget and hold the funds in cash. Much better than taking them out of the market after they've declined by 35%."
—John Stubbs, Director, Wealth Management,
Richardson GMP Ltd.

The 2008 financial downturn was a crisis of liquidity. One investor I met in Alberta was a poster child for what **illiquid markets** can do. This man received a modest fixed pension each month but as a real estate developer, he relied on his investments almost exclusively for business and personal cash flow. He had a traditional investment portfolio, which was heavily **margined** (he borrowed money against his stocks so the cash balance in his account was negative). Dividends from his stocks in that account were used to pay the interest on a bank loan that was **secured** by several real estate development projects he was involved in. It was a little more complicated than that but to clarify it for the illustration, those were the major components.

The value of your stocks must be twice as much as the money you borrow on **margin**. In addition, each of the eligible securities must be $5 per share or more and trade on a recognized stock exchange. In other words, if you borrow $100,000, you should have **margin** eligible securities worth over $200,000. Your total portfolio may have a market value of $300,000 but if you cashed it in and paid off the **margin**, you would walk away with the net $200,000 in your jeans.

During the 2008 financial crisis, not only did stock values get chopped in half but also the share price of many companies, formerly considered to be **blue chip**, dropped below the $5 threshold. For the Alberta investor, the first issue to deal with was to cover the **margin call**. He could do this by depositing cash, if he had it, or by selling enough shares to bring the ratio of securities to debit back in line. Unfortunately, it was unsavoury to sell stocks at decimated prices but he had no other assets to fund the **margin call**. We also helped matters by switching out of stocks whose prices had dropped under $5 per share in favour of those equally beaten up but above that crucial level to qualify as a **marginable** security. The next concern was funding the interest payments to the bank.

At one point of panic, he even tried to wholesale his real estate, to no avail. There were no buyers of anything back then, especially not a half-completed real estate development in the throes of devouring extensive **capital** in order to reach completion and marketability. Fire-selling illiquid assets, when there are no buyers in the first place, is a last resort. Squeezed by carrying costs of the loan, several **margin calls** as the market plunged day after day, no other cash flow and the majority of his assets in illiquid real estate, he felt the squeeze indicative of what makes and breaks millionaires and billionaires overnight.

The story has a relatively happy ending, though. Ultimately, my objective was to mitigate the quantity of shares to be liquidated, eliminating the **margin** borrowed and buying him ten years with cash flow from the remaining securities to fund his bank loans. Whew. I felt that given a ten-year window to complete the real estate development and watch the world right itself, he would have different options. Five years later, the world looked much different for him.

In the heat of the crisis, the profound liquidity issues drove bad as well as good investments to huge losses alike. When markets become illiquid, all investments are subject to massive sales as investors clamour for cash. When two assets are correlated, they behave the same. I have been arguing that hedge funds and alternative strategies have **low correlation** to each other and to traditional asset classes... usually. During times of severe illiquidity, however, all asset classes behave the same. That is to say, when everything is being sold in a market, everything drops in value. Everything is correlated. The only strategies that perform differently in this environment are those that don't own assets at all. Hedge funds and alternative strategies that didn't get caught in the liquidity squeeze or that were short or neutral to the market look like rock stars today.

Counterparty Risk

Every deal has a buyer and a seller. The **counterparty** is the other guy either buying from or selling to you. Most traditional asset classes live in a world where exchanges are accessible and regulated but not all derivatives enjoy this standardized marketplace. The core of counterparty risk is that the fellow on the other end of your transaction will not or cannot hold up his end of the bargain. As a retail investor, this issue comes into play far more often with hedge funds and alternative strategies as asset classes and strategies become more and more complex and unconventional. Keep in mind that both players are counterparties to each other. Both take the risk that their opposing business partner may drop the ball.

> *"Counterparty risk is when you arrive late and all of the bar stools are taken."*
>
> —B. B. Evans

The issues of counterparty risk have never been more newsworthy than after the bankruptcy of Lehman Brothers in 2008. The interrelationship between banks and institutional lenders is a delicately balanced house of cards. The lending between financial institutions is so profoundly integrated that the demise of Lehman Brothers, a mid-sized U.S. bank that didn't even hold customer deposits, was the chink in the armour that brought depositors from around the world to the doorstep of their bank's local branch.

To offset the debt swapped among financial institutions worldwide would assume that each party had the ability and willingness to honour their payments. Only one missing link sends the entire suspension bridge to the waters below. If the butcher cannot pay his employees, the employees cannot buy bread and the baker cannot buy flour. If lender D cannot collect interest and **principle** from C because C cannot collect from B because B cannot collect from A, it doesn't matter that A doesn't have clients of his own. As soon as the world even suspects that one bank may fail, a loss of confidence results in a run on every bank worldwide. It wasn't until intervening governments guaranteed bank deposits, that markets were assured and steadied. Unfortunately, that didn't come before a complete seizure of the international interbank lending systems.

As it applies to hedge funds and **alternative asset classes**, counterparties play an important role in executing trades, many of which are not transacted on controlled exchanges and without guarantees. In recent years, regulators were pushing to create systems for these securities for increased transparency, dependency and liquidity to these trades.

Manager Risk

Even great managers make mistakes. Manager risk could be split into human risk, strategy execution risk and the risk of a manager leaving. Hedge funds and **alternative strategies** are highly specialized. Nowhere else is manager risk a bigger issue than in a specialized investment strategy. The ability of another manager to successfully take over a strategy is far lower, the more unique a strategy becomes. Also, the more complicated a strategy is to execute, the higher the possibility that human risk will come into play.

Just be aware that the risks exist when it comes to these highly focused investments.

Chapter 5

Be Careful With Mutual Funds and Other Pooled Products

You cannot prevent the birds of sorrow from flying over your head, but you can prevent them from building nests in your hair.
—Chinese Proverb

Jump in the Pool

Pooled investments represent the entire spectrum of the good, the bad and the ugly. Unfortunately, many investors and even investment professionals are marketed into thinking that a mutual fund is a mutual fund is a mutual fund and past performance is a good approximation of the merits of a new investment. As Dirty Harry said, "I know what you're thinking: Did he fire six shots or only five? Well, to tell you the truth, in all this excitement, I've kinda lost track myself. But being this is a .44 Magnum, the most powerful handgun in the world and would blow your head clean off, you've got to ask yourself one question: 'Do I feel lucky?' Well, do you punk?"

There are more mutual funds than there are stocks in Canada. That number doesn't even include **ETFs**, structured products or **Separately Managed Accounts (SMAs)**. So where do you start? What do you look for? Are pooled products right for you? Do you feel lucky? Well, do ya?

Mutual Funds

In 1932, the first Canadian mutual fund, the Canadian Investment Fund Ltd., was formed. According to the Investment Funds Institute of Canada (IFIC) the fund held assets of $51 million in 1951. In 1996, the name of the fund was changed to Spectrum United Canadian Investment Fund. By the end of August 2002, the mutual fund had morphed into the CI Canadian Investment Fund having $2.6 billion of assets under management. Today, the fund is offered on a **Front End (FE)**, **Deferred Sales Charge (DSC)**, **Low Sales Charge (LSC)** and **Fee Class** basis.

To most Canadian investors, mutual funds hit the retail investment scene in the early 1990s when the major Canadian banks expanded their offering from one or two **equity funds** to a whole lineup of options. Prior to that, mutual funds were relatively exclusive and unheard of by the general public. The fees were substantially higher then, too. Today fees still range from 1–3.5% or so.

Mutual funds are the kibbutzim of investment portfolios. If you've visited Israel, you already know that the kibbutz is an agricultural based social community. Every member assumes a role in the community and all share in the collective production of the group. Participants in a mutual fund co-mingle assets in a single mandate. The PM of the fund invests the money by purchasing a select group of stocks, bonds or both, as outlined by the fund's **prospectus**. A Canadian Equity Fund is restricted to owning Canadian stocks in the portfolio. A **Bond Fund** is restricted to investing in Canadian bonds. A Canadian **Balanced Fund** can hold a combination of stocks and bonds. You get the idea. Each investor owns an interest in the aggregate pool of investments, rather than a specific number of each of the stocks or bonds in the portfolio. Each investor shares mutually in the income and growth of the total portfolio.

Corporate Funds are a class of shares operated under one corporation with a variety of fund strategies. Since the funds operate under one tax structure, investors can move between the strategies, within the same share class and not trigger a taxable event by the transaction.

Most mutual funds calculate the value of each unit, the NAV, at the end of each day that the market is open and securities are traded. The NAV is determined by adding the values of all of the securities in the pool, minus the management fees and expenses, then dividing by the total number of units owned among investors. Once the trading day is over and the NAV has been calculated, new investors can buy new units and existing investors can redeem the units they own. Usually the NAV is calculated each day, however, some funds do so less frequently, therefore having fewer dates to get in and out of the investment.

There are two types of mutual funds, **Corporate Funds** and **Trusts**, one of which has certain tax advantages. When a mutual fund trust investor sells her units of one fund to invest in another, say to switch from a bond strategy to an equity strategy, she must claim the **capital gain** on the growth in the investment value. By comparison, **Corporate Funds** are mutual fund shares, each offering different investment strategies, operated under one corporation. Since the funds operate under one tax structure, investors can move between the strategies, within the same corporation, and not trigger a taxable event by the transaction. You could invest in a Canadian Equity Fund at $6700 and switch into an International Equity Fund when your investment value is $7000, you would normally be responsible for a $300 **capital gain** when you redeem the units. However, if you invest in a **Corporate Fund** and switch to another strategy within that corporate class grouping, you will have no deemed disposition and no capital gain to claim.

In the case of the ugly sister, your second investment in a traditional mutual fund trust would have an **ACB** of $7000 since you already claimed your $300 gain when you sold the investment in the first fund. In the **Corporate Fund** investment, your cost base is still $6700 since you stayed within the corporation. You must claim the **capital gain** when you eventually redeem the investment, deferring taxes that would have otherwise been owed. A tax dollar paid today is far more expensive than one paid in future dollars, making the tax payment deferral a clear advantage. With inflation, money becomes less valuable over time because the cost of goods increases.

A tax dollar paid today is far more expensive than one paid in future dollars. With inflation, money becomes less valuable over time because the cost of goods increases.

On top of that, **Corporate Funds** can offset pending **capital** gains and losses among their family of funds within the corporation. The managers can offset gains in one investment with **capital losses** realized on a totally different fund within the group. Share the wealth and the savings. Tax distributions aren't an increase in value but merely taxes owed. If you can avoid or delay claiming a **capital gain**, that's smart!

Mutual fund companies issue and redeem shares at the request of investors. There is no cap on how many units the fund will issue, unless the mutual fund company decides to limit its units. Usually, the mutual fund manager limits new deposits when it becomes too popular and he cannot find enough feasible investment opportunities with the amassing assets he already has to manage. This could transpire when the market size is limited and there are not enough strategic options available. Also, the manager is constrained by the fund's directives outlined in the **prospectus**, which may be limiting.

The Canadian stock exchange is inadequate for PMs who control mutual funds with several hundreds of millions or billions of dollars. The **S&P/TSX** is only 300 stock names and you can imagine that it would be difficult to be strategic if you are restricted to only owning 10% of any one company, to find enough companies to invest in. That is one of the reasons that large mutual funds have a difficult time outperforming the market index in small markets.

Liquidity is one of the most prevalent issues with any large mutual fund. If a fund manager cannot find product to buy, it's an issue. Not being able to sell a position when there are limited buyers to take it off their hands or when the fund holds too much of a single security, is an even bigger issue.

You knew that at some point you'd have to get your calculator out. To bore you with the details, here is how your investment is calculated. The number of units and partial units you purchase is merely a function of how much you wish to invest. If a fund has a NAV of $9.34 per unit and you invest $10,000, you buy 1070.66 units. When the PM receives your $10,000, he buys the best stocks or bonds available but you participate with the other investors in your proportion of the whole portfolio.

Many mutual funds offer a variety of series, each of which charges fees differently so that they can be used in various types of accounts. The mutual fund carries the same investments, but the way the fees are charged differs. Below is a chart listing the differences between the class series.

Mutual Fund Fee Structures

Class	Description	Initial or Deferred Fees (in addition to ongoing management fees, administration costs or MER)	Advisor Compensation
A	Front End (FE)	Negotiated amount up front, usually 0–5%	The negotiated initial fee plus 1% trailer paid annually
B	Deferred Sales Charge (DSC)	No initial commission but a declining redemption fee over 5–7 years	5% up front plus 0.5% trailer paid annually
C	**Low Load** or **Level Load** (LL)	0-2% initial fee and declining redemption fee over 1–3 years	The negotiated initial fee plus 1% trailer paid annually
F	Fee-Based Account Purchase	Slightly lower MER than A, B or C	None, as the fees are generated by the account rather than the fund directly
G	Institutional Class	Lower MER than all other classes based on minimum investment amounts from $1M to $5M	Negotiable

Mutual funds in general carry a list of pros and cons. You can invest an entire portfolio in mutual funds, but just because you can, doesn't mean that you should. In the landscape of investment options, they play an important role but their benefits are specific to certain situations. Generally speaking, these funds provide diversification and easy access to professionally managed solutions for investors who have limited amounts of **capital** to invest. If you have $10,000 or less, you can't practically buy more than a couple of stocks at a time. The commissions are too prohibitive. If you purchase 10 different stock positions totalling $1000 for each position, paying $125 per trade, your investments would have to rise by 12.5% just to break even! Investing in a well-managed mutual fund is one-stop shopping. Investors gain exposure to 100 or more actively managed individual stocks or bonds with one transaction. In addition, mutual funds offer exposure to markets that are difficult to access otherwise and the fact that they're professionally managed provides a hands-off strategy, appealing to many investors busy with families, careers and other pleasurable pursuits.

Mutual funds are also flexible enough to handle small monthly contributions. If you're adding to your investment account on a regular basis - every payday, for example - you could easily add the funds automatically to a mutual fund.

There are problems, however. Lack of transparency, high fees and inherent **capital** gains issues are important concerns. As an investor with larger portfolios to manage and the ability to access other investment options, awareness of these faults is valuable in critically evaluating your opportunities.

Transparency is a major issue. Whether you've been accused of being a control freak or not, everyone wants to know what they're invested in. Even if you don't understand every detail, you want to know where your money is and what it's doing. Despite being an investment professional, I cannot tell you what securities are held in a mutual fund until the fund company reports its results and holdings at the end of the month or quarter. Even then, most fund companies only publish the top 10 or 25 positions held in the portfolio (on their proprietary website for those interested in digging it up). If you want more detail than that, you'll need to request that information from the fund company's head office. As you probably already know, the information provided on your account statement is limited to some abbreviated version of what the fund is called, the current NAV of the fund and an acronym indicating the fee structure (DSC, LL or FE) that you purchased.

Fees, conveniently a four-letter word, are another issue. I'll get into the various fee structures available with mutual funds, but regardless of which structure you buy, management fees are often higher in mutual funds than many contemporary investment options, including other professionally managed portfolios and ETFs. Also, tax issues arise when you invest in mutual funds within a taxable account. The inherent **capital gains** tax issues are discussed later in this chapter.

To find out specifics on any mutual fund, visit the fund company's corporate website as a useful source. You'll typically find the **prospectus**, historic returns of the fund, the fund objectives and mandate, as well as information on the managers themselves. For standardized analysis of mutual funds, including performance rankings among similar funds, you may enjoy digging through third party sites such as www.fundlibrary.com or www.theglobeandmail.com/globe-investor/funds-and-etfs/funds/ (or Google "globe investor funds").

SMAs

If mutual funds are kibbutzim, **SMAs** are Freehold Land Stratas. They operate much like a gated community. While homeowners own their real estate directly, all of the property owners collectively contribute strata fees to the management company responsible for making day-to-day operational decisions regarding common areas, landscaping and general management. Similarly, with an SMA, investment participants own stocks and bonds directly, but there is a PM in place making the strategic decisions to buy, sell, reallocate **capital** and steer the overall direction of the money.

*The role of the local office is to outline an **IPS**, determine your **asset allocation** among various mandates, negotiate fees charged and select the investment mandates that are appropriate for you. The local office services your account, addressing questions and generally taking care of you personally.*

Typically, investment firms offering **Separately Managed Accounts (SMAs)** act as an intermediary between the client and the PM, as opposed to managing the investments directly. Even when the firm offers in-house management for some of the portfolio mandates, most of the mandates are outsourced to other professional asset managers. For example, ABC bank may have an SMA program with 13 portfolio options managed by third party investment firms and 5 managers who work directly for the bank.

Practically speaking, the SMA platform doesn't vary significantly from one investment firm to another. Most offer a collection of managers, the majority of whom appear on SMA platforms across the board. In some cases, exclusive access to an asset manger or specific strategy is held by only one firm, but more likely the reason you will choose to deal with one firm over another is the relationship and trust you garner with the contacts you have locally or because of your existing banking relationship with the firm's parent bank.

As a consumer, a single SMA strategy, or several, can be added to any of your investment accounts. Rather than dealing directly with the people managing the money, you build a relationship with an IA or PM at your neighbourhood office. To save confusion, PM in this case refers to the local representative.

Each SMA investment strategy typically requires a minimum of $100,000. For smaller portfolios, you can complement one SMA strategy with a handpicked selection of bonds or ETFs managed directly by your local IA. With a larger investment, you may decide to diversify your portfolio among various SMA mandates (a stock portfolio, bond portfolio or a combined portfolio) with different **investment styles** or select only one style that you believe in.

*Style diversification was popularized in the late '90s when investment heat maps were used in marketing SMA strategies. The theory was that it was impossible to know which investment would outperform the other so diversification among momentum, value, growth and **small cap**, as well as geographic regions and different types of assets, would give you a smoother investment ride.*

Selecting the right strategies to hold is an art in itself. In portfolios that invest in stocks alone, there are several options. Mixing **investment styles**, such as **growth**, **momentum** or **value strategies**, or adding specific regional exposure and unique themes to your overall portfolio, can offer diversification even within the sole asset class of equities, when the strategies have low correlation to each other. If all investments went up, that would be great, but generally speaking, combining various investments evens out your **volatility** by having a bit of zig and a bit of zag in the same portfolio. That being said, there is nothing wrong with holding one investment style or strategy that you believe in, even if it's invested in only one asset class.

Deep value investment strategies outperform **growth and momentum strategies** in different market conditions, and vice versa. The first invests in securities that are severely underpriced by the market and the latter invests in those that have prices outpacing a rising market. Style diversification was popularized in the late '90s when investment heat maps were used in marketing SMA strategies. The theory was that it was impossible to know what investment would outperform the other so diversification among momentum, value, growth and **small cap**, as well as geographic regions and different types of assets, would give you a smoother investment ride.

That theory held true until all asset classes dropped simultaneously during the financial crisis of 2008.

The key role of the local investment representative (IA or PM) is to bring in new clients and to develop and manage the investment firm's relationship with you. The real advantage of this personal contact is that you benefit from a tailored set of services. She may not manage your assets directly but by knowing you individually, she is equipped to draw up your IPS, select the appropriate investment styles and mandates, address your cash flow needs, advise you on financial decisions, allocate different asset classes among your taxable and tax-sheltered accounts, rebalance your **asset allocation** and often offer financial planning services. This is also the person that will negotiate the investment management fees you pay, within parameters set out by the firm.

Low correlation is where investments behave differently during normal circumstances. One goes up when the other goes down. Of course, if they all went up, that would be great, but having zig and zag in the same portfolio evens out the volatility.

The local IA will also tout herself as integral for another reason: to act as the police or watchdog over the investment managers. She will hire or fire them if they deviate from their investment mandate or have prolonged underperformance. In practice, however, this almost never happens. Moreover, it may be poorly advised to ditch a manager or investment after a cyclical period of lagging performance. In today's market, professional money managers are zealously scrutinized for following their methodology and investment discipline, so much so that it's unlikely for major portfolios to stray from the shackles of their **prospectus** and investment style. With that in mind, historic data illustrates that investment sectors and management styles perform differently under various market conditions and over different parts of the economic cycle. Rarely does one style or asset class outperform others for long. It's shortsighted to replace an underperforming mandate with one that performed well during the last part of an economic cycle. To sell a good manager's portfolio after a lagging performance means that you're likely going to miss his outperformance.

A sell-low-buy-high approach won't make you rich.

ETFs vs. ETNs

Most investors have heard of **exchange traded funds (ETFs)**. Some have heard of **exchange-traded notes (ETNs)**. Many do not know the difference and get caught with their proverbial pants down. Not proverbial pants but their pants down proverbially speaking. Nevermind.

What you need to know is that there are important differences between the two. ETFs are better for some types of exposure and ETNs for others. Before we jump in the drivers seat, let's pull up the car and peak under the hood.

The price of the ETF and ETN units represents the aggregate price change of the particular market that they follow. They're both designed to replicate the performance of a commodity, such as oil or gold; a sector, including transportation or agriculture; or an entire index, like Japan or Canada or the emerging markets. It can be as broad as an entire stock exchange, as unique as a particular group of hedge funds or as specific as a single commodity, such as West Texas Oil futures. For example, the **S&P/TSX** index tracks the collective market values of the 300 largest publicly traded companies in Canada. Although the **S&P/TSX** is reported daily, the only way you could invest in it would be to separately buy the proportionate number of shares of each of the 300 companies. A daunting and expensive task. Moreover, theoretical indexes, such as the **DEX** broad bond index, are based on mathematical calculations rather than actual securities, making them impossible to invest in.

The impracticality or impossibility of accessing these markets all changed when large investment firms introduced units to reproduce them. With their purchasing power and **volumes**, it became feasible to execute the large number of trades required to replicate difficult markets and to manufacture exposure to notional ones using other securities. Today, investment firms are able to approximate the returns of theoretical indexes like the **DEX**.

When offering an ETF, the institution goes to the market to purchase the actual underlying investment pools to produce the desired results. Conversely, with ETNs, the institution offers an obligation to pay the equivalent return rather than owning the assets directly. It facilitates meeting this promise with the use of derivatives such as **options** and swaps. In both cases, investors now have the ability to participate in many formerly unreachable markets with one easy transaction.

ETF or ETN investing is somewhere between investing in stocks and mutual funds. Both are exchange-traded, similar to publicly listed stocks, yet the issuing investment firm offers the units continuously, similar to a mutual fund. Due to this continuous offering of units, its market price is not driven by supply and demand. The ETF's price on the market reflects the NAV of the underlying index while the ETN's price reflects the note's value in relation to the performance of the underlying investment. The only time this is not true is under extreme conditions of illiquidity, when investments cannot be sold at all. But then again, in those situations, worrying about your ETF or ETNs is like worrying about your umbrella when the river banks are spilling over.

Options *are a derivative contract that gives the owner the right to buy or sell an underlying security at a set price, on or before a certain date.*

While the values of the ETFs and ETNs are derived from the underlying investment, the units trade on the market with a small spread between the buy and sell trading prices. It costs a few cents more to buy a unit than it does to sell it. Theoretically, both should be the same since they reflect the NAV of the underlying portfolio, yet that is rarely the case. Nevertheless, this small disadvantage is more than offset by the benefit of trading the units all day long during market hours. In comparison, mutual funds can only be bought or redeemed after the market is closed and the mutual fund company calculates the NAV. Given this, ETFs and ETNs are more nimble for those who wish to buy and sell intraday (during trading hours).

Of note, any securities traded on an exchange are subject to commissions unless the transactions are executed in an account that pays annual fees instead. Mutual funds may or may not have fees associated with buying or selling them, which is covered in the section about them above.

Exchange Traded Funds

As mentioned earlier, ETF providers directly purchase the underlying basket of investments, or a close proximity to it, in order to produce the investment's return. ETFs provide investors with a one-trade opportunity to gain exposure to a complicated investment strategy for a very low management fee and small trading commission. Whether the investment firm replicates the return exactly depends on how closely the portfolio mirrors the actual index or commodity.

> **Tracking error** is the difference between an ETF's performance and the returns of the investments it endeavours to replicate. Fees, trading costs and timing are the most obvious culprits, but some investments, such as commodities, may not be traded during the same hours as the ETF.

Try as you may, it's impossible to track anything exactly. **Tracking error** is the difference between an ETF's performance and the returns of the investments it endeavours to replicate. Fees, trading costs and timing are the most obvious culprits, but some investments, such as commodities, may not be traded during the same market hours as the exchange the ETF is listed on. Ideally, if you're investing in a commodity ETF, the best strategy is to trade the units during times when both the ETF and the underlying commodity are traded.

Block trades, where a large quantity of a particular security is executed for multiple accounts at once, are another anomaly. If you plan to either buy or sell a large quantity of a particular ETF, it's best to call the issuing investment firm to tell them what, when and the quantity of the ETF you're planning to trade to ensure that they're prepared to absorb the trade on the market and liquidity is adequate. Investment firms issue their ETFs to designated brokers who invest in the underlying securities and swap the assets for the ETF units. The designated brokers then offer the units on the **secondary market** (stock exchange) to investors who trade them. It's the designated brokers who provide liquidity to the ETFs so that investors can buy and sell as many units as necessary. This also results in the units closely mirroring the NAV of the underlying investment. The only real trouble comes when they're unable to buy or sell any of the securities that make up the ETF.

ETFs are ideal when they offer good representation of the investment you're interested in. If the securities are freely available, ETFs are a good proxy for that portfolio, as long as the fees are low and the **tracking error** is kept to a minimum. Since they represent an interest in a real pool of assets, the issuer is less important than the liquidity of the underlying securities. Not unimportant, but less. The designated broker ties these risks to the saleability of the underlying investments. This is a substantially different risk than the ETF issuer's ability to make payments, as you'll discover is an issue with ETNs.

More recently, ETFs have expanded the scope of options that they replicate. Not only can you invest in market indexes and commodities, but you can also participate in actively managed portfolios. Regardless of the underlying investment strategy, all ETFs operate in the same fashion.

> *"The bifurcation of ETFs will continue in Canada between managed and index replicating options. Not only can you have high transparency but you can also buy and sell them during the trading day, which is a huge advantage. We will continue to see more and more wrap program ETFs available from prominent money managers. As a 'one ticket' solution, it will save trading costs for smaller investment accounts."*
> —J.P. Lavoie, Vice President Sales, First Asset

Exchange Traded Notes

An exchange-traded note (ETN) is a simple promise to pay an amount according to the performance of something else. Straightforward, right? Both ETFs and ETNs offer returns based on some other investment. Although they're meant to produce essentially the same result, they each have small iniquities that may impact your investment outcome.

ETNs offer superior access to complicated and theoretical strategies due to the fact that they don't actually buy the investment itself to reproduce the returns. Due to this, ETNs are the preferred access point for exposure to sophisticated strategies and inaccessible markets. Moreover, the costs of computer-generated and highly active trading strategies are prohibitive for an ETF. Sometimes ETNs avoid this entirely. By satisfying their obligation under a contracted formula, ETNs can replicate sophisticated hedge fund strategies, computer-based trend-following strategies, commodities and **volatility** exposure that are not easily tracked by an ETF.

Furthermore, ETNs avoid the issues of **tracking error**. As a simple contractual obligation to pay a return imitating the performance of the underlying investment, tracking error becomes immaterial. The small mis-pricing that an ETF is subject to due to minuscule timing errors, transaction costs and fees, simply doesn't exist for an ETN.

Also, the contractual structure of ETNs is more tax efficient than their counterparts. For example, with a U.S. Master Limited Partnership (MLP), ETNs do not incur double taxation. MLPs are structures similar to the oil and gas trust units formerly prolific in the Canadian market prior to tax changes notoriously made on Halloween 2006. The MLPs distribute high cash flows from commodity-based producers in the U.S., which can result in higher taxation for Canadian investors if MLPs are purchased directly. Much of the punitive taxation is avoided through the use of an ETN as the income is based on a contractual obligation rather than the commodity-based cash flow.

Nothing is perfect, though. With any contract to pay comes credit risk. ETN investors own a debt obligation—a loan of sorts—from the company supplying the strategy. That means the credit quality of the issuer and its ability to pay you back is paramount. There is no sense in making a great investment call on a profitable strategy if the issuer can't return your cash or the profit due. Credit quality and default risk are measured for ETN issuers the same way as for corporate bonds.

There is no sense in making a great investment call on a profitable strategy if the issuer can't return your cash or the profit due.

In summary, ETNs are clearly the winner in situations where the investment you'd like to imitate is theoretical or impractical to invest in. Also, ETNs are slick with handling tax issues, but be careful about accepting the risk of issuer default. You are only trading the liquidity risk of the underlying investment for the singular risk of the group providing the ETN. To mitigate credit risks, ETFs are the best choice.

Either way, both ETFs and ETNs offer excellent access to a variety of markets. In the early part of this century, ETFs and ETNs gained popularity primarily for the low management fees, ease of use and immediate diversification. The burgeoning interest spurred demand for increasingly specialized and narrowly focused mandates. Where money flows, investment managers follow. Even at low marginal fees, they're happy to collect small individual amounts if the scale and **volumes** warrant.

Today, both ETFs and ETNs are offered by a growing number of investment firms and are swallowing a big slice of the mutual fund market pie. Investors and investment professionals alike have adopted the trend for the low management fees and the ingenious selection of offerings. Now, between ETFs and ETNs, a wide range of commodities, industries, specialized investment styles, hedge funds, entire markets and broad asset classes are easily accessible investment options.

Structured Notes

Combining unlikely ingredients can sometimes result in unexpected and useful applications. When fluorosurfactant, the persistent environmental contaminant perfluorooctanoic acid, is placed in an emulsion polymerization process to make the solid, polytetrafluroethylene (PTFE), and it's expanded through heat, it transforms into a stretchy, microporous structure that revolutionized everything from gaskets to medical devices and fabric. In 1969, the beginnings of Gore-Tex were born.

Structured notes are manufactured investments with a bunch of ingredients including how the investment pays off, its maturity date and the fees you'll pay. Every note created is as different as offspring. Each note is designed to meet a specific need but due to this individuality, ask the mad-scientist about it before you take it home.

Equity-linked deposits and **Principle Protected Notes (PPN)** gained popularity in the 90's by an aging demographic vigorously pursuing anything with high distributable income, especially when it came labelled with the word, "guaranteed." What we found out over wild market rides was that these early versions are not the riskless securities that they were touted to be. Linked notes that guarantee your **principle** investment and promise returns that follow some volatile investment lock-step (such as the **stock market index**), marketed themselves as providing a risk-free way to get exposure without the risks.

Fortunately or unfortunately, your mother was right: when something sounds too good to be true, it usually is. Guarantees don't come for free. What investors didn't realize was that they were holding a three to seven-year bond backing their guaranteed capital, together with a highly **leveraged** derivative to replicate the market's return. Most of their money was invested in the **discounted** bond that matured at par to guarantee the principal of the note. After the fees were paid to the firm that built this vehicle and the bonds were purchased, not much money was left over to invest. This is especially true when interest rates are low and the money needed for the guarantee is high. The remaining sliver must be highly **leveraged** in order to replicate the promised return.

In the event of high **volatility**, the **leveraged** part of the portfolio is dramatically affected and in extreme cases, the derivatives literally become worthless. When this happens, all you're left with a **strip bond** yielding nothing but the low interest rate returns originally meant to deliver your guarantee at maturity. Abracadabra and all of the expected income or growth disappears with a poof of smoke for effect.

Other strategies followed with slightly different methods in an attempt to deal with the low interest rate environment and the high cost of the bonds locking in the guarantee. These work on a system where the amount of cash in the note increases or decreases depending on the market value and **volatility** of the invested components. As the value of the investments drop, a formula increases the amount of cash on hand to satisfy the guarantee. Without actually having to buy the bond until it was necessary, the portfolio retains more investment flexibility. Unfortunately, these are subject to a similar fate of the former version when higher levels of **volatility** creep in. Ultimately, the objectives are not met and the investor is left with no monthly payments, no inflation protection and no growth. The sock drawer solution.

The manufacturers went back to the drafting table. Structured product developers were forced to be more creative and it's this creativity that is increasing the complexity of structured notes today. Hand in hand with increased complexity comes the need to be vigilant. As an investor, you need to understand what you own.

Today, structured products are more realistic and interesting but their sophistication introduces concepts that you may or may not be comfortable with. By using a combination of **options** and other derivatives, manufacturers are able to create solutions to suit a wide range of investment views. Unfortunately, with language like, "*5% participation in the additional performance of the reference index over the indicated coupon rate for that valuation date,*" or "*If the asset return is negative and the final level of the reference asset is less than the barrier level on the final valuation date, the maturity payment amount will equal the actual index* return (which will be negative by the decline in the reference asset)" many investors shy away from these structures. In some cases, unnecessarily so. By the way, both of those quotes are from actual, current notes available.

Although these are more complicated than their predecessors, the language is much more moderate and descriptive (for marketing, of course). Thankfully, we are rarely looking at unilateral guarantees that don't guarantee much anymore, and now the focus is on a practical set of inputs.

These new-age notes are a potpourri of strategies in one jar. Imagine that you are seeking a medium-term investment, you have a neutral or slightly bullish view of the price of West Texas Crude oil, you want to enhance the returns of oil over the period of the note yet you also want to protect yourself in case oil drops by no more than 20%. Easy! This can built! Assuming that the price of oil increases marginally over the term of the note, your investment will pay off in multiples of that increase. If the price of oil drops within the barrier protection (20%) you won't lose any money either.

There is a price to pay though. This scenario must cap the total increase on the investment. That's the trade off. Also, if the price of oil drops below your 20% safety zone, you will lose as much money as if you owned oil directly. It's safe to say, the terms of these notes are exact and an excellent way to find specific exposure to unique scenarios.

> "The low interest rate environment that has prevailed for years now means that investors need to look elsewhere for returns. By utilizing these alternative investment solutions, they can do so without jeopardizing their principal and mitigate the risk of market volatility."
> —Tasha Konkin, Vice President Financial Products,
> Bank of Montreal

Notes can be created for exposure to a long or short interest in a commodity, index, currency, a single stock or basket of stocks. You can enhance your upside return if you think the underlying investment will be stagnant. Also, you can give yourself protection against a potential decline in market value entirely or for a specific drop zone. By using **options** to manage the investment side of the note, there really is no limit to the possibilities and combinations of return outcomes that can be developed. With a minimum of $5 million commitment, an individual

PM can request that a note be completely tailored to meet explicit parameters. For someone with a particular investment stance, these cleverly designed tools are built to suit.

The notes are offered in the same way as a new issue, with fees embedded in the original price to pay for manufacturing them. In addition, the notes carry ongoing management fees that pay a **trailing commission** to the IA who maintains your account. Certain notes, however, are created to accommodate fee-based portfolios, eliminating those ongoing **trailers**.

Investment firms that sell these products also provide **after-market liquidity**, meaning that they'll buy the shares back from you if you need to sell them. The difference between the NAV of the investment and the amount (**bid**) offered by the firms to take it off your hands is called the spread and acts ostensibly as a convenience fee. Intuitively, you realize that the difference is never in your favour so if you invest in these structures, generally plan to stick with them until the maturity date unless there are tax reasons to abort the position prematurely. Regardless, it's nice to know there's an escape-pod if you need one.

Strategy

All of these pooled options can be combined into one account if you so wish, but don't get too complicated. Most ETF, ETN and structured notes are **passive investments** meaning that once the positions are established, there isn't anyone at the helm changing investment decisions. Despite that, you can manage how much of any of them that you own at any given time. Other portfolios, such as mutual funds and SMAs, are actively managed for the duration. Similarly, you can limit or expand the quantity of these portfolios as you see fit over time.

Contango

Contango is one of those words that you come across in your life that is entirely fun, mostly misunderstood and impressively playful to say, especially at a cocktail party. Despite the specific reference, it describes a situation that is becoming increasingly important now that ETFs are part of the regular investment landscape. The word isn't recognized by spellcheckers, at least not on my desktop computer, but I promise it's a real word.

Imagine that you produce natural gas. Once it's out of the ground, someone may buy it from you straight away. That's called the **spot price**. Think of it as selling the gas on the spot. Not to trivialize this, but you'll never forget the term if I compare it to when your mother emphatically ordered you to do something immediately. "Clean up your bedroom, on the spot."

Funds from the matured contract are then used to buy the new future contract, which is more expensive. This is where the natural erosion of capital happens, as the value of the contracts decreases as time passes.

Play along and imagine that you have extra gas that you'll need to store until more demand generates. Storage costs can be hefty depending on location, time, existing storage utilization and accessibility. It would make sense that natural gas prices under this scenario are higher in the future than the **spot prices** are today. There are more inputs than storage and expected sale prices that drive future costs but the future price is logically going to be higher than the current price per barrel, under normal conditions.

Investors, speculators and commodity business managers can lock in future prices, including the cost for storage and expected commodity price increases in the short term, by buying **futures contracts**. Remember that ETFs attempt to replicate the change in the value of a commodity or market. If an ETF is replicating a commodity by investing in **futures contracts**, they could buy the 3-month future contract, which matures at the **spot price**. Like counting down to Christmas, the contract maturity dates roll closer to today and the future and **spot prices** converges. Funds from the matured contract are then used to buy the new future contract, which is more expensive due to the other considerations that go along with dealing with the physical commodity. This is where the natural erosion of **capital** happens, as the value of the contracts decreases as time passes.

As a side interest, the opposite of **contango** is **backwardation**. By definition, **backwardation** is when the contracts to buy a commodity in the future are less than the spot or present value of the commodity. This happens when the market anticipates a drop in the price of the commodity so the future price reflects that. Another fun word to throw around between martinis.

Short the Short VIXY

I had a great conversation with some speculative traders at a trade show in Chicago in 2010. I was particularly interested in the nuances between the numbers of ETFs that replicate different aspects of the **volatility index (VIX)**. The **VIX** itself is a measure of **volatility** in the market derived from the price S&P500 option **premiums** using the Black-Scholes model. You don't need to know that, but I thought I'd throw it in for entertainment. Remember, there's no exam at the end of this chapter.

Stick with me. To keep it simple, the price you pay to buy an **options contract** is determined by three easy to understand ideas:

1. The **intrinsic value** of the **options contract**. If you own an **options contract** and you can make money by executing it right now, that's the intrinsic value.
2. The length of time (**time value**) until the **options contract** expires. The more time there is, the greater the random chance is that the **options contract** will be profitable.
3. The **volatility** of the security that the **options contract** covers. The more the price of the underlying security moves around, the greater the statistical chance that the **options contract** may be profitable.

The total amount you pay for an **options contract** (the **premium** or sticker price) is the total of these three items, each of which can be mathematically separated from the others. It's the third variable that the **VIX** follows. More specifically, it's the **volatility** on the S&P 500 **options contract,** used for its broad representation of the U.S. stock market. When the **VIX** rises, the 500 largest publicly traded stocks in the U.S. have risen and fallen more voraciously. When the **VIX** drops, these companies' prices are more stable.

There are a bunch of ETFs that represent different variations of the **VIX**. One imitates the short-term **VIX** futures. Another gives investors exposure to the mid-term **VIX** futures. Certain ETF versions provide twice the exposure to the short-term **VIX** futures and even inverse or short the short-term **VIX** futures! So, when you come across the mathematical rebalancing issues with inverse ETFs, two times **leveraged** exposure ETFs and those who roll futures in **contango**, you'll realize that holding any of these investments long-term will be a disaster. They're intended for extremely short-term trading. It isn't even recommended to hold these positions overnight and it isn't recommended for almost everyone with an ulcer or eyelashes.

Beyond that, bantering about the implications of being long the short VIX and short the medium-term long **VIX** is great fun for an esoteric group of theorists. Add a bit of gin and bitters and you'd have a party!

Fees

Building wealth is a two-pronged strategy: making money and keeping money. Making money may be tricky, but keeping more of it in your pocket is far easier than you think. A wealthy friend once said, "You won't be rich for long if you keep spending it."

Control what you can. You'll never be able to accurately project investment returns on stocks, bonds or businesses any more than you can predict the monetary value of sweat equity. On the other hand, costs are clear, known and controllable. It's the same with death and taxes. Both are inevitable. One you can mitigate. When the net benefits warrant, which is most of the time, controlling taxes and fees is valuable. Death and investment returns can be influenced but not controlled. Choosing healthy meals and keeping fit are as valuable as researching and valuing good quality investments.

Fees can have a profound impact over time. To convince you, compound 0.5% of fees on $100,000 for 20 years and you'll fill a duffle bag with 73 kilograms worth of loonies minted in 2000. By saving 0.5% on your fees, it could mean the difference between comforts and skimping, especially when you're projecting over longer periods of time, as we do in retirement planning.

You'll never be able to accurately project investment returns on stocks, bonds or businesses any more than you can predict the value of sweat equity. On the other hand, costs are clear, known and controllable.

Here's the alternate. Recently, a couple that was referred to me to turn their portfolio around had lost 20% in the last year and was not happy with their accounts. Concurrently, they were dealing with other stressful issues so their frantic responses were completely understandable. I first spoke to them on a Wednesday evening and they insisted they needed to meet with me the following day. I had some difficulty, but was able to accommodate the request. Later that afternoon they emailed me copies of their statements and the fees they had been charged. The demanding need for immediacy should have tipped me off. When someone shows you who they are, believe them.

They asked me to tell them what stocks to sell right away in order to transfer the funds. Being a long weekend, I spent time going through the entire list of stocks in their portfolio, fleshing them through my models. Ultimately, I recommended selling certain companies right away, rather than the entire portfolio.

I was a bit surprised to receive their next email requesting a reduction in the fees on their accounts. The one truism is that if you are a demanding client and expect above normal service levels, asking for lower fees is inappropriate. Control what you can, including fees, especially if you're being gouged. If you're being charged a reasonable fee for the value of the service, balking at it may result in an undesired effect. Bartering fees isn't a sport in and of itself. When they are too high, barter! If they aren't, consider that you may undermine what you receive in return.

There is a happy ending to the story. Luckily for all, this family decided to transfer their accounts elsewhere but not before demanding that I pay for their transfer-out fees too. I would have taken money from my kids' piggy banks if I'd had to. Sometimes, it just isn't the right fit.

It's important for practitioners to maintain a level playing field to avoid client biases. It's quite acceptable to charge lower fees for clients who have a more assets under management than for smaller accounts. Larger accounts require a diminishing amount of work per dollar invested so the fees should reflect that. More specifically, there is still only one person or group of people to contact regarding tax documents, trades, strategy maintenance, etc., regardless of the size of the account. Issues only seem to arise with gross inadequacies.

As a consumer, it's useful to understand convention. There's a danger in paying too high a price as much as there is in paying too little. For practitioners, it's best to standardize the process and provide transparency. Pay for value. Charge for value.

With mutual funds, the management fees embedded in the fund cannot be changed but various classes of funds are provided accommodate different types of accounts. For example, F class funds are designed for fee based accounts; G class for institutional quantities; A class is the plain-Jane version for commission type accounts. You may, however, insist on FE, zero commission investment into them, so that you don't have to pay a fee to invest in the fund and you don't have a penalty to get out. Many investment practitioners offer mutual funds this way.

In today's marketplace, fee-based accounts can expect to pay management fees somewhere in the neighbourhood of 2% if your portfolio is under $200,000; 1.75% for portfolios between $200,000 and $500,000; approximately 1.5% for between $500,000 and $1,000,000; and 1–1.25% for over a million. Fees are negotiable for multimillion-dollar accounts and there are special cases, such as money market or bond only investment portfolios, which may carry smaller fee levels.

Conflict of Interest

One of my biggest bones of contention is with **Deferred Sales Charge (DSC)**, commonly offered as a fee option for mutual and segregated funds. All excessive fees are cause for concern but in terms of a conflict of interest, DSC is the most outdated practice in the investment and insurance industries today. The bottom line is that the investment professional is paid 5% upfront for locking you into a withdrawal fee-schedule for up to seven years!

I mentioned convention, and charging DSC was a business practice widely condoned in the past. Times have changed. Similarly, mutual funds used to have astounding annual management fees compared with what they are now. Imagine the difference of charging 2.5% management fees on long-term stock returns of 8–9% compared to a **bond fund** generating interest at 2–3%. That is an expected net return of approximately 5% and *zero*, respectively. In the case of the **bond fund**, that categorically cannot be called investing!

With any kind of pooled investment platform, an IA who offers them is paid in a couple of ways, depending on how you purchase the fund. For **commission-based accounts**, investors can purchase most segregated or mutual funds one of two ways. In a **FE** purchase the advisor can charge you up front a 0–3% fee that comes right off of your investment amount. A portion of that fee is given to the advisor and the investment firm retains the rest. Once the funds are invested, the FE fund pays an ongoing **trailer** fee of 1% to the investment firm, of which the advisor receives roughly half.

DSC means that you don't pay a fee up front but if you decide to take your investment out of the mutual fund family (such as AGF, Fidelity or Mackenzie) you will be subject to a declining penalty fee schedule. The mutual fund company coughs up a fur ball representing 5% of the amount you invest and pays that to the investment firm that then splits the commission with the advisor. If you wish to withdraw your money from the fund in the first year after your initial investment, the fund company will recoup that entire fee paid to the firm and advisor by charging you you 5–5.5%. Each year the withdrawal penalty is less, eventually reducing to zero once the fund matures. You're permitted to withdraw 10% without fees each calendar year, meant to facilitate lifestyle needs that you may have. Also, while your funds are invested, an ongoing management and administration fee is charged, 0.5% of which is remitted to the investment firm and is split with your advisor.

Justification for recommending an investment in a DSC mutual fund is too often the standard response, "It's a long-term investment anyway." What if there is a change in the management of the fund? For example, star portfolio manager Brandes Investment Partners, formerly managed the widely followed AGF International Value fund. In 2002, Brandes decided to stop managing the funds for AGF and offer funds directly to Canadian investors. If you had purchased the AGF funds on a DSC basis, you could not move your assets over to the newly established portfolio without paying a steep penalty. Similarly, if a family emergency or unexpected event transpired, you wouldn't be able to take your money out of the DSC mutual fund without incurring a large penalty fee, especially in the inaugural years of the investment.

Even worse is the moral hazard of what this type of fee structure has bred. DSC funds typically offer a 10% amount released from the fee schedule every calendar year in order to facilitate income required by investors from their accounts. What has transpired with this loophole, however, is that a few unscrupulous IAs withdraw these free funds along with any matured DSC assets and reinvest them for the expressed purpose to generate additional commissions. Often these funds are redeemed in January, as soon as they become available, to reinvest them and regenerate the 5% commission on the trade as they jam your funds in to a new DSC fee schedule. I have seen advisors set up spreadsheets to track the maturity dates of DSC assets with the sole intention to garner new fees.

While this practice isn't illegal, investment firms and mutual fund companies dissuade it, as it's clearly counter to a client's best interest. The trouble with the practice is that it's possible to legitimize the trade by putting the newly released funds into a different portfolio or new investments. Flipping investments to generate commissions or fees with little or no real benefit to the client is called **churning**, even when the fees are hidden.

In recent years, mutual fund companies have tried to bridge this gap in the market by offering a **LSC** purchase option. In this structure, the client doesn't pay any up-front costs and the fund company pays the advisor and his firm a 2% fee instead of 5%, as well as a 1% **trailer** each year similar to the FE option. The period for which the client is locked into the declining fee schedule is much shorter, typically three years. Obviously, if you are investing in pooled funds, doing so on a FE, zero commission basis, or a no-load basis (where no FE or DSC commissions are levied) is ideal. If your advisor offers this to you, it's a good indication that he runs a quality practice, embracing changing times.

Not All Fees are Created Equal

On an investment of $10,000 into a DSC fund, $10,000 is invested on your behalf and $500 is paid to your IA from the fund company. If you withdraw the investment after two years, you may pay a penalty of up to $550. After four years, $400, and so on. Also, 10% of the value of the assets can be withdrawn without any fees assessed each calendar year, and after seven-years, the deferred fee schedule ends and your fund withdrawals are completely free. The advisor receives a **trailer** of $12.50 quarterly (assuming that the investment value doesn't appreciate or depreciate for simple calculations) during and after the DSC schedule.

For that same investment into a FE load, the fee paid to the advisor is taken from your total purchase amount. You can negotiate this fee with your advisor based on the size of the purchase and level of service, right down to 0%. On a $10,000 investment into a FE mutual fund with a 2% fee, your advisor is paid $200 and $9800 is invested on your behalf. The fund company pays the advisor a $24.50 **trailer** quarterly and none of the invested funds are subject to withdrawal penalties.

The **LSC** option emerged in the late 1990s. On a similar investment into a pooled fund under this fee structure, $10,000 is invested directly into the fund. The fund company pays $200 commission to the advisor and a $25 quarterly **trailer**. The client is subject to withdrawal penalties for the first 3 years, except for the 10% free amount each calendar year. While this is a step in the right direction, the same conflicts of interest between advisor and the client that you find in a DSC scenario are still present.

In the event of a no-load or zero commission FE fund investment, $10,000 is directly invested and the advisor is paid a $25 quarterly **trailer**. The client is not locked in or subject to withdrawal fees.

SMA Fees

Separately Managed Account (SMA) platforms are similar among investment firms. The cross-pollination of managers offered at one institution versus another makes the major components of the platforms more or less homogenous. As mentioned, one firm may offer exclusive access to a particular manager; however, most carry offerings from the better-known investment firms.

The similarities among SMA platforms extend to fees charged. As with fees on anything, knowing the convention is the best way to understand the landscape and whether you're being fairly charged or not. All firms assess the percentage of fees to be charged based on the total value of the investment, with higher account balances commanding lower percentages. There are slight differences, however. Among firms, there are small variances between how much is charged for how many dollars being managed.

The fees themselves are surprisingly low given all of the people involved. They have to be or the investment would be rendered profitless.

Also of note, is that the fees are chopped up among several layers of interested parties. Firstly, the investment manager holds back and divvies up a certain amount to cover the management firm's costs and the PM's compensation. The second interested party is the company that analyzes the investment mandates and the manager's performance, often outsourced to a third-party consultant. The last piece of the fee is divided between the investment firm and the IA who manages the client relationship. The fees themselves are surprisingly low given all of the people involved. They have to be or the investment would be rendered profitless.

Drawdowns are Depressing

Closed end products refer to those manufactured investment pools that are issued by an investment company. They have a finite maturity date and typically trade on an exchange or may by redeemed by the issuer. Fees on **closed end products** sliced off of the initial investment, the moment they're issue by the investment firm. Although investors don't pay directly, the cost of creating them is scooped off of the top of the money they put into it, on day one. There is a major complaint among advisors who have participated in newly issued **closed end products** over the years. "Why purchase these pools when they're newly issued if they're going to trade below the issue price right out of the gate?" Common sense dictates that investors should wait until the new units hit the market and buy them at the cheaper, **secondary market** (stock exchange) price.

The fees embedded in these new products pay for the efforts and costs of manufacturing them and bringing them to the marketplace. The people spending time designing and executing the product don't work for free and the transactions carry costs.

An investor participating in the new issue averts trade commissions usually charged if he waits to purchase the notes on the stock market, but the commissions he saves are often offset by the fees embedded in the issue to pay for the costs of bringing it to market. What happens, however, is the value of the initial investment may naturally drop by the amount of the fees charged. If your portfolio is managed where you pay for each trade you make, this is justified. If your portfolio is managed on a fee schedule instead of being charged commissions on each trade, you may be better off to wait until the issue is trading on the stock market after the NAV of the investment, post fees, is reflected by the **secondary market** trading price.

The tricky part is that a drop in price doesn't always happen, so you may want to evaluate whether the risk of the price dropping is present or not.

The other issue is that some closed-end funds and structure products may trade at prices less than their NAV from time to time. This can be frustrating to existing investors but it's also an opportunity to buy investments below their value. Some of these products offer annual redemptions at the NAV, which provides an **arbitrage** opportunity. If they trade below the NAV and you can redeem it at the NAV, that's an opportunity to make money when executed on large scales.

Drawdowns are a normal part of **new issues**. Stay on top of what options work best within the structure of your account and don't lose out on extra fees.

Inherent Capital Gains Tax

Mutual funds have been around the investment scene for decades. If a mutual fund manager bought shares of Royal Bank of Canada stock 30 years ago, it's possible that the fund still holds those shares today. It's a strong company that has stood the test of time. The shares over this period have increased significantly, accounting not only for price increases but also stock splits that results in multiplying the growth of the share price.

If the manager decides, for whatever good reason, to sell the stock this year, the taxable **capital gain**, calculated from the original purchase price, must be distributed by December (net of any losses in the fund during the year) to all of the unit holders. If you held the mutual fund for many years you'd expect unrealized gains that have accumulated over time to be distributed. Yet, the truth is that if you purchase the mutual fund, literally the day before it distributes a tax receipt for **capital gains**, you will receive a tax slip proportionate to your share of the overall portfolio. Despite the fact that you only owned the fund for a day, you mutually participate in the portfolio in every way, even with the distribution of taxable events.

Now, let's hail the managers of these funds. They're a pretty brilliant group and realize that this issue exists. As well, they try to mitigate tax implications on an ongoing basis. They do their best to minimize taxes by offsetting gains and losses through their active management of the fund.

Corporate investment structures were developed to widen the opportunity to defer taxes. The best scenario is to have the PM make money for the fund holders—but if you didn't enjoy the profit, it would suck to have to pay taxes on those gains. The two-pronged opportunity for corporate investment structures to defer taxes is an obvious advantage to investors.

Sell Before Maturity

In the case of some structured notes, if held to maturity, the gain you make on your investment may be declared as interest income, being the most punitively taxed money. Every dollar that you receive as interest is fully taxable as income in your hands. Alternatively, if you buy and sell an investment that appreciates in value, the difference in the purchase and sale price is a **capital gain**. You're only required to include 50% of the appreciated amount in your income, essentially reducing potential taxes on half of your returns. This issue is immaterial in a TFSA, RRSP or RRIF, since those accounts are sheltered from tax. In a margin or cash investment account, it's preferable to trade a note on the market prior to the maturity date if the appreciation in value is received as a **capital gain**, rather than interest income at the maturity of the investment.

Return of Capital

Return of capital is an intuitive phrase used to describe receiving your own invested **capital** back. I know what you're thinking: why would you take your own money back? Doesn't that decrease the value of your investment?

The answer is yes! That's exactly how that works! It's also a savvy tax strategy...as long as the investment grows.

Here's how it works. The investment manager distributes income from the after-tax dollars that you originally invested, before distributing the taxable money that the investment

Return of capital is an intuitive phrase used to describe receiving your own invested capital back. I know what you're thinking: why would you take your own money back? Doesn't that decrease the value of your investment? The answer is yes! That's exactly how that works! It's also a savvy tax strategy...as long as the investment grows.

itself earns. Ultimately, they defer taxes on the gains made on the investment by postponing the distribution of those funds to you.

Each return of **capital** payment you receive from the investment reduces your original investment amount, lowering your **ACB**, the amount that you measure your future growth from. Take the example that you invest $15,000 and receive monthly payments of $100 for three years. Assume that the market value of the investment grows to $14,000, when you ultimately sell it. You will have received $3600 in return of **capital** payments reducing your **ACB** to $11,400, deferring the **capital gain** of $2600, to the end of your investment.

The benefits of this structure are that tax payments on the funds are postponed and once it's realized it's taxed as a **capital gain**, with an advantaged 50% inclusion rate, meaning only half is taxable as income.

The drawback is that the distributed cash is actually withdrawn from your own investment. Receiving your own money back on an investment that isn't producing a return can mask the poor performance of the investment for some time. More importantly, you erode your wealth.

Guaranteed Risk

As a reminder, guarantees on structured products are conventionally designed in two ways. With a $1000 investment, a **strip bond** (refer to chapter 3 regarding fixed income) is purchased in order to guarantee that the initial investment will be available at the maturity date. With the remainder of the investment, the investment manufacturer can be as aggressive as is needed to replicate the returns of some investment, typically a stock index.

With the majority of the funds, say $875, the manager purchases a bond that will mature on the same day as the note with a value of $1000. The remaining funds are used to invest in the derivatives (**options** or futures), which are naturally **leveraged** to an underlying portfolio or **stock market index** that the note plans to replicate. The remaining $75 or so is allocated to execution, marketing, commissions and other costs.

In practice, these animals work fantastically if nothing eventful happens. For investments that were designed to protect against a downturn in the investment market, they fall short of real protection. They crumble when extreme events happen. When there's a severe or sudden shock, the **leveraged** part of the strategy implodes, leaving the investor with a promise to repay her original investment at some future date. Nothing else.

> *"If you want a guarantee, buy a toaster."*
> —Clint Eastwood

Many risk-averse investors who think they're protected against inflation are given a false sense of security. In extreme circumstances, the protection may or may not be intact, but in every case, the protection against inflation is worthless. What wasn't understood prior to the financial meltdown was that at best, these investments end up as nothing more than a merger interest-bearing **strip bond** when markets become volatile and the **leveraged** part of the portfolio blows up.

Again, guaranteed notes are only as good as the guarantor. Some of the so-called guaranteed notes issued prior to the financial crisis dropped in value to close to zero. Not exactly the risk-averse nature they were intended to be.

Today, manufactured investments are far more interesting, as much as they're complicated. All sorts of option strategies from Himalayan **call options** to collars and forward swap contracts (I'll spare you the details) can be combined for various risk-reward results.

If you don't understand them, don't invest in them. If neither you nor your advisor can explain how the investment structure works, in layman's terms, don't invest in it.

If you don't understand them, don't invest in them. If neither you nor your advisor can explain how the investment structure works, in layman's terms, don't invest in it. Transparency is important and understanding the implications of how investments behave in various scenarios is important.

Invest in quality, not in guarantees that may or may not be all they're cracked up to be.

Double and Short

The ETF market opened up investment options that formerly could not have been replicated by the average investor or advisor. Execution costs and access to certain strategies were prohibitive until these structures were introduced. It was only a short matter of time before the strategies themselves became more and more sophisticated. As with any strategy pushing the corners of the envelope, the risks involved are often not well understood until the structures are put into place and operate for a period of time through various market conditions.

What we discovered since the launch of the **double exposure** ETFs and ETNs was that the daily rebalancing of the **leverage** had an impact on the performance of the ETF over time, with a larger effect for more volatile underlying markets or securities. A negative impact.

The double exposure is set up so that your investment reflects twice the market movement of the underlying investment. For example, a two times natural gas ETF gives you twice the returns on the price change of natural gas for the day. The double short exposure works the same way, but opposite.

The problem arises because of the **leverage**. The portfolio must be reset daily in order to continuously double the underlying portfolio's performance each trading day. For every $100 invested, there is $100 of borrowed money for a total $200 investment. The **leverage** produces double exposure to the basket of securities but due to the daily rebalancing of the portfolio, gains as well as losses impact the investment value, twice as much. Mathematically, when underlying portfolio drops the **leveraged** exposure to the underlying portfolio erodes twice as much **capital**, diminishing the funds available to invest on the following trading session. **Leverage** is then rebalanced and decreased lock-step with the lower amount of **capital**, reducing the overall amount to invest the next day. Over time, this deteriorates the value of the ETF, regardless of the performance of the underlying portfolio.

For interest's sake, below is a performance comparison of a plain-Jane ETF with its **leveraged** version.

Comparison of Regular and Double Exposure ETF

Day	INDEX (Regular ETF)				Double Exposure (2× ETF)			
	Open Value	Close Value	Day %	Total %	Open Value	Close Value	Day %	Total %
1	$100	$99	-1%	-1%	$100	$98	-2%	-2%
2	$99	$98.01	-1%	-2%	$98	$96.04	-2%	-4%
3	$98.01	$97.03	-1%	-3%	$96.04	$94.12	-2%	-6%
4	$97.03	$96.06	-1%	-4%	$94.12	$92.24	-2%	-6%
5	$96.06	$100	4.1%	0%	$92.24	$99.80	+8%	10%

Note that on day two, the double exposure investor only has $98 to invest in the new investment. By day five, the regular ETF investor still has $100 but the double exposure investor only has $99.80 even though the underlying investment that the ETF follows is the same value. The double exposure investor lost regardless. The return on day five would have to be .12% higher than the non-leveraged ETF in order to return to the beginning level. Over time this effect becomes increasingly exaggerated, especially when the underlying basket of investments has a high variability of returns (**volatility**). The "some days up, some days down" type of **volatility** creates great issues with these structures in the way they're calculated.

The following paragraph is a bit of an investment tongue twister. If you wish to refill the glass of Argentinian Malbec you've been sipping, now would be a good time.

A short exposure ETF suffers the same fate as an ETF that tracks commodities with futures in **contango**. So, a short, **leveraged** ETF tracking a commodity with futures in **contango** is thrice the problem! And they do exist. If you were to short them, you may find a profit. Unfortunately or fortunately, retail investment firms disallow these trades, due to the fact that the risks are too great for almost everyone. Roulette is more fun and often more profitable, even with one of the worst odds in the house.

Back down on earth, a reasonable way to evaluate whether the ETF in question is subject to these issues is to graph the numbers. Graph the ETF and the underlying investment that it's supposed to represent over the same time period. Visually, you'll easily be able to determine whether it's doing what it's intended to do. Having both charts in the same pane paints a clear picture of the relationship between the two variables. With a double exposure ETF, you'll likely see some of the same peaks and valleys but it will inevitably drop in value over time, despite any upward movement in the underlying investment.

Above is my version of Rorschach inkblots used by some psychiatrists to help patients express their inner driving thoughts. More or less, they are mirrored images that were created from folding a page in half and squishing the ink so that it approximates a balanced picture when the halves are spread open. Ideally, an inverse ETF would be able to produce the exact opposite price movement to the underlying investment. The concept is simple enough, yet no investment tool to produce this effective has been manufactured to date. The formulas and structures available simply don't work in the real world…yet.

What is the first thing that comes to mind when you see each of those images? Do you prefer the image on the right or the left? Are you better at analyzing your investments or your psyche?

Chapter 6

This Investment Account Will Change Your Life

> Stay committed to your decisions,
> but stay flexible in your approach.
> —Tony Robbins

What do you need?

I know what you're thinking. *"How can the type of account I choose actually make me money?"*

Well, perhaps not make you money, but it will save you money. The main differences between types of accounts offered by banks and investment firms are in the way the investments are taxable or not, whether you end up in a penalty situation or miss out on the benefits of government programs and which ones charge fees. Over the next few pages, I'd like to encourage you to alter your use of tax shelters and shift how you think about saving for retirement. By exhausting government benefits to your advantage and strategically allocating your investments among these accounts when it most benefits you, you'll find more money for travel, healthcare, wine, early retirement, tee times or manicures.

What? Men need manicures, too!

The federal government's efforts to mould Canadians' saving and spending behaviours drive the rules of these programs and how these types of accounts operate. Our government's fiscal policy makers perform a balancing act between influencing the way Canadians behave with their money, raising funds for the operation of the country and getting re-elected. The rules change over the years, so make sure you know where the gettin's good.

Registered Retirement Savings Plan

As life expectancy continues to expand and the number of years spent in retirement along with it, the Canadian government realized it needed to ease the developing reliance on public social systems. The Registered Retirement Savings Plan (RRSP) was one such initiative introduced in 1957, according to the Canada Revenue Agency (CRA). The strategy of incentivizing retirement saving with current income tax deductions has evolved over the decades, including increased limits and removing loopholes.

Today, you may have as many RRSP accounts as you wish as long as you do not breach the aggregate contribution limit of 18% of your reported earned income from the previous tax year. You may carry forward any unused contribution amounts to future tax years indefinitely, until they're used. The annual contribution limit is capped at $24,270 in the 2014 tax year and is adjusted annually for increases in the cost of living. If you participate in a pension plan through an employer or if you have an individual pension plan (IPP) managed for self-employed people, contributions to these plans reduce the amount you can add to your RRSP. Corporate pension plan contributions reduce your RRSP contribution limit by the pension credits reported on your T4 income slip.

You may contribute your maximum amount plus $2000 to your RRSP without claiming all or any of the amounts contributed in that tax year. Instead you can claim the amount over several years, ideally focusing on reducing taxes during higher-earning years. The sooner you shelter your investments from tax, the better.

Whenever you file a tax return and report earned income (as opposed to passive income such as rental income) you will be given an assigned amount that you can contribute to your RRSP. Every taxpayer also has an **excess**

contribution amount of $2000. While you may contribute this amount to your RRSP, you may not deduct that amount from your income. This grace amount helps to avoid inadvertent over-contributions and the hugely punitive penalty of 1% per month (12% penalty per year). on the overage.

Although you cannot deduct the $2000 over-contribution from your income, you effectively shelter income earned on the money transferred into the plan from income taxes. You may also contribute $2000 in your children's RRSPs and shelter additional investment income earned on those funds from taxes. Although it's only a small amount, the long-term advantage of sheltering this money as it compounds for decades is profound, especially if your children are young. $2000 invested at a 5% tax-free return will be worth $6772.71 after 25 years and $14079.98 after 40.

> "I hate RRSPs! They have never made me any money."

The profitability of an RRSP is entirely dependent on the investments that you chose within the account so you can never say that your RRSP didn't perform well. Okay, the investments didn't perform well, but don't take it out on your poor RRSP account. It's just a tax shelter.

Treat your RRSP as a wrapper for your investments and an important vehicle for managing the income taxes you pay over your lifetime. If you can defer or reduce your taxes, you should. Avoid, reduce or defer income taxes in that order. I don't mean tax evasion, but you might as well study up on the various programs to keep as many of your hard earned dollars in your jeans. There are important details about how RRSPs work which determines the best way to manage how much and when you remit taxes.

Tax sheltered accounts (RRSP, RRIF, RESP and TFSA) are simply wrappers for the investments that you select. Each of the accounts has various rules but for the most part, you can select a wide variety of investments for your plans, such as GICs, stocks, bonds, mutual funds and ETFs.

When it comes time to consider making an RRSP contribution, you are at liberty to make full or partial contributions to your own plan or those of your spouse or common-law partner (as a spousal contribution) at any time during the tax year. Wait for it...I'm setting up a useful strategy.

Contributions applied to any tax year must be made no later than 60 days into the ensuing calendar year. That includes contributions made in previous years but not yet claimed on your tax return. You can claim the deduction against current income or carry forward the deduction to future years. This poses an be an interesting opportunity for a person whose income varies from year to year or whose income increases substantially over a few years. She can shelter investments assets from taxation now by making eligible contributions and then strategically apply the RRSP deduction against her income in higher-earning years down the road.

Contribution limits are finite. Like Aeroplan® points accumulated through Visa® purchases and loyalty miles with Air Canada, they're gone once you spend them. Withdrawals from your RRSP cannot be replaced. If you receive an inheritance or some other windfall, you could dump the entire amount into your RRSP account if you have accumulated the contribution room from past years of earned income. You may elect to claim the entire RRSP contribution receipt in that tax year or you could spread it out over several years. If the receipt equals a substantial portion of what you earn in a year, it would make more sense to only use a portion to reduce your income and save on the highest tax rates over a few years instead. Remember that lower income levels attract lower tax rates.

You cannot make new contributions to your RRSP after the year in which you turn 71 but you can claim previous contributions against your income after this date.

Once you contribute to your RRSP, your contribution limit is exhausted and you will have to accumulate a new contribution limit from earning income. Even if you withdraw funds from your RRSP the following year, you cannot redeposit those funds into your tax sheltered RRSP account until you generate a new contribution limit from additional earning income. The only exceptions to this are under the Home Buyers' and Lifelong Learning Plans to be discussed shortly. As Henry David Thoreau, American author, poet, philosopher, abolitionist, naturalist, tax resister, development critic, surveyor, historian and transcendentalist, is quoted as saying, "Never look back unless you are planning to go that way."

Are There Benefits to Spousal Plans Anymore?

A spousal RRSP is exactly what it sounds like. It's a plan owned by your spouse to which you can make contributions. The tax receipt for the contribution is issued in your name but the investment is made in the name of your spouse. A common-law partner may also qualify to have a spousal RRSP for these purposes.

Regardless of the number of spousal plans your spouse has, the last money in, is the first money out and if you take funds from a spousal RRSP within three years of *any* spousal contributions, the withdrawals are taxed as income in the hands of the contributor, completely defeating the purpose of using the spousal plan. To be on the safe side, ensure that contributions made to a spousal plan are deposited well in advance of three years prior to when you plan to use them. This goes for funds converted to a spousal RRIF from a spousal RRSP also.

Today, however, spousal RRSP plans have been all but rendered useless for those who plan to retire after age 65. Recent changes in the legislation permit spouses to split retirement income from their RRIF and pensions. Spousal plans are still useful for income splitting before age 65 by converting RRSP money to a RRIF during early retirement as long as couples respect the restriction on the timing of withdrawals made on recent deposits by the contributing spouse.

Retirement Income Options

Save, save, save. You've spent all these years amassing an RRSP. Now what? You will have to make a decision as to what to do with your RRSP by December 31 in the year in which you turn 71 if you haven't done so sooner. When you finally transition from the RRSP accumulation phase to the spending years of retirement, you have three choices of how to handle your RRSP:

1. Use your registered RRSP investments to buy a registered annuity
2. Convert your RRSP to a RRIF
3. Withdraw all of the money in your plan, pay the income taxes on the whole wallop of it (and live like a rock star for a short period of time)

A registered annuity is a contractual promise to pay a string of pre-tax monthly deposits for the rest of your life. Annuity contracts offer a variety of payment terms and even may guarantee that certain amounts are paid to your estate in the event of premature death. For example, you could select a term that pays a certain monthly income for the rest of your life but for at least 20 years, whichever comes last. That is to say that if you become deceased before the 20 years is up, the balance of payments for the guaranteed period is owed to your estate.

RRIF payments can be split between spouses for tax purposes once you reach age 65 regardless from whose account the funds were withdrawn. RRSP withdrawals cannot be split.

There are some drawbacks. Once you execute the contract, you have no control over your assets because they no longer belong to you. You've essentially traded your money for a piece of paper guaranteeing certain income. You and the issuer are bound by the terms of the agreement. If you become ill or other life events create a need for larger amounts of **capital**, you'll need to access other sources for funds since an annuity contract is irreversible.

Also, the lifelong contractual payments that annuity issuers agree to pay you are determined partially by mortality rates and actuarial data but are also heavily influenced by prevailing interest rates. Given extended life expectancies and profoundly low interest rates, the payments calculated on these agreements today are egregiously unappetizing, making it difficult to justify this as an option for your RRSP assets.

At best, registered annuities are a partial solution with appeal to those who expect a long life and do not want the burden of managing money. Since the terms of an annuity are unchangeable, you would never spend all of your assets on a contract of this sort, but in some cases, it may be an amenable solution for part of your savings.

Most investors choose to roll their RRSP investments into a RRIF. There is little difference between how an RRSP and a RRIF operate beyond the fact that an RRSP is meant for accumulation while the RRIF is designed for withdrawals. Otherwise, they are sisters. Both plans shelter investment income from tax; investments eligible to be held in either plan are the same; and both plans carry a named beneficiary which plays an important roll in estate planning.

You may convert your RRSP to a RRIF at any time (yes, even if you are 25!) and you may also revert back to an RRSP, if it makes sense to, any time prior to the end of the year in which you turn 71. When rolling from one registered plan to the next, you don't need to sell or wait for your investments to mature. They simply roll over in kind, on a tax-deferred basis.

If you begin drawing money from your registered plan on a regular basis, converting your RRSP to a RRIF will save you transaction fees. It's purely a matter of convenience to have your withdrawals automated and to save the processing fee charged on ad hoc RRSP withdrawals. If you're not working for a couple of years or if your income is dramatically lower for some other reason, you may decide to convert all or part of your RRSP assets to a RRIF and begin taking taxable funds out of the plan. If you return to work subsequently, simply roll the assets back into an RRSP as long as you're younger than 71 years of age. Moreover, RRIF payments can be split between spouses for tax purposes once you reach age 65 regardless from whose account the funds were withdrawn, while RRSP withdrawals cannot be split.

Similar to an RRSP, a beneficiary or list of beneficiaries may be named on your RRIF. When your spouse is the beneficiary, the assets in your plan roll over to his or her registered plan on a pre-tax basis, in its entirety. In the case of someone other than your spouse being named, the funds are deregistered and your estate pays taxes on the full amount as income prior to being delivered to that person.

Keeping the tax money until it's due the following year means that you will have the use of those funds for a longer time. While it's in your hands, you can lower finance costs or increase your returns by investing over that period or by reducing your debt, at least temporarily.

Minimum amounts are required to be withdrawn annually from a RRIF beginning in the year subsequent to rolling your investments into the plan. Once you convert your RRSP to a RRIF, the value of the account on December 31st multiplied by a prescribed percentage (based on your age below) to determine the minimum payment you must take out of the plan the following calendar year.

Determining Your Minimum RRIF Withdrawal

Age	Factor	Age	Factor	Age	Factor
Under 71	1/(90-age)	78	.0833	86	.1079
71	.0738	79	.0853	87	.1133
72	.0748	80	.0875	88	.1196
73	.0759	81	.0899	89	.1271
74	.0771	82	.0927	90	.1362
75	.0785	83	0.958	91	.1473
76	.0799	84	.0993	92	.1612
77	.0815	85	.1033	93	.1792
				94 or older	.2

You may elect to take more from your RRIF; however, any withdrawals beyond the minimum prescribed amount will require that withholding taxes be remitted to CRA. These are prepaid taxes on the entire sum that you take out. By limiting withdrawals to the minimum prescribed amount, it's your choice whether to have your investment firm collect and remit taxes on your behalf or not. You may also decide to have additional taxes withheld at source beyond those automatically collected if it helps you with your cash flow planning, especially if you're in a high income tax bracket. If you only withdraw the minimum prescribed RRIF payment, you're generally better off to elect no taxes to be withheld. Keeping the tax money until it's due the following year means that you'll have the use of those funds for a longer time. While it's in your hands, you can lower finance costs or increase your returns by investing over that period or by reducing your debt, at least temporarily. Practically speaking, however, few Canadians are this fastidious with their cash management. If paying the taxes up front assures that you won't have a surprise tax bill next April, pay the taxes when you make the withdrawal rather than waiting.

In the event that you transfer your RRIF from one carrier to another, the former investment firm must pay your minimum prescribed withdrawal for the calendar year prior to delivering your account to the new institution.

In the event that you transfer your RRIF from one carrier to another, the former investment firm must pay your minimum prescribed withdrawal for the calendar year prior to delivering your account to the new institution. This could significantly impact your investment strategy and planned withdrawals for the rest of the year by having to take those funds into your hands right away. You may elect to take the withdrawal in kind instead of in cash, by moving securities from your RRIF into a non-registered investment account without selling them. By doing so, your funds remain invested while still complying with the prescribed withdrawals governing RRIF accounts. To facilitate a payment in kind, contact your IA or investment firm to process this manually, in advance of the payment date. Alternatively, cash payments may be directed to your bank account directly or to a cash or margin investment account.

Locked-In Registered Accounts

As recent as a couple of decades ago, the relationship between workers and employers was career-long and far more loyalty based than it is today. With the reality of extended working lives and our keen interests in pursuing entrepreneurial endeavours, mixed with corporations' increasingly tight grip on expense management, the notion of working for the same company for an entire career is diminished, if not entirely extinguished.

Another signpost of our transitory work environment is the demise of the **defined benefit pension plan**. The real boon of these plans is in the compounding of returns in the later years of a long-term career and the security of knowing what your payments will be once you retire. However, with the periods of extreme **volatility** and illiquidity in recent decades, corporations now realize that the risk of these plans is squarely on their shoulders. By guaranteeing the payments that their retired employees receive without knowing how investment markets will perform or when the next crisis will unfold, is a tricky prospect.

In addition, employees have realized that changing employers throughout their career wreaks havoc on the benefits of their compounded returns and the eventual retirement income they hope to receive. The portability of defined pensions is almost non-existent compared to that of RRSPs.

With the advent of employment headhunters, an entrepreneurial work culture and major employers' staff reduction policies, defined benefit plans are going the way of eight-track tapes and camcorders. Due to the lessened investment risks and a better alignment with the demands of the workforce, corporations are happier to offer **defined contribution pension plans** and employer-assisted RRSPs instead. Outside of provincial or federal employers, you would be hard pressed to find an organization offering defined benefit pension plans any longer.

The main difference between a defined benefit pension plan and a defined contribution pension plan is that the latter tells you what you will receive at retirement in hard numbers, based on actuarial tables and expected rates of return. With a defined contribution pension plan, you know the amount of your contributions and the market value of the plan. At best, you're provided with expected payout amounts at projected dates based on assumed portfolio returns.

Employer-assisted RRSP accounts (group RRSP plan) administered through a third party investment firm, where contributions are taken directly off your pay cheque. In most cases, the corporation offers an incentive to make contributions by matching a portion or all of the contribution you make to your plan, to a maximum limit. The group RRSP option usually gives you the control to decide among a group of mutual funds offered through the third party investment firm and in many cases, the ability to transfer part of the plan, once a minimum vesting period has passed, to the RRSP provider of your choice. The benefit of pensions over RRSPs is that contribution limits are higher so you can shelter more funds from the taxman and accumulate more for your retirement years. If you're self-employed, you may be eligible to set up an **Individual Pension Plan (IPP)**, which is just as it sounds, and get the best of both worlds: higher contribution limits plus full investment control.

When you leave an employer who provided a pension plan, you're given several options of what to do with your pension assets. You may be able to leave your funds in the existing plan, allowing the managers to continue on and begin collecting your variable or defined payments at a predetermined retirement date either immediately or in the future. Alternatively, you may elect to transfer the funds into your own care under a locked-in registered account governed by the provincial or federal legislation under which the pension plan originates. Each of the provincial and federal regulations set out rules for locked-in retirement savings and locked-in retirement income funds. These provide the minimum and maximum withdrawals allowed each year and any restrictions to transfer all or part of the locked-in amounts to a regular

RRSP or RRIF. It also gives the conditions under which you may access the funds beyond the prescribed withdrawals.

Instead of transferring your pension to a locked-in plan, you are able to purchase a prescribed annuity. It's the least flexible option since it's simply a contract to provide a guaranteed string of payments into the future. As with other annuities, once the contract is purchased, there is no way to alter the contract despite changes to interest rates or the economic environment and there is no option to take the funds out in a lump sum in the event of illness or death.

The other option of leaving the funds in the pension plan is something to consider if it's a defined benefit pension plan offering inflation protection. These plans are valuable and while you have little flexibility in the selection of withdrawal and investment options, the value comes in that the financial risk is assumed almost entirely by the company or agency governing your previous employment.

Maintaining control of your registered savings is in your best interest as long as you feel capable. You decide when and what to invest in or you are always at liberty to seek professional management. You maintain control of your investment options as well as the fees paid. Legislation that governs locked-in registered retirement plans have provisions for unlocking small accounts so that you can roll those funds on a pre-tax basis into your open RRSP. Both the provincial and federal locked-in legislations allow for a one-time rollover to a regular RRSP either when you convert the funds to a locked-in retirement income fund, you are terminally ill or you are in financial need.

A locked-in RRSP is ultimately converted to a locked-in RRIF. Both RRIFs and locked-in RRIFs prescribe a minimum annual withdrawal amount but only locked-in plans also limit a maximum withdrawal amount each year. Having a bedtime is one thing but being told when to wake up is quite another. Without consideration for taxation, it's usually best to withdraw the maximum from any locked-in plans due to their prohibitive nature, leaving other, more flexible registered assets for the future. When the value of your plan drops below what is deemed to be a small account size, roll the remaining funds into your RRSP or RRIF. This amount changes annually and varies depending on the legislation governing each plan. Consult the provincial or federal terms to which your plan is subject and free up the funds as soon as you're able.

Tax planning is also part of the decision to deregister any assets but the goal of this strategy is to bring those assets into your control when you are able to use them. You can shelter assets in an RRSP or TFSA if you have room available but if you leave them in a locked-in plan, there are restrictive covenants that will prevent you from using any funds in excess of the maximum withdrawal limits. The preference is to maintain flexibility and latitude in managing cash flows rather than leaving it in the hands of regulators to decide.

Tax-Free Savings

Introduced in 2009, Tax Free Savings Account (TFSA) is one of the most accessible estate planning tools available to Canadians. Regardless of whether you have a will or not, the money in your TFSA passes directly to your designated beneficiaries, without the need for probate. This is important for a couple of reasons. The funds pass directly to your beneficiaries on a tax-free and probate-free basis, providing immediate liquidity to your heirs and saving a bunch of money for your estate. Also, the assets in your TFSA distributed according to the beneficiaries named on the account rather than through your will, are therefore not subject to any caveats filed against your will and they are not part of the publicly filed information with your will.

*If you're married, make sure that you establish your TFSA so that your spouse is not only the beneficiary but also the **contingent owner.***

If you're married, it's even better. Ensure that assign your spouse as the **contingent owner** in order to take advantage of a unique opportunity to have the funds in your tax sheltered TFSA remain in a TFSA when it's rolled over to your spouse, should you become deceased.

Originally, Canadians over the age of 18 could contribute up to $5000 to their plan each year, with the limit increasing by inflation in $500 increments. The contributions are cumulative so in 2014, you'd be eligible to place up to $31,000 ($5000 for each year from 2009 to 2011 and $5500 per year thereafter) in a TFSA account. Although you cannot deduct TFSA contributions against your income, any income or growth on the assets within the TFSA is not taxable. Also, you can take the funds out of the plan in cash or in kind at any time without being taxed on the withdrawals or on the profits made on those investments. If you had invested an allowable amount of $15,000 in the first 3 years and the investment grew to $18,000, you can withdraw all or part of these funds at any time either in cash or securities and re-contribute any amount withdrawn to your TFSA in the following or subsequent calendar years. In addition, new contribution amounts become available each year for funds to be contributed and these contribution limits can be carried forward indefinitely, if they're not used in any calendar year.

Similar to an RRSP, a TFSA is just an account type; like a wrapper. The investments that you make within the plan determine what your returns are. Also, the same types of investments that are eligible to hold in an RRSP are eligible to hold in a TFSA. Typically, publicly listed stocks, bonds and mutual funds, GIC's, term deposits, etc. are eligible. Also, be careful not to day-trade or trade with extremely high frequency in your TFSA or CRA may deem that activity in eligible to be sheltered from tax and your efforts are ineffective.

Margin vs. Cash

Margin is the proportion of a whole, as in a perimeter or a partial deposit to purchase something. An investment margin is the same idea. Borrow to invest so that you only use a proportion of your own funds. The margin is the amount you can borrow against the securities in your account. So in a margin account, you can withdraw funds or invest in additional stocks and bonds without coming up with more money. There are maximum amounts that you can borrow, interest is charged on the amount borrowed and only some securities are eligible to be margined (used as security). It's essentially like an overdraft on your investment account with your investments in the account held as security.

You must be careful when utilizing margin. If the value of your margined securities drops, you may be forced to sell some of them, even if they are at temporary or unrealistically low market prices, in order to cover the margin call if you can't come up with cash from another source to address the shortfall. For example, if you have a portfolio of stocks that qualify for a 50% margin and they're worth $250,000 market value, you can withdraw $125,000 from your account. You may also use this amount to buy additional investments. If these new investments also qualify for margin, the total amount you can borrow increases, turning your original $250,000 into exposure of a half a million dollars worth of stocks.

Imagine your account has margin eligible securities that are offer up to 50% loan to value ratio, with a current market value of $250,000. You may take out up to $125,000 to buy that home in cottage-country your husband has been nagging you about. Subsequently, the market value of the stocks drop by 10% and your securities are worth $225,000. You have to come up with $12,500 in cash or sell $25,000 of your shares to cover the shortfall, not accounting for trading commissions or fees. The reason you have to sell more shares to cover the margin is that once you sell the shares, they're no longer available to provide security, lowering your overall margin available. You can see from this illustration how the leverage of margin can quickly overwhelm you like a tsunami if markets continue to decline for prolonged periods and your other cash options are limited. By using margin, less of your invested **capital** is needed for the same amount of exposure, so you can multiply your returns. Keep in mind however, that your losses will be exponentially if you are forced to cover your margin by selling off securities used to secure your margin debt in the first place. Alternatively, you may use margin more conservatively by not drawing the maximum allowed, providing latitude to accommodate market prices changes.

Cash accounts do not allow for negative cash balances. For this reason, I often recommend that clients open a margin account whether or not they plan to borrow to invest, simply for the flexibility of facilitating payments and withdrawals. With a margin account, you can take funds from your account when you need them while you strategically time the liquidation of investments to cover the withdrawal or wait for dividend and interest payments to be made. This allows you to take advantage of market timing; allows more time to sell illiquid positions; or gives you an opportunity to time the sale of assets into a new tax year without preventing the ongoing use of your funds when you need them.

Strategy

There are more accountants than I care to count who are categorically against RRSPs. I didn't get it until I remembered that they're consumed with navigating taxes, at times to their detriment. Granted, I have my shortcomings as well and I won't begrudge other professionals speculating on what those may be. That being said, I feel so strongly about this that I've been at loggerheads for years on this issue with accountants, whom

I respect tremendously. Ultimately, unless you have income flowing through a corporation, most people are better off with an RRSP than not.

Then there are individual investors who emphatically oppose RRSPs for an entirely different reason, hung up on statements of wanting to unilaterally avoid paying any taxes at all, even in the future and even when the strategy is clearly to their advantage. It's possible that their position is more a political stance than a financially logical one. Coupled with these camps is the ongoing debate about RRSPs versus TFSAs. Like eight-year-old boys pulling wings and legs off an insect, we have been collectively fascinated by the circular debate without gaining much progress.

Allow me to indulge in the debate. If you could have an interest-free loan, would you think that was a good idea? Not only interest-free, but you wouldn't have to make any payments on the loan and you wouldn't have to pay it back for an extended period of time. You wouldn't pay tax on the money you make on this plan, either, while you continue to accumulate and invest. When you sell your investments to live on, you return the loan (which sounds much better than paying tax). Depending on your circumstances, you may not even have to return all of it, if you're in a lower tax bracket. Furthermore, if your investments fall in value, you wouldn't have to pay all of the loan back because the amount you pay back is directly proportional to the amount your overall investments are worth.

That is exactly what an RRSP is. Think of your tax bracket as the percentage that the federal government will lend you. If you're at a marginal tax rate of 40%, for every dollar you contribute to your RRSP you only use 60 cents of your own money to invest. That's brilliant.

Moreover, when you pay back the 'loan,' you do so well into the future. Future expenses are much cheaper because the value of the dollar is worth less. The cost of goods is more expensive in the future. Inflation makes paying a dollar in taxes today far more expensive because you can buy so much more with a dollar today than you will be able to 10 years from now. So in effect, you use this borrowed money at a much higher value than when you pay it back in *real dollars*. The bonus? If you're in a lower tax bracket in the future, the benefits are compounded in your favour because you pay back less in absolute dollars and real dollars.

The only drawback is if you make a lot of profit on your registered assets. The only drawback is if you make a lot of profit on your registered assets. Just checking to see if you read that correctly. It's true. The more money you make on your **leveraged** investment, the more you have to remit to Ottawa when you take funds out.

That repeated sentence is facetious. Making too much money is never a drawback!

Are you convinced yet that RRSPs are a brilliant idea? Good. Get on it. The federal government takes part of your investment risk and helps you maximize your retirement savings for free. Many Canadians should take advantage of this vehicle and don't.

Those who have little or no current taxable income, may be the only group of people for whom the usefulness of an RRSP is debatable. Also, people who have businesses at a much lower tax rate may have an argument for keeping money in their corporations rather than taking it in their personal name and contributing it to an RRSP, but if you need the cash flow, taking out an RRSP to offset taxable income that you need, may be a smart solution. That money has to come out of the corporation at some point and it's not **leveraged** while it's in there, unlike an RRSP. But I digress…

Too Much Money in Your RRSP

There is a point when you may accumulate more money in your RRSP than you can strategically take out and it doesn't make sense to keep adding funds: a problem that anyone would want. Conceding this, there is a balance between current and future taxes paid, but generally speaking, most people err on the side of underutilization of this vehicle.

If you convert your RRSP into a RRIF and start withdrawing the minimum amount required at age 72, (assuming a 6% return on investments and 2% inflation) you would have to accumulate $1,750,000 to have your withdrawals crest the breakwater of the highest federal tax level of $132,406 per year. That doesn't take into account other income. Practically speaking, deferring taxes with an RRSP should always balance your current with future income and spending needs. It's easy to suggest that excess **capital** be harboured in an RRSP tax shelter, especially early in your life when taxes can be deferred for decades and income stays tax-sheltered for all of those long years. Notwithstanding, there is equilibrium. You don't want either current or future income top heavy with taxes any more than you save for a tee time in 2042 at the expense of feeding the coin-op laundry and splurging for pizza and beer night this Friday.

Note that as you come closer to your retirement date, the value of the tax-free compounding in an RRSP diminishes. If you're in a relatively high tax bracket and still have 10 or more years to save, back up the RRSP truck and load 'er up. As a rule, the earlier you contribute the better.

Effective Income Splitting

Registered accounts of all kinds are an excellent way for spouses to split assets and income. If one spouse makes substantially more income than the other, investing funds into the lower income spouse's tax sheltered account comes without any tax attribution. All of the interest, dividends and **capital gains** within these plans are sheltered, and are therefore not taxable in either spouse's hands. By doing so, the couple can reduce the overall taxes paid. This is also true for contributions to a child who has RRSP contribution room or is eligible to open a TFSA. The same rules apply insofar as there are no taxes payable on investment income due to the shelter so there is nothing to attribute back to the source of the funds. The child is, however, the owner of the assets.

Be careful with contributions to a spousal RRSP. Withdrawals taken after three calendar years are counted as income in the RRSP owner's name, usually the lower income spouse, saving overall taxes between the couple. If you withdraw the funds from a spousal plan earlier than three years of the last contribution to any spousal RRSP account, the withdrawal will be taxable as income in the contributor's name, defeating the efforts of the tax strategy.

Recently, the rules about income splitting between spouses during retirement years have become more generous. When you are over age 65, you are able to split your retirement pension income with your spouse. This includes private pensions and CPP payments, as well as income from your RRIF. Note that it does not include RRSP withdrawals so if you wish to avail yourself of this income splitting, you will have to convert your plan (or part of your plan) to a RRIF rather than making withdrawals directly from you RRSP. While this recent update has rendered spousal plans all but useless, it's still worthwhile for couples planning to retire earlier or who wish to income split for other reasons prior to age 65.

If you have a younger spouse, you may be the envy of others but not for the reasons that may first pop into your mind, rather, because you're afforded a couple of tax planning opportunities. At the end of the calendar year in which you turn 71, you cannot contribute to your RRSP any longer, regardless of whether you have contribution room or not. You can, however, contribute to your spouse's RRSP until December 31 in the year that your spouse turns 71. Similarly, an executor cannot contribute to your RRSP after your death but can contribute to your younger spouse's RRSP to shelter assets.

Prohibited Investments

In an effort to thwart crafty ways to de-register investments held in an RRSP, TFSA and other registered accounts, the Canadian government implemented a series of anti-avoidance measures in the 2011 budget including harsh penalties for noncompliance. Canada Revenue Agency – 2011 Budget Questions and Answers: http://www.cra-arc.gc.ca/gncy/bdbt/2011/menu-eng.html. One of the main changes to RRSPs is the list of prohibited investments, introduced in TFSA accounts two years earlier. Non-qualified investments fall into two broad categories: certain significant obligations, or non-arm's-length debt obligations, and equity positions.

More specifically, the first categorical exclusion prohibits any debt obligation of the annuitant (owner) of the registered plan, except for mortgages insured through Canada Mortgage and Housing Corporation (CMHC) under the RRSP mortgage program. Business or personal bonds, loans or other indebtedness fall under this umbrella.

The second broad category includes situations where the RRSP holder owns a significant interest, either on his own or together with non-arm's-length people in a public or private company. Generally, a significant interest equates to 10% or more of a class of shares of a corporation or related corporation or a similar proportion of the **fair market value** of a partnership or trust. Although an insider falls within the parameters of these restrictions, the restrictions are farther reaching and more constrained than traditional insider definitions.

Tax Schemes

Over the years, schemes to avoid paying taxes on RRSP or RRIF withdrawals or to augment the value of the RRSP contribution receipt have come and gone. Typically, the slick promoters offer tax-free RRSP withdrawals often using of offshore debit cards, credit cards, bank accounts or loan agreements. They've also been known to offer access to locked-in RRSPs or RRIFs or dangle the promise of unrealistic returns on investments. One example from recent memory, is an offer to contribute art by assigning it to a corporation or other vehicle and then contributing that to an RRSP. Art is already difficult to value (isn't beauty in the eye of the beholder?), so in order to maximize the contribution, the value is buried among transactions. These are bogus tricks. If it walks like a duck and it quacks like a duck, it's a duck.

Anti-Avoidance

Anti-avoidance rules were enacted to thwart even more crafty plots that schemers dream up to devalue their RRSP. By contributing stocks and debt that the owner has control over to an RRSP, these slicksters could effectively make non-taxable RRSP withdrawals by devaluing those investments while inside the plan. Also, it used to be that you could substitute an investment held in your taxable account with a different asset in your RRSP trust without tax consequences, as long as it had the same market value at the time of the switch. What the crafty folks were doing was swapping company shares that they controlled into the RRSP and other assets out, for an equal value. They would then reorganize or revalue the stock that they put into the RRSP at or near zero, thereby reducing the value of the RRSP and future withdrawals and taxes, as well. Clever but unfortunately for the rest of us, the ability to legitimately swap securities between accounts was taken out of our arsenal of asset management tools.

> *"The point to remember is that what the government gives, it must first take away."*
>
> —John S. Coleman

Investments where the account holder has control over the securities, no longer qualify to be held in registered accounts if they are acquired after March 22, 2011. Qualified instruments are now limited to **money market instruments** (short-term debt securities), GICs, government and corporate bonds, mutual funds and securities listed on a designated stock exchange, such as stocks, closed-end funds, ETFs, ETNs and many structured notes, etc. Private shares and direct ownership of real estate, for example, no longer qualify and must not be held within an RRSP or RRIF. Similarly, your own debt and the debt, share or interest in a corporation, trust or partnership where you own more than 10% of the value or any deal not executed at arm's length, are prohibited.

All non-qualified or prohibited investments held in a registered account that were obtained after March 22, 2011, or those owned prior but were first deemed prohibited after October 4, 2011, are subject to a 50% tax of the fair market value of the property or securities. Set at an amount that is meant to eliminate any clever trading scheme, the tax repercussions for unknowing investors can be brutal. According to the 2011 Budget Questions and Answers section of the CRA website, this tax may be refunded especially in inadvertent cases that are resolved promptly and the questionable property is removed from your RRSP or RRIF.

If you earn income on non-qualified investments in your RRSP or RRIF, you are responsible for claiming this taxable income, even though it was earned inside the tax shelter.

Although most institutions have been proactive in identifying and notifying account holders who are subject to the new rules, they cannot be aware if you and your family (non-arm's-length group of investors) collectively own more than 10% of a company, especially if you deal at different institutions. It's your responsibility to identify this issue if it exists. Also, if you earn income on non-qualified investments in your RRSP or RRIF, you are responsible for claiming this taxable income, even though it was earned inside the tax sheltered account.

In addition, you are no longer allowed to swap assets between your RRSP, RRIF and TFSA sheltered accounts as mentioned before. Previously, there were options to swap funds between a non-registered account (such as a margin or cash investment account) and your RRSP, RRIF or TFSA. This was particularly useful for rearranging and managing investments that you did not wish to sell by substituting one with another of equal value between your registered and non-registered accounts.

When TFSA accounts were first introduced, there were opportunities to substitute securities with taxable accounts at a range of values. This allowed for small benefits to be earned by choosing a favourable price. When the price of a security fluctuated dramatically in a day, **capital gains** could be avoided by sheltering the security at a lower price after it had appreciated in value by swapping the shares into the tax-free account at the previous day's closing price, the opening market value or some average price that was lower than the current trading value. It didn't take long for that mechanism to be shut down.

Another evasion strategy discovered was the slick trick to move securities between tax-sheltered accounts. When an investor has the ability to affect the price of the shares by trade **volumes**, internal controls and management of the asset, slipping these securities into a TFSA while the security price is being driven upward and swapping it back into a taxable account to enjoy the benefits of a **capital loss**, is clearly a manipulative tax strategy. Bill C-13 focused on eliminating these types of unfair advantages. The CRA website's answers to questions regarding the bill itemize these unfair advantages as follows:

- Increases in the fair market value of a security due to transactions or series of events that would not have occurred in an open market
- Payments in lieu of payments for services or a return on investment, disposition of property held outside of the RRSP or RRIF, swapped transactions between accounts, or withheld income on a non-qualified investment paid from an RRSP or RRIF
- Direct or indirect income reasonably attributable to prohibited investments held in an RRSP or RRIF even if it's paid to someone else who is a non-arm's-length person

If you have a prohibited investment in your RRSP or RRIF, get it out as soon as possible or face what feels like the equivalent of being mugged in Toronto's Moss Park. Charged at a rate of 1% per month, the penalty fees are meant to be punitive. The simplest way to avoid the issue is to swap the ineligible investment in your registered account with another eligible investment (such as cash, bonds, mutual funds or publicly listed stocks) of equal value held elsewhere. There are no tax consequences for swapping the assets since the market value of the registered account is preserved even-steven and most institutions don't charge fees for this type of transaction.

If you don't own any eligible securities to swap for the prohibited ones, it gets a little trickier. Worst-case scenario, you may be forced to sell the prohibited investments. Unfortunately, most of these types of investments are illiquid, as many private shares can be. Finding a buyer (also referred to as finding a bid) for investments not listed on a market or exchange can take time, if at all. In the event that the security cannot be sold, it isn't unreasonable to borrow funds against a line of credit to offset the value of the prohibited securities in the swap transaction. If you already have access to a line of credit or home equity (**secured**) line of credit, borrowing against the existing facility is an easy solution. Alternatively, you could consider margining securities to access **capital** by borrowing against the market value of other securities in your margin account. Keep in mind that borrowing to facilitate the extraction of prohibited investments increases your risk level as you will be encumbered by debt and likely unable (at least in the short term) to liquidate the asset that you were required to remove from your registered plan.

Home Buyers' Plan

If you have not owned a home in the last five calendar years, the Canadian government will help you do that by allowing you to finance part of the purchase with a temporary withdrawal of up to $25,000 from your RRSP. Your spouse may also be eligible to participate separately as long as he or she did not own a home or live in a home owned by you in the last half-decade.

To be eligible under the First-Time Home Buyers' Plan, the home must be your or your disabled relative's principle residence. Also, qualifying individuals must be Canadian citizens who have not owned the home for more than 30 days before the withdrawal is made. You must buy or build the qualifying home by October 1 in the year after you make the withdrawal, you must complete a T1036 form and the withdrawal must be made from your own RRSP plan. You cannot withdraw from a group RRSP or a locked-in plan and any contributions made in the previous 90 days cannot be withdrawn under this plan.

Following the purchase of the home and the RRSP withdrawal, you may then re-contribute 1/15th of the funds back into your RRSP each year beginning the following year, in the usual manner. When you file your tax return, you designate all or a portion of your RRSP contribution as repayment of your Home Buyers' Plan. If you do not make the repayment, that amount is added to the calculation of your income in that tax year and the ability to re-contribute that amount is lost.

In addition to first-time homebuyers, this program is open to persons with a disability who don't necessarily qualify as a first-time homebuyer. If you are a person with a disability looking for a more accessible location or more functionality in a home or you are assisting a relative with a disability to obtain a more accessible home, you may also qualify under the program. The CRA website has an excellent questionnaire available to determine whether you or your spouse (or common-law partner) qualifies for this program: http://www.cra-arc.gc.ca/tx/ndvdls/tpcs/rrsp-reer/hbp-rap/

Lifelong Learning Plan

If you're reluctantly planning to go back to school on a full-time basis, the excuses are getting more difficult to overcome. The Lifelong Learning Plan allows you to tap into your retirement savings without the financially punishing tax issues that a straight withdrawal from an RRSP entails. As long as the educational program that you enroll in qualifies, you sign up before the end of the calendar year in which you turn 71 and you are a resident of Canada with an RRSP, you are likely eligible to participate.

Human Resources and Skills Development Canada lists qualifying studies; however, generally they are those offered by a university, college or other educational institution that normally qualify for the education deduction on your income tax return. The program must be at a post-secondary level, last at least three consecutive months and require students to spend at least 10 hours per week working in the program, including practical training. You must have received a written offer to enrol before March of the year following the withdrawal from your RRSP. You generally have 10 years of equal instalments to repay the amount to your RRSP beginning no later than the fifth calendar year after your first withdrawal. So all of you 69-year-olds thinking about booking a dorm room and attending study hall might want to get on it before the time on this clock runs out.

RRSP vs. TFSA

Since the TFSA account was introduced in 2009, a great debate ensued about which account—TFSA or RRSP—is better. An Internet search revealed a myriad of analytical papers and complicated calculators arguing for one over the other. Being analytically inclined, I prefer a mathematical approach to ascertain which account works better for a given set of inputs however, as the number and subjectivity of variables increase, so does the opportunity for error. Several available calculation tools ask for your province of residence, age, current income, estimated income after you retire (a pretty far-off estimation), estimated OAS and CPP, pension, RRIF income when you retire (and whether you will split it with your spouse for tax reasons), RRSP contribution, age at which you will convert your RRSP to a RRIF, estimated returns, expected number of years to make contributions and several other inputs. Whew. If we knew half of that information accurately, we wouldn't need the calculator. Here are the general comparisons to assist in gauging the best option for you.

Comparison of Tax Sheltered Savings Plans

	TFSA	RRSP
Limits	$5000/year (or as determined by inflation) plus amounts carried forward from previous calendar years plus amounts withdrawn in previous calendar years	18% of your earned income in the previous tax year to a maximum of $24,270 for 2014 plus amounts carried forward from previous tax years
Tax	Contributions are not deductible; no tax payable on withdrawals or income earned within the plan	Contributions are deductible against income; withdrawals are taxable as income
Dates	Contribute any time after January 1	Contribute during the tax year or 60 days into the ensuing tax year
Excess Contributions	Carry a 1% penalty per month	Carry a 1% penalty per month for amounts over the $2000 lifetime overcontribution limit

	TFSA	RRSP
Re-contribution	You may re-contribute the full amount withdrawn in any previous calendar years	There are no provisions to re-contribute funds withdrawn unless they were made under the Lifelong Learning or First-Time Home Buyers' Plan
Beneficiaries	The value may roll over upon your death to your spouse (as a successor owner) or be paid out tax-free and probate-free to named beneficiaries	The value may roll over upon your death to your spouse's registered plan or be paid out tax-free to a named beneficiary; other named beneficiaries may receive the proceeds on a probate-free basis but the estate will be responsible for taxes on the withdrawal of the funds from the plan upon your death
Eligible Investments	Include listed stocks, mutual funds, hedge funds, GICs, bonds, **debentures**, preferred shares, etc.	Include listed stocks, mutual funds, hedge funds, GICs, bonds, debentures, preferred shares, etc.

Note that these comparisons do not take into account that you have additional free cash flow from an RRSP because of your current income tax reduction.

General rules of thumb are:

- The higher your taxable income, especially in the highest marginal tax brackets ($130,000 or more), the better an RRSP is over a TFSA
- The closer you are to retirement, the better a TFSA is over an RRSP
- The higher your income will be in retirement, the better a TFSA is over an RRSP

In any given tax year, if you're in the highest marginal tax bracket, it's best to use the RRSP first and any additional available investable assets should be sheltered in a TFSA. If you're near retirement and you have a modest income, the TFSA should be the go-to option. Also, consider what you plan to use the funds for. The foregoing discussion assumes you're looking at which option makes more sense for retirement income. TFSAs are also an excellent vehicle for short-term saving for a specific purpose, a **sinking fund** to repay future debts or obligations or creating an emergency contingency because they are far more flexible for withdrawals than an RRSP.

A sinking fund is used to set aside money periodically, in order to protect you against a potential, future disaster, as an alternative to insurance; or to retire debt.

To find out your RRSP and TFSA contribution limits, refer to your most recent tax assessment or contact the Tax Information Phone Service (TIPS) at 1-800-267-6999. You will need to provide your Social Insurance Number (SIN), month and year of birth and the total income amount you entered on line 150 of your previous tax return. If you call after May 1, you will need to know the amount from the preceding tax year and if before, the one prior to that.

Ideally, if you can maximize both of your RRSP and TFSA accounts, the discussion becomes a moot point.

Estate Planning with Registered Accounts

RRSPs, RRIFs and TFSAs all offer an opportunity to name a direct beneficiary on your account in the event of you become deceased. You may list more than one beneficiary and allocate your assets proportionately among the beneficiaries to inherit the funds. With RRSP and RRIF accounts, there is a distinct advantage to naming your spouse as the beneficiary because those assets automatically roll into an RRSP or RRIF in your spouse's name, maintaining the tax shelter. In every other case, funds must be withdrawn from your plan upon the date of your death before being paid to the beneficiary, adding the market value of the withdrawal to your

An executor can make contributions to your surviving spouse's or common-law partner's RRSP in the year of your death or in the first 60 days after the end of that calendar year. Your maximum contribution amount must be respected but the amount contributed may be deducted from your income on your final tax return.

total taxable income on your final tax return. That typically translates into a good deal of ink spilled across a cheque destined for Ottawa.

Similarly, the benefits of naming beneficiaries on your TFSA mirror those of your RRSP and RRIF accounts. Firstly, you can elect a single beneficiary or multiple beneficiaries on your TFSA with funds allocated on a percentage basis to each person named. As mentioned earlier, these funds will be transferred to the beneficiary outside of your will and therefore avoid probate. Beyond the fact that circumventing probate eliminates probate fees on the assets in a TFSA, it also means that the assets in your TFSA will not be disclosed publicly and are not subject to a challenge (filing a caveat) against your will. This makes TFSA accounts an excellent tool for complicated estate planning. Heck, taking care of a secret mistress has never been easier. Moreover, the funds are passed tax-free to the beneficiary at the date of the annuitant's death.

Be mindful when executing an estate. **Capital** growth, interest and dividends generated by investments in the TFSA are taxable after the owner becomes deceased, except in the case where the spouse is named as a **successor annuitant**. In that case, the funds stay in the tax shelter and roll over to the spouse's name, increasing the total amount that the individual can hold in a TFSA. There are so many tax advantages to having a spouse that I might have to consider getting remarried.

Fees

Most full-service investment firms charge an annual trustee or account fee for RRSP, TFSA and RRIF accounts. Banks and credit unions typically do not charge an annual fee but the investment options within their plans are limited to proprietary products such as their GICs, term deposits and mutual funds.

If you have a discretionary or fee-based investment portfolio, usually the annual fees on your registered accounts are waived.

Currently, most full-service investment firms offer RRSPs at an annual fee of $125 plus tax or a TFSA at $50 plus tax which allows you the freedom to invest in most eligible investments. If you have a **fee-based account**, including a discretionary platform account or **SMA** platform, RRSP, RRIF and TFSA accounts do not attract the annual trustee fees.

Alternative Minimum Tax

Canada Revenue Agency wasn't named by accident. The middle word is material. When crafty taxpayers avail themselves of every legitimate tax-reducing strategy, CRA steps in with a baseline minimum income level on which you must pay taxes. "Drats!" is the expletive used by villains whose evil plot has been foiled.

Practically speaking, most tax payers need to watch out for this when making a sizeable RRSP contribution and claiming the deduction all in one-year, resulting in a substantial offset of most of their income. If you're considering catching up and exhausting a large accumulated RRSP contribution limit or any other sizeable taxable transaction, it's worth your time and effort to consult an accountant prior to execution to ensure that you do not fall into the clutches of the evil alternative minimum tax level. In fact, if you're contemplating any sophisticated tax strategy, the money you spend on a good tax opinion is worth every nickel.

Chapter 7

What's Wrong with My Retirement Plan?

Retired is when you are first tired of working, then tired of not.
—**Anonymous**

The New Face of Retirement

Freedom 55 was the 1980s hallmark marketing slogan for a major insurance company in Canada. I recall thinking at the time that it was quite an achievement to devise a way to retire earlier than age 65. I was barely working age at the time. The commercials featured an attractive, mature couple sporting a sly smile indicating they'd outsmarted the majority with a simple investment strategy. It seemed it was now available to all Canadians! It was a brilliant plan to be free from the shackles of the work regimen a decade sooner. How clever!

Formerly, 65 years old was the arbitrary birthdate to receive publicly funded Canada Pension Plan (CPP) income. It was ingrained in our culture as the accepted date to hang up your briefcase, if not by choice, then by force. Retiring before or even after this date was unusual if not unfathomable. This campaign, however, worked its way into the

According to a report by Investors Group in 2009, 1/3 of Canadians now expect to delay retirement and many plan to work past 65 years of age.

folds of our cultural grey matter and in time became the golden ring of achievement. Leading-edge Baby Boomers adopted early retirement as entitlement, in recognition for their hard work, almost as though none had been done previously.

In a collective movement, Boomers were corralled into an early retirement trend. Marketing notions of the work–life balance and private sector downsizing compounded the early retirement shift and gave birth to the active lifestyle for middle-aged folks. This played a major role in the alteration of Canadian culture for a tried yet brief period. The sobriety of an extended life expectancy soon took hold of pre-retirees grappling with a low and declining interest rate market and volatile investment strategies.

In 1996, the employment rate for those aged 55 plus dropped from 30% levels recorded back to 1976 to a low of 22%, only to rebound to 34% in 2008. Similarly, as Statistics Canada reported, the expected number of years a 55-year-old planned to continue working rose by a whopping 30% from 1996 to 2008, usurping former retirement projections.

This trend isn't over yet. According to a report by Investors Group in 2009, 1/3 of Canadians now expect to delay retirement and many plan to work past 65 years of age. Anecdotally speaking, the discussions I have with clients rarely include a defined retirement date. I find myself imploring them to pick an arbitrary age for planning purposes, despite their heel marks in the carpet under my desk. This may be partially due to the high percentage of entrepreneurs and professionals I work with, but I believe it extends far beyond that. Some individuals are just afraid of running out of money or feeling purposeless.

Many other people, however, truly enjoy their work and for those reasons cannot fathom giving it up. It defines them. In fact, the majority of people who feel this way report that they don't intend to stop working entirely, barring any significant health issues. The conversations taking place usually focus on the financial ability to retire rather than setting a planned date to stop working. People want the trapeze net set up but they also want to continue swinging. Some professional and entrepreneurs only intend to slow down by hiring in management roles to replace some of the work they perform rather than selling their business entirely. By working fewer hours or working on their own terms as a consultant they continue to provide expertise on a project-related basis. Even non-professionals talk about scaling back hours rather than ceasing work altogether or propose that they could provide consultative work based on their years of experience.

Outside of the desire of many pre-retirees to become consultants, the demand for this herd of independent contractors remains to be seen. Imagine what the marketplace would look like at a future Chamber of Commerce luncheon filled with 70-year-old, vaguely-defined business people handing out inkjet-printed business cards with the occupation *"Consultant."* Oh, you're one of those, too!

The second impetuous for delayed retirement is our ever-extending life expectancy. Generations approaching peak earning years and beyond have become acutely aware of the fact that our retirement funds may have to extend into our 90s, thanks to advanced healthcare, regular medical testing and a shift to active living. The fear of running out of money has increasingly drawn more people to at least formulate some modular retirement plan. Reported by Human Resources Development Canada (HRDC), 20% of Canadians shockingly count solely on government pensions, inheritance and lottery winnings to fund their retirement. Alarmingly, outliving your money is a bigger risk than premature death.

> *"Fifteen, there's still time for you*
> *Time to buy and time to lose.*
> *Fifteen, there's never a wish better than this*
> *When you only got a hundred years to live"*
> —Dave Matthews Band, "100 Years"

The third leg of the stool rests on marginal or absent investment options stacked on top of poor guiding principles over recent market cycles. During the inflationary post-Great Depression decades, double-digit interest rates elevated a delusional expectation for stable projected returns. In popular retirement planning schedules, many investment projections were based on the lofty, prevailing rates of interest of the 1980s and 1990s. If you extrapolated the value of an RRSP at an investment rate of 8% or 9%, you may find your forecasts grossly overestimate the actual value of your investments in 2010, after the financial crisis.

Today we are more educated, or should I say, street-smart. The projections used are more conservative, partly due to professional liability concerns and partly due to a new market reality. During the years of high interest rates, if an IA or financial planner provided investment growth illustrations based on a low return expectation, potential clients darted out the doors leaving a helicopter of papers spinning on the desk behind them. In those days, we would have been better off dressed in a purple robe with a cone-shaped hat adorned by golden moons, our hands swooping through the air above a smoking glass orb. Clients, whose preference is for a rosier picture, as if it held predictive karma, are now sobered by the obvious problems of recent market cycles, post-2008. While you don't need to expect the worst-case scenario, cautious realism is more advisable than optimistic abandon.

The truth is that many workers were caught up in the soothing lullaby of the retirement estimates that they had not revisited in a long time. The false assumptions that they or their advisors made years earlier coupled with poorly stewarded investment decisions, navigated plenty of 60-somethings straight back into the work force. Like a bunch of old seamen heading wearily back into the salty waves for another catch, their promised Freedom 55, 60 or even 65 was sinking with the level of the stock market. To add insult to injury, many of them had never enjoyed the market rally leading up to the 2008 collapse.

I'd like to think that we are all older and wiser for the journey. Our projections are based on more conservative numbers. We review and amend our expectations with new information and with increased regularity. The understanding of investment vehicles has expanded and fees have narrowed. Federal economic leaders from around the globe have a better understanding of the impacts of fiscal and monetary policy on **Gross Domestic Product (GDP)**. Yet despite this, 75% of Canadians who knew what they held in their portfolios reported that they still did not think they were on the right track, according to Statistics Canada.

GDP is the value of all of the goods and services produced within a country's borders over a certain time period.

Bless the Government Programs

In Canada, our social system is well established for the benefit of citizens. Between public healthcare, Old Age Security (OAS), Guaranteed Income Supplement (GIS) and the Canadian Pension Plan (CPP), most Canadians have some form of safety net in place despite themselves.

A good place to start when planning for retirement is to understand which government programs you are eligible for and how they work. Begin by setting up your *My Service Canada Account* through the Service Canada website: www.servicecanada.gc.ca/eng/online/mysca.shtml. After specifying a username, a temporary password is mailed to your home address for security. Once you receive it, you can login to the site and find useful information about your CPP contributions, projected retirement payments and other helpful details and calculations.

Canada Pension Plan

In 2013, if you were eligible to collect the maximum CPP benefit at age 65, you would receive $1012.50. The most recent changes proposed in Bill C-51, which received Royal Assent in December 2009, require anyone who is under age 65 and earning pensionable income to continue contributing to the plan. After age 65, you may elect to cease contributions even if you continue to earn pensionable income. By today's rules, your earnings do not need to drop before you can collect early benefits. You can, however, continue to make payments to the plan even if you begin collecting funds from CPP, which will result in the receipt of **Post-Retirement Benefits (PRB)**.

PRB contributions result in increased payments even for persons already receiving the maximum pension amounts. The additional benefits are up to 1/40 of the maximum pension (up to $25.31 per month in 2013) for each year of additional contributions. The exact payment depends on the earning level of the contributor.

The Bill also introduced an increase to the general dropout rate to 17%, so that in 2014, you can remove 8 of your lowest income years from the CPP benefit calculation. This change will increase your CPP benefits as well as your disability and survivor pension benefits for your beneficiaries, which are based on your retirement benefit calculation.

Canadians are still permitted to collect CPP benefits early but with increased clawbacks for each month prior to their 65th birthday that they begin receiving payments. In 2013, the reduction is .54% per month gradually increasing to 0.6% per month in 2016 and thereafter. At this rate, if your regular benefits at age 65 totaled $12,150 you could take a 36% cut in annual payments to receive $7776 per year at age 60.

Similarly, deferring payments will increase your benefits by .7% for each month that payments are delayed. If you delayed payments until you were 70 years old, your annual benefits jump from our arbitrary $12,150 (in 2013) payment to $17,253.

If you continue working, your employer matches your mandatory 4.95% PRB contributions until age 65. You may continue contributing $2529.45 based on the upper income limit of $51,100 per year (in 2013) if you work until age 70, which will increase your benefits in the future. Currently, a rough estimate of PRB payments expressed in today's dollars (adjusted for inflation) are $218 per year at age 61, $302 if you begin payments at age 65 and $429 annually when you start at age 70, according to the Canadian Retirement Income Calculator offered by the Service Canada website.

Comparison of CPP Payment Options

Age	Discounted CPP Benefits at Age 60	Maximum CPP Benefits at Age 65	Enhanced CPP Benefits at Age 70
60	$7776		
61	$15,552		
62	$23,328		
63	$31,104		
64	$38,880		
65	$46,656	$12,150	
66	$54,432	$24,300	
67	$62,208	$36,450	
68	$69,984	$48,600	
69	$77,760	$60,750	
70	$85,536	$72,900	$17,253
71	$93,312	$85,050	$34,506
75	$124,416	$133,650	$103,518
80	$163,296	$194,400	$189,783
81	$171,072	$206,550	$207,036
81 reinvested at 6%	$327,491.75	$326,730.50	$269,224.79

The preceding chart illustrates what you would collect aggregately under the early and deferred CPP collection options assuming full contributions based on the maximum earned income of $51,100 (in 2013) collected after 2016. For simplicity, these numbers are unadjusted for inflation and are only intended to compare cash payments based on these straightforward assumptions.

Some people maintain that it behoves you to collect pension income as soon as possible as you can't predict your mortality and the rules of collection may change down the road. Without considering the effect of inflation and tax, the chart illustrates that the total payment received by a pensioner who defers receiving benefits to age 75 will be larger once the person survives to age 80. However, an investing pensioner would have substantially more by taking the discounted payments earlier and investing them at 6% (not including taxes).

If you do not have any eligible survivor benefits, it may make sense to collect your CPP benefits early. No one knows when they'll decease and government legislation may change at any time, with possible implications on when and how much you can collect.

The value of having the funds at your disposal cannot be discounted whether you spend the money or invest it. The effect of compound interest is undeniable. Each situation can vary dramatically due to taxation, expected mortality and inflation, so ensure that you consult your *My Canada Service Account* and obtain professional advice.

Old Age Security

Old Age Security (OAS) sounds more like something to avoid than to be grateful for. Perhaps it should be renamed the Golden Years Bonus Cheque or the Canadian Bridge Retirement Payment. There is something about the term "old age" that causes uneasiness, as if it comes with a lifetime supply of anti-wrinkle cream.

In March 2012, the federal budget proposed an amendment to the age at which retirees can collect OAS payments. Beginning in April 2023, the eligibility for OAS increases from 65 to 67 and the Survivor Allowance increases from 62 to 66 years of age. On the heels of the extended collection dates for Canada Pension Plan (CPP) income only three months earlier, the message is clear. The bubble of Canadians set to rely on our social system could burst our financial capacity with the same unfortunate, inevitable realization that those last 10 pounds are here to stay. It's time to relinquish those size-28 Levi's to the charity pick-up bin.

> *"The problem with socialism is that eventually you run out of other people's money."*
> —Margaret Thatcher

These measures, however, are meant to ensure longevity and sustainability of our system. Even with the modifications, Canadians can still expect to receive continued OAS payments. You may recall that in 1965, the government made a popular move to reduce the collection age for OAS from 70 to 65, and in 1972 introduced inflation indexing to benefits so that retired Canadians could keep up with the cost of living. The spousal allowance was introduced in 1975 with same-sex and common-law couples' recognition following 25 years later.

When Do I Have Enough?

Retirement planning night is popular with both the Kelowna and Vancouver Women's Investment Clubs. Before each of the meetings, members are asked to submit their most pressing question regarding retirement. Knowing the calibre of women, the concerns that recently came back were not surprisingly well thought out and poignant. While there were a wide variety of issues, certain trends were evident among respondents. Far and away, the number one question was, "When do I know if I have enough money to retire?"

Time is the single biggest issue impacting your financial retirement plan. Over the extended time spent in retirement living, costs march exponentially higher. Although the Bank of Canada recently set an inflation target of 2%, it has averaged a whopping 4.47% over the last 40 years. Compound your cost of living at these rates for a few decades and you have a hefty bill to fund. According to the most recent Statistics Canada survey, 50% of Canadians live longer than their life expectancy at birth and 35% of women aged 60 in 2011 will reach their 9th decade.

Canadians are rightfully concerned about outliving their money. To plan properly, begin to evaluate your situation by collecting your own basic data. While average life expectancy is easy to reference, you'll want to consider your own heredity and adjust for differences in your family and personal circumstances.

The Statistics Canada CANSIM table, last modified in September 2011, indicates that the average life expectancy for men born between 1950 and 1952 was 66 years of age, steadily increasing to 78.5 for those born in 2006–2008. Similarly for women, those born in 1950–52 could expect to live an average of 71 years, gradually rising to 83.1 years for those born 56 years later. Keep in mind that these are average numbers, which means that mortality at younger ages offsets those of us who live longer. Consider your genetics and lifestyle when you start your planning. Then budget for an extended lifespan. I like to think that the Dave Matthews Band has it right and we should anticipate living for 100 years. Planning at least to age 95 for many people makes practical sense unless there are strong reasons not to.

If you have unused RRSP contribution room but your income is low in that tax year, it may still be to your benefit to contribute funds to your RRSP so that they can be invested within the tax shelter. The income tax deduction can be carried forward indefinitely and used to offset future, high-income years.

The second crucial input to your plan is the rate of inflation. Historical averages may be skewed by anomalies during the 1980s so you may want to adjust long-term averages by a grain of salt. Also, the Bank of Canada Board of Directors' monetary policy has an objective to maintain inflation at approximately 2%, which justifies favouring rates closer to that level. For these reasons, an arbitrary figure for projections may be a realistic choice despite the historic mean rate of 3.14%, measured between 1914 and 2012. It's up to you but be cautioned not to underestimate this number. That would paint an unrealistic projection on how long your funds will last in an inflation-adjusted future. A payment of $1000 drops to a real value of $545 at 2% inflation over 30 years. The impact of a higher inflation number as well as a longer time frame lowers the value of future figures dramatically.

The last figures to collect are a list of your current savings and other assets and whether they're held in taxable or tax-sheltered accounts. You will also need to estimate the amounts that you can invest annually as well as your current lifestyle spending habits. A reasonable proxy for your retirement income needs can be determined by projecting your current spending levels into the future depending on how you expect your retirement to look, adjusted for inflation and changes in your healthcare needs, debts and activities.

If you are in a modest income bracket of $40,000–$60,000, government plans will replace 30–40% of this during your retirement and that income is inflation-adjusted. If your income is higher, the government plans will be less impactful as a replacement. They'll only fund approximately 20% of your pre-retirement income due to the maximum payouts leaving a large gap that you'll need to fund yourself.

Beyond age and inflation, the risk of running out of money is highly influenced by the rate at which you withdraw your funds. Individuals who take out more than 6% of their portfolio per year are likely set to deplete invested **capital** rather than solely drawing on income, at least in some years. Based on a variety of outcomes, it's generally accepted as ideal to plan on a 4% withdrawal to sustain wealth.

Armed with these numbers, you can find several Internet-based calculators to project your retirement income or if you're handy with a Hewlett Packard 12C, sit down and start plugging in the digits. Failing those tool-time-Bob do-it-yourself strategies, your financial professional or your local banker should be equipped with appropriate software to pull off the feat. Better still, a CFP or CSWP can provide a more comprehensive analysis integrating other assets, various dates for balloon payments, liquidation events and possibly a Monte Carlo simulation of an array of possible outcomes of your own. Now, doesn't that sound like a party!

How Much is Too Much in My RRSP?

There is an answer to this question. Withdrawals from a RRIF can become burdensome in retirement if you have too much accumulated in your plan. Not only can your income in retirement be pushed to the highest marginal tax rates, but you may also be subject to a clawback on your OAS payments due to poor planning. If you're paying high taxes you might not receive OAS at all because you have too much money. But is it right to complain about having too much money?

Interestingly, the question about how much money in an RRSP is too much is most often asked by individuals in a medium income range trying to forecast the reductions to their OAS payments in retirement or those who are averse to paying any taxes whatsoever. The RRSP is a tax shelter to be used to earn investment income while you're gainfully employed. Consider the implications from a practical standpoint. It isn't difficult to project what your income will be at retirement and whether that level will be above the point where OAS is reduced, if that is your major concern. If you're one of those individuals who amassed profound wealth, RRSPs are not likely the vehicle you will rely on in favour of more sophisticated vehicles including **trusts** and corporations. The short answer is if you have $900,000 saved in your tax shelter and no other income, your OAS payments will start being clawed back if you begin withdrawals at age 71, given a 6% return, minimum required RRIF withdrawals and current OAS clawback income levels. If you have a spouse with whom to split income, those factors will change again.

The answer more correctly will depend on what you're trying to achieve. If it's current tax sheltering while in high-income employment years, keep socking it away. If it's avoiding tax, spend every penny you have.

When I die, I want to drop dead with nothing more than a Canadian nickel and some pocket lint. After all, we Canadians are now all penny-less.

Other Ways to Save for Retirement

As a country, Canada has done well instituting safeguards for basic financial care during retirement. Beyond that, retirement financing is up to each individual and your ambition to create an enjoyable existence in your twilight years. When we turn our attention to retirement planning, there has been good marketing and legislated tax reasons to focus on RRSPs and pensions but there's more than one way to slay a dragon.

After the 2008 financial crisis, the use of private pensions has come under scrutiny. If you work for company XYZ, they also manage your pension plan and your share purchase plan is invested in XYZ, you have significantly concentrated risk in one company. With the threat of meaningful employers declaring bankruptcy in the United States, the downturn in the markets pressuring managers of small pension plans with funding deficits and a growing body of retirees coupled with a reduced workforce, more than a few experts wonder how the funds will hold up. Increasingly, individuals are choosing to control their own retirement savings to ensure they safeguard against funds in these pools depleting prematurely.

The Interest Free Loan

"I'm counting on my pension since my RRSPs have been a disaster."

Why have your RRSPs been a disaster? High fees? Ill-managed and ill-suited investments? Poor returns? All of the above?

The benefits of controlling your retirement investments are the same as the drawbacks. You have control of both the risks and the responsibility! For every reason that pension plans are better than RRSPs, RRSPs are better than pension plans. Personally, I prefer to hold the control over investments myself but not at the expense of features such as inflation protection that some **defined benefit pension plans** have. If you have the aptitude, the flexibility of managing your own investment direction, risks, fees and diversification are worth the chances of underperformance, lack of control, underfunding and corporate bankruptcy. I'm not suggesting that you should go without professional management but that you take the reins for some of the steering committee decisions if you have the confidence and understanding to do so.

Differences Between Retirement Vehicles

	Pension (Defined Contribution)	RRSP
Contributions	Higher contributions are allowed compared with RRSPs.	Contribution of 18% of earned income to a maximum of $24,270 in 2014 plus carry forward of any unused contribution room.
Withdrawals	Restricted depending on the provincial or federal legislation that governs your company's plan.	Full access to withdrawals at any time.

	Pension (Defined Contribution)	RRSP
At Death	There may be survivor benefits that have been established once you enter the payment stage. Otherwise benefits are forfeited upon death.	Assets can be rolled over tax-free to a spouse or infirm dependent child or assets passed to your named beneficiary on an after-tax basis or through your will.
Investments	No control over the investments. Also no responsibility over the investments.	Total control over investment decisions, risk level and strategies.

> *"If I have a good pension plan, should I even bother to put a minimal amount in an RRSP each year, instead of say, paying down my mortgage?"*

The decision to invest in tax-sheltered savings beyond a prescribed pension plan depends on your taxable income level, cash flow and other **capital** resources. If you're in the highest marginal tax bracket, you have several years for the funds to compound within an RRSP and mortgage rates are low, you're likely better off to contribute to your RRSP. Another consideration is whether your mortgage is tax deductible or not. If it is, paying it down may make less sense than you think especially if interest rates are low and you have capacity to comfortably meet the payments.

At this point, an investment in a TFSA starts to become an interesting consideration, as well. But outside of saving for short-term investments or if you have a low taxable income, RRSPs win out over TFSA contributions by simply reframing RRSPs as a way to borrow to invest for retirement on an interest-free basis from the Government of Canada at the rate that you pay taxes.

For some strange reason, there has been a popular push to refute the RRSP. If I had a toonie for every time I heard someone tell me she didn't believe in RRSPs because she hated paying taxes, I would have enough to buy a Blenz franchise and live the barista's dream.

Let's cut to the chase. Whenever you can defer paying taxes, not only do you have the use of money in your hands for a longer period of time but due to the effects of inflation, a dollar of taxes paid today costs you more than a dollar paid in taxes in the future. The reason this works is because money is worth less in the future. Remember what a handful of old copper pennies used to buy you at the corner store? Mmmm... soft banana marshmallow candies, black licorice pipes and a Lik-M-Aid.

Contributing to an RRSP will defer paying taxes on current income. Moreover, if your future lower income drops you into a lower marginal tax rate, the amount of taxes you pay drops in absolute terms as well. By investing in an RRSP, you are credited with the amount of income tax you paid on the amount that you contributed to the plan. Think of this as borrowing to invest for your retirement, interest free from the CRA for as long as you keep the funds in the plan. When you take the money out, you repay the pseudo interest-free loan. Reduce, defer and postpone taxes whenever possible. Equal only to a true interest-free loan.

TFSA Retirement Plan

"I plan to move $5000 a year into my TFSA and have been doing so since 2009 when they started and kind of ignored RRSPs. Is this wise?"

Chapter 9 discusses various types of accounts and provides details on the functionality of TFSA versus RRSP accounts. Generally, if you have low or no earned income, a TFSA is the best choice, hands down. If you have too much money in your RRSP and pension plans, a TFSA is the best place to add more dollars. If you have no other contribution room for RRSP or pension contributions, put your money into a TFSA.

Another benefit is in the event that you need money in the short-term. Funds in a TFSA are easily accessible without immediate tax implications. You can even re-contribute the money withdrawn in future calendar years so the ability to shelter that amount is never lost, unlike an RRSP contribution, which is lost once contributed regardless of withdrawals. If you don't have other savings, the TFSA can be more flexible for these reasons.

Generally, if you have low or no earned income, if you have too much money in your RRSP and pension plans or if you have no other contribution room for RRSP or pensions, a TFSA is the best place to add money, hands down.

Funding Retirement with Real Estate

There are other routes to financial security beyond the clear benefits of the RRSP and good ol' fashioned saving. Some courses are by hard work, some by happenstance and some by dumb luck. Does it surprise you to hear that a good number of individuals are literally counting on a 'great North American retirement plan' complete with a lottery win or strategic lawsuit? Despite the odds of 13,983,816 to 1, there are a shocking number of pre-retirees who hold firm to the lottery dream as the answer to all of their financial worries. Marginally better off are those holding out for a long-lost uncle leaving them millions. For the same reasons they fear running out of money and there are good reasons to think that your parents, grandparents and long-lost uncles may have the same concerns. And in this age of divorce, I suspect that match.com is fertile ground for hunting sugar daddies.

> *"Personally, we will rely more on our business and real estate for our retirement but I wonder if you have any thoughts on these sectors of the market and the impact they have on overall savings."*

The dropping interest rate cycle has been fruitful for investors in real estate. **Leveraged** investments that generate rental income in particular have quietly built the wealth of many families across Canada. Those who had the foresight or luck to buy in, hold on and have the mortgage paid off by retirement, use the free cash flow to fund retirement expenses. As long as the location is good, the rental market is stable, market values sustain themselves and you don't mind the grunt work of fixing broken dishwashers, this has been a good place to put long-term investment money. Has been.

Thirty years of dropping interest rates will come to an end and being close to zero in 2012 means that there is more room for rates to rise than to continue falling. North American monetary policy makers continue to appease us with a low interest rate commitment for the near-term years, but beyond that, if the inflation cycle pits itself against us, something will have to give. It's in our economic interest to keep inflation at reasonable levels. There are more tools in the war chest to stave off a rampant rise in the cost of living but interest rates have long been the feasible lever of choice.

When the tide changes, the price of real estate will drop along with the affordability of higher mortgage payments. Coupled with demographic issues in North America's retiring population, the key to keeping real estate growing is squarely on the shoulders of the birth rate and immigration. The increased accessibility of the Internet certainly won't help urbanization either, as the sprawl of commercial properties and jobs with them expand to less expensive locations driving overall pricing levels down. The one resistance in pricing at the bottom is found in the comparable cost of construction, which will bring a **notional value** to developed properties. You can see this happen in certain locations including resort towns replete with accessibility challenges and short building seasons, but even these areas will deteriorate if extreme downward pressure persists.

The reasons that real estate, as an asset class, has done well are twofold. The use of **leverage** has turned a 3–4% return to 7–8% and the dropping interest rate has created a 30-year real estate market rally in the same way that bonds and other interest sensitive investments have been on wheels. It's easy to imagine, however, that if there comes a time when no one wants to own, the residential rental market will be reasonably robust. People need to live somewhere and if they're displaced by affordability to buy, they'll rent. This balancing act will play out over the next decade with the internal rate of return on investments in real estate, including the **capital** values, the cash flows' ability to meet obligations and the alternative option to rent. Of course, overall demand will play a major role including immigration, non-resident purchasers and population trends. Other considerations that play a part in how this unfolds include lifestyle choice, pride of ownership, affordability and desire to maintain control over personal environment. Believe it or not, choosing paint colour is important to some people! Just keep in mind that this asset class has more risk today than at any time in the last half-century. The other way to spin the real estate retirement wheel is to downsize. Condo living and even versions of assisted living have great appeal for retirees who travel, want lower maintenance or an expanded social life.

Comparisons between Real Estate and Equity Investing

	Real Estate	Equities
Leverage and Borrowing	Up to 75% secured.	Up to 50% margin and subject to margin calls.
Historic Long-term Returns	Approximately 3–5%.	Approximately 7–9%.
Tax	Residence is tax-free, commercial and investment property are capital gains.	Dividends have preferential tax treatment. Capital appreciation offers a 50% inclusion rate.
Marketability	Valued annually with the provincial assessment authority but sale prices depend on comparable and other listings.	Valued minute to minute during market hours.
Maintenance	High maintenance to property and improvements.	If self-managed, monitoring for buy and sell opportunities is important at least quarterly when earnings are released, if not more frequently.
Fees/Costs	Maintenance costs, deterioration, strata fees, property taxes, real estate commissions for buying and selling.	Commissions to buy and sell are approximately 2% at a full-service brokerage.
Risks	Risks are due to liquidity, lack of interest or changes in the market or if the ability to obtain capital dries up (higher interest rates or lack of lending).	Value of businesses (including publicly traded shares) is dependent on economic activity and the viability of the business.

"I have a lot of equity in my property but you have to live somewhere in retirement and my property will be difficult to sell. When is a good time to sell a unique property?"

Moving to a smaller residence that you own or lease frees up **capital**, lowers maintenance costs, reduces property taxes, alleviates stress, increases your security (with gated communities, condos and assisted living) and reduces the time and money you spend maintaining it. The decision isn't always an easy one to make. If you have lived in a home for many years, there are emotions surrounding a decision to move, never mind the disruption of organizing, packing and reducing the stuff in all of those closets.

A year ago, my sister and her husband sold the home in which they'd raised their two grown boys. My sister is a local version of Martha Stewart without the incarceration stint. A professional musician, she ran a music school of a hundred students out of her basement and the pride of ownership was evident throughout their home. When she and her husband decided to sell, it was a little alarming to everyone who knew them well. They held good reasons given that their children were now grown, but their former lifestyle of yard work, car tinkering and a music school would have to be sorted out. They were smart enough to rent initially and try out the drastically different lifestyle before committing with **capital** dollars. It turned out to be a brilliant decision.

On top of that, a soft real estate market may make selling difficult, especially if your property is unique or in a higher price range. Be prepared to follow your arduous decision to sell with a languishing tolerance for property showings, other disruptions and pricing decisions that you may not be entirely comfortable with.

Not to make it sound overly simplified, but the best time to sell real estate is when there is a buyer. If the value of real estate is location, location, location, the ability to sell is timing, timing, timing. I'll follow that up by saying that all it takes is one buyer. Pricing property is crucial and the right marketing approach is a key to selling illiquid assets such as real estate.

Reverse Retirement Savings

Paying down debt is valuable. Reflecting on the advantages of **leverage**, it isn't contrary to pay down non-tax-deductible debt. Some pundits have gone so far as to call it bad debt and good debt but in a low interest environment, I don't see affordable debt of any kind as bad. The only real issue is when a situation changes and debt becomes unaffordable due to changes in market rates, job loss, excess **leverage** or something else out of your control. Keeping debt manageable is ideal but being able to pay it out entirely is perfect. Not actually paying it out, but being able to. It can be a useful way to augment carefully laid plans to earn equity but not for disposable or depreciating goods. The idea that we are entitled to travel after a hard day's work or that we should have the same car as our neighbour was a marketing scheme as savoury as when former U.S. president George W. Bush proclaimed home ownership for all Americans precipitating the housing bubble and the **ABCP** market collapse in 2006.

There are psychological reasons to pay down debt as well. Lower debt and lower risk often result in lower stress. Those who have suffered job loss and financial setbacks can account for the emotional impact of strangling obligatory payment levels. High debt is a rope that under the right circumstances loops itself around your neck in a noose. Paying down non-deductible debt frees up monthly cash flows in the future, which leads to either lower risks needed in the future or the liberty to take on more calculated, structured opportunities. By having monthly income available, either you can spend it, invest or borrow to invest.

One of the most rewarding ways to save for retirement is to do so naturally, if you're so fortunate. Owning a successful business provides income during your working years; often something to sell when you retire or a legacy to pass on to children and family members. Without a plan, however, the prospects of selling a private business are tricky. If real estate is not easy to sell, you can imagine how the perfect buyer would have to come along to buy a small business. Business people sometimes groom employees or family, but if planning for retirement happens too late, the succession plan is a piecemeal approach and often less than successful.

In some cases, however, the transition from small business annuity during working years warps into a balloon payment at retirement. This is brilliant and not profoundly different from a 10-year overnight success.

Leverage Your Lover

Not only do people who are in loving relationships tend to live longer, there are financial advantages, too. Income splitting with a spouse is one of those key advantages.

> *"Marriage was one of the first non-biological factors identified as improving life expectancy. The explanation given was that married people tend to take fewer risks with their health and have better mental and emotional health. Marriage also provides more social and material support ('material support' is a term for things like someone to take you to the doctor or care for you when you are sick)."*
>
> —Mark Stibich, Ph.D.,
> "Being Married Improves Life Expectancy"

Even though you have to convert your RRSP to a RRIF at age 71 and begin withdrawing funds the following year, if you're still working or if you have unused contribution room, you can still contribute to a spouse's RRSP and use the tax deduction. As people continue working into later years, this may become a good way to defer income; however, the advantages of making contributions are diminished, as the years available to compound investment returns are less. The real benefit to making a contribution to a younger spouse's plan is to postpone and possibly reduce aggregate tax payments as pension income is split between spouses.

Also, if your spouse has lower income, consider investing **capital** into his TFSA. The funds do not attract income tax so it isn't attributable to the higher income spouse. I'm personally out looking for a younger spouse right now!

The other side of the relationship coin is the tough situation if you have a spouse who is a spendthrift, has destructive vices or has a medical condition such as dementia. Controlling your own financial security and the safety of your financially stable retirement can require the finesse of a psychologist and support of the medical community.

> *"My real worry is how to control a spouse who loves to spend money in certain areas and will not consider a budget. I would like to pay off my mortgage before I retire and I'm not sure I can control the finances to do that."*

There is nothing wrong with setting up separate bank accounts for various expenses or even for each of you. In some cases, managing cash flow by forcibly constraining it is the only practical option. You could also try a "shock and awe" discussion with a frank financial planner. Seeing the numbers on paper can sometimes be a rude awakening to someone who has always thought of money as easy to come by and hearing the message from a professional and someone other than you can make a big difference in its efficacy. You can also try other ways to bring expenses to the attention of a spouse by compiling them regularly, but the message usually sticks better when delivered by an outside party.

Keep in mind that the ways you and your spouse behave around money are not likely to change after retirement. Establish good habits now and create a supportive environment.

Another consideration is to introduce a marriage contract. You don't have to be getting married to employ this effective tool. You can set up a contract to divide responsibility over debts and assets to be included or not in your family asset division. A good lawyer can help you devise an agreement that is fair and takes into account your differences regarding savings and reducing debt versus a spendthrift approach. Separating or clarifying certain aspects of your financial affairs brings financial security to the saver in the relationship and can reduce stress from financial friction. It might even preserve a relationship ready to veer off course for no other reason.

Healthcare

By 2031, 23.4% of the population will be 65 years of age and older compared with 14.4% in 2011, according to Statistics Canada. Critical illness and long-term care for you or your spouse can significantly deplete your **capital** and your security along with it. There are three ways to approach this. Aptly named, both **critical illness insurance (CI)** and **long-term care insurance** are available to those who qualify. With critical illness insurance, your **premiums** are paid each year based on your application age, the amount of the policy, the insurance company and your coverage. Essentially, if you're diagnosed with a life-threatening illness defined by your contract, the insurance company issues a cheque for the value of the policy. You can then use those funds to find a cure, travel the world, pay for expenses or renovate your home for accessibility. Of course, the downside (or upside as the case may be) of having CI insurance is never being able to make a claim and being out of pocket for those **premiums**.

Long-term care insurance can help fund assisted living. These policies are fairly expensive as the likelihood of collecting on them is higher. There are several types of policies available and they range from assisted living in government facilities to having care and nursing within your own home. The payout on these policies is a monthly amount according to the original terms of your policy.

Lastly, a **sinking fund** is always an option. Self-funding gives you the flexibility to use the accumulated amount for other purposes not originally designated because they are your own investments. As a rule of thumb, depleting your saved **capital** by no more than 4% will usually leave **capital** available for unforeseen expenses including health related issues. As an alternative, a line of credit can be a lifesaver if you have access to financing—either on a **secured** or unsecured basis—but this option leads to other planning issues farther down the road.

Another consideration regarding healthcare comes into play when you move from one province to another. Remember that although Canada is one country, each province individually governs its public healthcare offering. Even private insurers vary their coverage and premiums. Before considering a major move to be closer to family, take a look at what the healthcare and ensuing financial implications are. In the end, the lifestyle decision will prevail but you need to have all the information at hand before making any significant changes.

Inflation Risk

One of the most important risks to your retirement plan is the risk of inflation. It's difficult to know how much the cost of living will rise over various time frames but it's interesting to note that between 1973 and 1982, the Canadian Consumer Price Index rose an average of 9.63% each year for a decade, according to Statistics Canada. More recently, inflation has been contained in the 1–3% range and it's the stated objective of the Bank of Canada to target a 2% inflation rate. Regardless, inflation over expansive periods of time will undermine our ability to pay for goods and services. The following table illustrates the value of $1000 over various periods of time at various rates of inflation.

Effects of Inflation

Inflation Rate	5 years	10 years	15 years	20 years	25 years	30 years
0%	$1000	$1000	$1000	$1000	$1000	$1000
1%	$951	$904	$860	$818	$778	$740
2%	$904	$918	$739	$668	$603	$545
3%	$859	$737	$633	$544	$467	$401
4%	$815	$665	$542	$442	$360	$294
5%	$774	$599	$463	$358	$277	$215

Qualitative Retirement Planning

In the same way that your home purchase is more closely aligned with your lifestyle needs than your investment needs, the financial side of your retirement plans is necessarily pinned to how you plan on spending your time. Creating a vision for the years that you're no longer building a career means that you'll have to redefine yourself as an individual or yourselves as a couple.

Give some thought to the following questions:

- Do you plan to work part-time after your proposed retirement date? If so, will it be in the same area, for the same firm, on a contract or freelance basis or by some other arrangement? How likely is it that these opportunities will be available to you at that time?
- Does your heredity imply any potential health issues that you want to be financially or psychologically prepared for during your retirement years?
- What are the three main activities that you enjoy now that you plan to continue during your retirement? What do you spend on those activities now? Outside of inflation, how do you see those costs changing? Consider membership fees, equipment, travel, supplies, organizational support, etc.
- What are the activities that you wish to participate in once you're retired that may be new or may be a version of some hobbies that you currently enjoy? What are the costs associated with those activities?

- Estimate your current expenses and use of free cash flow from your employment and/or investment income.
- What kind of home do you plan to live in? If you own a house, do you plan to downsize? Will you live in an apartment or assisted-care facility in due course? Do you wish to stay in the home you're in as long as possible with the employment of private nursing? Will you move in with family members?
- What city do you plan to live in?
- Will you be near family or established friends?
- Who do you think you'll spend time with?
- What are your expectations around your personal abilities and mobility?
- Are you outgoing or do you prefer more time on your own?
- Are you adventurous or tried and true?
- Do you depend on anyone to manage your finances currently?
- Do you have a spouse? If so, what are your expectations about your spouse's life expectancy and healthcare needs?
- Theoretically, would you prefer to change your lifestyle to fit your budget or make significant changes to your plan to live well?
- Are you a saver or a spender?
- Are you generous with your time or your money?
- Can you imagine yourself doing anything radical during retirement? If so, what might that be and how will it impact your finances?
- If you require medical or physical assistance, what avenue would you consider first? Relying on family (spouse, child or sibling) and are they willing and able? Hiring private care? Relying on social programming? Does assisted living have any appeal as a solution?
- Do you hold Critical Illness or Long-term Care insurance? Are you relying on your assets, the sale of your home or a sinking fund to provide for illness and infirmity?
- What assets do you have access to in order to meet your retirement goals?
- Which is the most important to you?
- That I do not have to rely on my children or be a financial burden on them.
- That I am able to fully enjoy my retirement lifestyle for as long as I have my health.
- That I maximize the time that I have in new adventures.
- That I keep enough money to be able to afford good quality healthcare.

Having formulated some ideas around how you plan to spend your golden years, do yourself a favour and write it down. This is your vision of you in the future. Without a clear understanding of what retirement looks like, you cannot begin to project the associated costs, the required assets or whether or not you have enough. Start with something like, "My ideal retirement will be filled with days of…" or "When I wake up the first morning of my retirement, I can see myself…" or "What I'm most looking forward to in my retirement is…." Include in your vision where you imagine living along with whom you plan to live or near whom you plan to spend time. Consider which activities and social engagements you want to participate in and how often. Add a list of places that you would like to go or spend time in with as much detail as you like. There is no way to do this incorrectly and when you're done, you'll be able to actually picture what this time will be like. Along with your financial advisor, you will then be in a position to project the **capital** needed to make it happen and control the risk of outliving your savings.

Sources:

Liu, Hui, and Debra J. Umberson
2008 The Times They Are a Changin': Marital Status and Health Differentials from 1972 to 2003. Journal of Health and Social Behavior 49(3): 239-253.

Statistics Canada
2005 Population Projections for Canada, Provinces and Territories 2005-2031. Statistics Canada Catalogue 91-520-X.

Chapter 8

Professionals Are Not Created Equally

> It's not whether you're right or wrong that's important
> but how much money you make when you're right
> and how much you lose when you're wrong.
> —George Soros

The first time I put pen to paper on this topic, a cathartic rant chastising investment professionals who have no business representing the industry for lack of knowledge or ethics, tumbled onto the page. After 20 years in this line of work, I've seen more that a few things that I wish I hadn't. You've probably heard a few investment horror stories of your own, if you haven't lived one or two yourself. Having exhausted my cynicism, I hope to impart sound advice and pragmatism crediting the many proficient colleagues who represent clients well.

This past summer, I had the pleasure (read: displeasure) of rebuilding a 10-foot by 30-foot engineered retaining wall that failed long before it should have. Working with tradesmen is definitely outside of my comfort zone…especially on a cost-plus basis where there's no absolute cap on the money you'll spend. As men come and go, the invoices multiply. The anxiety reaches a peak near the end of the project when you find yourself pleading to the construction gods for the workers to stop traipsing through your yard, for completion of the project and the cheque writing to stop.

The talented folks who came through my redevelopment performed excellent work and were committed all the way through. Regardless, the racket of paying for your dirt to be removed and then paying for new dirt to replace it (they called it engineered fill, crush and other fancy, expensive dirt terms) is enough to choke on. I can personally attest to how gut wrenching it is for a type AAA personality to pay for labour by the hour, watching the inefficiencies of trench digging. Between "too many men hanging around" and "the dirt racket," it was almost too much to take. By project's end, I believe I had good people working for me and I was pleased with the outcome. Nevertheless, I slept like a rock when it was all over.

With the same stigmatization as a lanky, blonde woman in a suit standing beside a smoking car hood in Latte Lovin' Larry's Garage and Tire Centre, (which I feel comfortable stating as the former), if you've ever had the sense that you're getting shafted in the investment world and wish you knew how it operated, I hope that you'll feel solid ground beneath you by working through the following chapter. I'm lucky that someone helped me out in the landscape construction world. Thanks, Matt.

A structured approach is always helpful in fishing the right professional out of the sea of personalities and accreditations. Moreover, adopting a structured process will equip you with the best ways to manage and maximize your professional relationship for the future, bar none. Between you and I, we could eradicate the unnecessary issues in the industry, at least as far as our arms can reach and start making consistent investment returns across the board.

Know Thyself

I made the mistake of meeting with a family lawyer in the throes of my divorce, expecting him to tell me what to do and how to do it. I found out the hard way that I should have understood what I wanted and then asked him to execute the plan. Similarly, don't expect to meet with an investment professional and have her tell you what you need or want. This approach will land you an investment strategy that is suitable to the advisor and may or may not fit your objectives.

While you may get lucky finding a professional relationship that accidentally fulfills your needs, more often than not you'll be disappointed sooner or later. By the fact that you're reading this, you realize that you can't cross your fingers and haphazardly follow a road that meanders in an unknown direction. Sometimes all it takes are a few ideas and some time to think about what you really want to ensure your long-term success.

The Ancient Greek aphorism "Know thyself" speaks equally to the dangers of gratuitous self-claims as much as it's a warning not to become wrapped up in herd mentality. Forward steps in unknown territory become calculated and sure with the awareness of your abilities and shortcomings, and a sense of direction. You already know confidence comes from being able to identify your skills, attributes and the depth that you bring to the table. Set the direction and you become unstoppable in your achievement.

A good place to begin is by identifying what you don't want. On a large blank page, draw a line through the centre vertically and horizontally to create four equal rectangles. Label the upper two boxes "All Past Investments" and "Ideal Investments." Then, in the two lower quadrants, entitle them, left to right, "What I Can Do" and "Hire a Professional to Do."

Reflect on your past forays into investing. List every investment that you've ever made including the ones you'd rather not remember. Fill the upper left side of the page with single word descriptions of investments you've made and note any strategies. You may include such investments as term deposits, bonds, GICs, stocks, mutual funds, real estate, commodities and gold. Feel free to add private ventures, flow-through shares, time-share properties, the lottery, endowment fund, art, antiques, Chinese imports, rental properties, sovereign debt, swaps, derivatives or a trusty lemonade stand. Tax strategies, RESPs and real education, insurance, TFSAs and the like are all game. It doesn't matter what you call the items in your personal list but that they're meaningful to you. Anything you think of is valid and useful here since we are going to draw qualities from these experiences to lay the cobblestones for future investing.

Past Inv.

- (real estate - Calgary house) (S) ✓
- GIC + term deposits (S) ✓
- Saving for college (S) ✓
- (oil stocks, bank stocks) (S) ✓
- Jim's ag business - part owner (S) ✓
- California time-share (R)
- That diamond stock (R)
- RSP + margin account mutual funds (R)
- Silver ETF (R)
- money market (S)
- lottery ticket (R)
- (CP shares before split) (S) ✓

Ideal Inv.

- Income
- stable growth
- profitable
- good return
- no stress

What I can do

- read business news
- decide what stocks I want
- ~~save~~
- budget
- file + ~~prepare~~ taxes
- buy ETF's + Mutual funds

What I want to hire out

- Financial Plan
- protect my savings
- research investments
- tax strategies
- manage daily investment decisions

Once you have an exhaustive list, put a checkmark beside those that were successful, either achieving what you'd set out to do or turning out to be ironically profitable in some other way. Then write an *R* or *S* beside each of those investments, to identify whether you felt it was a Risky investment or Safe one. This is purely subjective. Don't succumb to what you think it should be; rather, base it on your experiences, whether you perceive it was risky or safe. Finally, circle what you consider the three most comfortable, satisfying, best investments.

Next, think about what successful investing means to you, drawing on a variety of your experiences with success. In the upper right quadrant, list the qualities of the investments that you want to see in the future. Use adjectives such as aggressive, safe, income oriented, low maintenance, compounding, sustainable, ethical, stress-free, balanced, life enhancing, philanthropic, interesting, stable, exciting, fun, worry-free, profitable, home-run or anything that describes your ideals. Transfer any investments that worked out well from the upper-left box to the upper right, including the circled items. Add any you think are missing. There are no wrong answers.

> *"History never repeats itself, but it often rhymes, to borrow from Mark Twain's famous quote…a piece of advice which rings just as true in today's financial market as it ever has. A robust understanding of history reveals nothing is really new. Perhaps just another colour. While this will not prevent us from making some financial missteps in life, it will help us to avoid life altering, portfolio destroying mistakes and to be wise enough to elude the 'this time is different' trap!"*
>
> —Scott Ross, CFA, Portfolio Manager,
> RBC Dominion Securities

Now draw your attention to the lower left quadrant. Here, consider your capabilities and jot those skills down. Remember that we are only using one sheet of paper for a reason. This is meant to be an informal way to have you evaluate who you are as an investor and uncover the gaps. Moreover, I don't want to create a project that is so daunting that you won't approach it. Keep it simple and focus on your first reactions.

The list of what you are capable of may include the following:

- deciding the amount to contribute to my RRSP
- effectively selecting ETFs for my portfolio
- determining how much I need each year for a comfortable retirement
- balancing a cheque book
- hiring trustworthy professionals
- buying large-purchase items
- making money in my profession
- understanding my risk tolerance for managing personal assets

- watching market trends
- researching investment options
- defining my retirement plan
- executing a variety of buy and sell orders
- trading listed securities
- managing asset allocation

When your list is complete, stroke a line through those you have no real interest in or don't have the time to do well. Just because you *can* do something, even if you can do it well, doesn't mean you *should*. Leverage your time and skills to do the things that you do best in life. It's more valuable to be effective than competently busy.

Finally, you will populate the lower right box. You have already given thought to what you felt comfortable actively executing yourself and what you have the time and interest for, so this will be easy. Would you garner value from a professional taking over some sophisticated tax planning, intergenerational estate management or assessing your financial position in contemplation of divorce, marriage or another life event? You may wish to be hands-on and involved with investment decisions; make them entirely on your own; or prefer to leave all of the day-to-day decisions to a professional management team. Are you interested in sophisticated strategies using **options**, futures, flow-through shares or other derivatives? Think of the variety of financial aspects that can be possible and desirable for your lifestyle and write them down. When you're assessing the fit of your new advisor, this is the list of key services that you'll be looking for and asking whether or not they're able to provide you.

Deciphering Acronyms

This is going to sound like dating. It probably is a bit like dating. If only there was an investmentadvisormatch.com or iHarmony website. Recently, this list of professional financial accreditations and their acronyms came in handy for a judge I know who was presiding over a case about investment suitability. As a professional with expertise in law, engineering, teaching, mechanics, design, healthcare, biomechanics, shipbuilding, land development or other, how the heck could you be expected to know what the following acronyms in this long, long list stand for?

Advisors in the investment world come in all shapes and sizes, with a myriad of qualifications and qualities. Certain provinces in Canada recognize the Mutual Funds Dealer Association (MFDA) where members who sell mutual funds to the public are required to pass a proficiency test regulated by the provincial securities commission. For securities trading at an IIROC registered investment firm, IAs must pass the Canadian Securities Course (CSC), the Conduct and Practices Handbook (CPH), plus a 90-day IA Training Course (IAT). Also, they're required to complete the Wealth Management Essentials course (WME) within 30 months of approval for registration,

In recent years, IIROC has instituted continuing education requirements for all licensed securities professionals. During every 3-year cycle, each IA must complete 12 hours of compliance-related accredited course material and 30 hours of Product Knowledge or Professional Development, in the interests of remaining current. Securities professionals also can obtain specialty licenses for trading **options** and futures, financial planning and the like, which require additional examinations and licensing procedures. The best approach is to decide what you want your advisor to do for you before you set out to find one.

Below is a list of commonly used accreditations in the investment world. It's a decent reference tool when reading business cards, but education doesn't tell you anything about desk-side manner, application of skills or real investment performance. For that, you'll have to skip to the following sections.

Investing

CIM® – Chartered Investment Manager. It used to be called Canadian Investment Manager, at least what my certificate from the Canadian Securities Institute (CSI) reads from a few years back. This designation allows a professional to invest funds as an Associate PM and then a PM after a 2-year period. A PM can invest funds on a discretionary basis. The only other designation that qualifies for a PM designation is the CFA®.

FCSI® – Fellowship of the CSI is obtained once several Canadian Securities licenses are completed, a letter is obtained endorsing the application, a sponsorship is in place by an existing fellow and 7 years of investment experience are completed within the preceding decade.

CAIA® – Chartered Alternative Investment Analyst is a specialization in the hedge fund and alternative investment sector. It's a rigorous set of exams not easily passed.

IA – Investment Advisor, which used to be called stockbroker. The minimum qualifications are listed in the paragraph above.

CFA® – Chartered Financial Analyst. The charter is granted after the successful completion of all 3 levels of exams and 4 years of relevant employment experience. Each exam represents approximately 300 study hours and the pass rate is roughly 50% for each level. Annual filings confirming ethical obligations and membership fees are required to maintain the use of the charter.

Financial Planning

PFP® – Personal Financial Planner is the designation issued by the Canadian Securities Institute. It's a broad-based program.

CFP® – Certified Financial Planner is recognized as the central financial planning designation. The CSI regulates financial planning and planners are required to maintain ethical standards and ongoing education updating.

CSWP® – Chartered Strategic Wealth Professional is the CSI's answer to the CFP for sophisticated financial management strategies.

RFP® – Registered Financial Planner is offered by a privately run organization from the CFP group. The organization separately provides education and self-governance among members.

CPCA® – Certified Professional Consultant on Aging is another new designation. It's granted after successfully completing training focused on the aging demographic and their specific needs in areas such as pension information and healthcare.

MTI® Estate and Trust Professional – These professionals address sophisticated estate planning strategies for protecting wealth and transitioning it to the next generation.

FDS – Financial Divorce Specialist specializes in, you guessed it, planning for the financial aspects of a divorce. While this area of expertise is relatively new as a formal discipline, the Academy of Financial Divorce Specialists endeavours to form loose regulation around practitioners of this ilk.

Accounting and Tax

CA® – Chartered Accountant

CGA® – Certified General Accountant

CMA® – Certified Management Accountant

CPA® – Chartered Professional Accountant is the new amalgamation of the three separately labeled professional accountant designations, CMA, CGA and CA.

FCA® – Fellow of the Institute of Chartered Accountants

FCGA® – Fellow of the Certified General Accountants Association

Insurance

CLU® – Chartered Life Underwriter specializes in developing effective solutions to manage risk, estate planning and income replacement using insurance products.

RHU® – Registered Health Underwriter focuses on living health benefits such as disability income replacement.

Other

BBA, B.Com. or BMgmt– Bachelor of Business Administration, Commerce and Management are undergraduate programs in business as the first level of university. Usually general in nature, it typically covers 4 years of full-time study.

MBA – Master of Business Administration is a university graduate degree in business from the faculty of business or management. The degree often focuses on the management and leadership of businesses and financial management of corporations, which may be useful in assessing the investment prospects of publicly traded securities, depending scope of the program.

Matchmaking

So, there you sit in an armchair across from a professional-looking receptionist behind an oversized flower arrangement in the lobby of an investment firm. A fan of business cards splays across your hand. One professional you plan to meet holds a CFP® designation. One is underscored as a Senior Vice President! Other cards indicate CFA®, FCSI® and BBA and each state the individuals are IAs, PMs or Wealth Managers. Don't they all do basically the same thing?

Basic Planning

With the software available today, almost all investment professionals, even with minimal qualifications, provide rudimentary savings projections and basic financial plans. They may not, however, be interested in doing so. Most investors require some sort of projection at one point or another, but suffice it to say that even with old-fashioned stockbrokers, someone at any firm is likely able to get these calculations together for you. The questions are, at what additional fee, if any, how basic or complex of a plan do you need and will their software and expertise fit the bill. These are great questions to ask, which comes a bit later in the chapter.

It's Complicated

The financial planning industry has been embroiled in a tug-of-war between the Financial Planning Standards Council (FPSC) and the CSI regarding its series of accreditations, including the PFP® program that leads to a certificate in financial advising. If you aren't confused yet, the CSC recently launched a higher level financial planning designation called the Chartered Strategic Wealth Professional (CSWP).

FPSC was organized to regulate financial planners and manage CFP designations. Prior to this organization, there were no homogenous standards for financial planning and just about anyone could hang a shingle out and call herself one. According to the CSI website, the organization touts their Wealth Management Essentials course together with the Fundamentals of Financial Planning as a preparation for writing the CFP® exams.

If you're seeking a planning professional, the complexity of your situation will dictate whether a CFP® or a CSWP® is the route you want to take. A planner with a PFP® designation can certainly advise you on the basics and even develop a decent, straightforward plan. For more complicated issues, consider the high-level standards outlined by either the CSI or the FPSC.

If your situation involves multi-generational planning, sophisticated tax strategies or more complicated issues, including corporations, second marriages or **trusts**, you'll want to ensure you involve a tax and legal advisor for execution; ideally, someone who specializes in your area of interest. As with every profession, lawyers each practice a different area of law and even accountants can be specialized. Find a financial professional who has something specific on his business card that relates to your area of interest, whether **trusts**, estate or tax specialization.

Estate Planning

While estates are a specific area of financial planning, you may want to also consider having a life insurance broker (**CLU®**) wade into the discussion. Some IAs may also be licensed to sell life insurance, but unless they process life and disability policies as a regular part of their practice, you'll want to opt for an insurance specialist. Policies are complicated and various issuers and reinsurers have important differences in their offerings. Pick a professional who has their finger on the pulse of these changes for the most up-to-date solutions.

Divorce Financial Assessment

Along the Westside section of highway leading out of Kelowna, there are at least three billboards marketing divorce planning services among the zipline ads, real estate agents and one for Coors Light. This burgeoning area of expertise has developed from a culture of acceptance and the growing market of clients. No longer does the divorcée stigmatization from former generations hold the scandalous and mysterious allure that it once did in the movies.

Ascertaining the value of future cash flows between former spouses, analyzing the value of illiquid real estate, private companies and investment portfolios and before- and after-tax analysis takes the skills of a professional. Also, having a basic background in the legal implications that impact these financial calculations is imperative. An FDS may also be an investment professional or she may have a fee-for-service offering. The Academy of Financial Divorce Specialists has created this professional designation for advising on financial aspects of divorce, as well as providing basic background knowledge for the province in which they practice, each being quite different. In addition, a forensic accountant, CPA or CFA® will have the skills required to crunch the numbers accurately, and when combined with a divorce lawyer, you'd be well equipped from a financial aspect, especially for complicated transactions.

Mutual Funds

For someone who is just starting out and with a small amount to invest, the likely route is to find someone who can give you good advice on selecting one or two quality mutual funds. IAs at your local bank have basic mutual fund licensing which qualifies them to select the broad categories of mutual funds that their bank offers, usually on a **no load** basis. That is a decent place to begin. You probably cannot expect ongoing rebalancing of multiple funds unless you initiate these yourself, so choose funds that are broadly diversified rather than sector funds (such as a specific country) unless you plan to stay on top of it.

Outside of the major banks, a variety of independent companies, manage mutual funds for distribution through a variety of channels.

Some even have an internal, direct sales force but most are sold through external financial planners, via the Mutual Fund Dealers Association (MFDA) or IAs operating at IIROC licensed dealers and brokers. What you can expect is a more hands-on approach to administering and rebalancing your pooled investments. Depending on each company's compensation structure, many of these groups champion front-end commissions structures, even some with zero commissions charged. In this day and age, there's really no need to lock your investments into a high fee structure. Too many effective choices are available to tolerate the handcuffs of DSC purchases. If you find a planner or IA who offers mutual funds on a FE, zero commission basis who will actively rebalance your portfolio and you do not have much **capital** to work with, that may be a terrific solution. Mutual fund sales people obtain their educational requirements through the CSI and are typically registered under the MFDA or with IIROC as an IA.

Buying Stocks and Bonds

Licensing for an IA is as minimal as obtaining the CSI's Canadian Securities Course along with the Conduct and Practices Handbook course and poof, after a 90-day Investment Advisor Training Program anyone can hang out a shingle. The criteria to become an IA doesn't set one apart from another, so be discerning when you. Many IAs go on to advance their stable of accreditations and specialties, several of which are listed in the foregoing sections. IAs typically cannot produce a track record, so asking for testimonials from a client with a similarly sized account is a good idea and if you can obtain more than one recommendation, your comfort level will be higher. You'll also need to determine what kind of practice your IA manages. Some hire out the management of the investments to mutual funds or SMAs, while others prefer to buy and sell stocks and bonds directly. Some offer option and future trading as well as hedge fund and exempt market investments for sophisticated and **accredited investors**. Generally speaking, your IA must call you with any recommended changes to your portfolio for which you must give the final approval.

Ensure you understand the commissions and fees being charged, as there can be a wide range among practitioners.

Portfolio and Discretionary Management

If you have a portfolio of over $200,000, your opportunities to access more sophisticated strategies and investment professionals increase dramatically. A PM is the only professional who can handle discretionary money management.

In Canada, a PM can follow one of two paths. The CSI offers a course route beyond the CSC, through the Investment Management Techniques and the Portfolio Management Techniques courses. Each of these requires 30 hours of self-study followed by successful examination. Alternatively, the CFA® designation is internationally recognized and comes after three separate levels of rigorous testing. The CFA Institute recommends 250 hours of independent study for each of those levels and passing rates for every 8-hour exam is less than half. Most pension fund managers, mutual and hedge fund managers, stock analysts and corporate financing specialists hold a CFA® charter; however, some charterholders operate private practices, especially outside of major centres where other professional financial roles don't exist.

The role of a PM in the private wealth arena is split into two primary areas. The first is the investment councillor. Typically, investment councillors operate from the arm of one of the big banks and offer actively managed portfolios through third parties. I realize there is duplication in the PM reference so stick with me. The PM that you work with gets to know you and your objectives and essentially manages the relationship with you. They will select the portfolios and pools that are appropriate for you and actively rebalance the funds placed with each mandate, and will, from time to time, hire or fire the various managers of those mandates by withdrawing your funds. Each of these pools or portfolios will in turn be managed by a PM who buys and sells the stocks and bonds that make up the investments in your account.

In other cases, a PM is an investment professional who operates your account on a discretionary basis. Not only do they develop an **IPS** and allocate your money among various asset classes, they also buy and sell the securities accordingly for your account directly. Each decision made to buy and sell the various positions is done within the constraints of your IPS rather than contacting you every time a position is traded. Many PMs will manage accounts with block trading, where accounts holding a position will be sold or purchased all at once. This allows the PM to be more efficient and nimble in a live market and the process is equitable for accounts of all sizes. With the efficiency of this type of platform, it's conceivable to manage a greater amount of assets and number of clients and the risks of a certain client falling through the cracks is all but eliminated when portfolios are managed concertedly.

Options, Futures and Derivatives

Derivative trading can be an effective way to protect your investment portfolio as much as it can be to increase your **leverage**, risks and returns. The strategies are typically complicated and require specific education and registration through IIROC. If this is an area you're interested in working with or having access to, ensure your IA or PM has a derivatives license. Even if the professional is licensed, make sure that you know what you're getting into and that so does he! Not more than a few years ago in B.C., an investment professional who had designed what he thought was a relatively conservative strategy got caught in a mess. When option pricing went through the roof during the financial crisis (recall that the cost to buy and sell **options** increases as **volatility** increases), he was not only unable to effectively execute the strategy but he was powerless to unwind existing positions given existing market conditions.

New Issues

New issues from public companies, especially those that garner high demand, are difficult to access. If this is an arena that you want to play in, ensure that you're with a firm that does a great deal of underwriting and has an extensive corporate finance department. The large investment firms are the most active and can provide greater access to the major issues presented to the market. Even when a firm participates in the syndication of a new issue, if the local branch and advisor with whom you deal isn't generally active in **new issues**, your local IA may not receive enough allocation of the issue. Also, if you're interested in the over-subscribed **issues** that are well publicized and garner more interest than there are shares, be prepared to take some of the lesser quality **new issues**, as well, to keep your place in line when the really great ones come along. This is a game that is not appropriate for most investors, but if this is up your alley, have a long hard discussion with your prospective advisor about what **volumes** of **new issues** her firm actively participates in and how the firm allocates the **issues** among clients. There are many middlemen in this game.

Alternative Strategies and Hedge Funds

When it comes to non-traditional asset classes and strategies, IAs are usually relegated to outsource specialized hedge fund strategies rather than creating strategies themselves. The nature of hedge funds and **alternative strategies** is complicated and they typically require a huge amount of **capital** and large numbers of transactions to execute their strategies profitably. The variety of hedge funds available in the market isn't necessarily open to investment at all firms. Some prohibit certain strategies deemed too risky, unproven or lacking transparency. They are usually purchased through an **OM** document, which ultimately means you must be accredited in order to invest.

Accredited investors are those who have one of the following: significant investible assets, high income or professional level investment education and experience. Some provinces allow access to these alternative funds even if you're not accredited, if you sign a waiver stating that you realize that you can lose all of your money. It's exclamatory, but the shock value makes investors think twice while protecting the investment manager, at the same time.

Understand the risks and how the portfolio works before you take out your pen. As we go forward, many hedge fund providers are moving to more accessible platforms similar to those of mutual funds and ETFs. This almost eliminates the cumbersome paperwork associated with OM offerings and opens the door to non-sophisticated investors. Despite the fewer documents required and the significantly greater accessibility to investors' wallets, the strategies mirror their OM counterparts, including the risks.

CAIA® charterholders certainly have a deep understanding of non-traditional asset classes, but CFA® charterholders also cover a wide range of alternative strategy topics in their deep body of study. Since you do not need any special license or accreditation beyond an IA to sell hedge funds, tread with caution. Be aware of fees and get a grip on the potential implications of how the funds behave in various market cycles.

Insurance

Only practitioners who hold life insurance licenses through the Canadian Association of Insurance and Financial Advisors (CAIFA) can offer life insurance products which include segregated funds, life insurance policies, disability insurance, critical illness and **long-term care insurance**. The requirements for a license include self-study programs and examinations followed by licensing and additional continuing education credits specifically in the field of insurance. The real trick with insurance is to find a professional who deals regularly or exclusively with the products that they offer. Given the nuances between policies and issuers and the ever-changing underwriting process, it takes a hands-on approach to stay current. It isn't enough to be licensed to practice this business.

The Litmus Test

The old adage, "three economists, four opinions," isn't far off. There are as many investment management opinions as there are advisors. Knowing what you want is half the battle. Finding the right advisor to meet those needs is quite another. Separating the wheat from the chaff takes some work but investing a little time now will pay off later. Referrals are a good place to start. When you're sitting on the other side of the desk, here are some questions that you may want to ask. Not to say that it is appropriate to barrage some interviewee with all of the following, these are meant to generate questions that are important to you. Choose a few key questions and use them consistently. Comparing apples to apples is easier than comparing cumquats to oranges.

How long have you professionally managed investments for clients?

It goes without saying that the longer the better. You may want to consider the IAs age and the likelihood that they are contemplating retirement. Find out if that's in her plans in the near term and if so, ask about her succession plan. Demographically, the industry as a whole is skewed to older advisors. What you gain in experience, you give up in longevity.

What credentials and licensing do you hold?

With the 30-hours-per-cycle of continuing education requirements, most IAs have depth of knowledge beyond the basic licensing requirements and today, there are a wide variety of ancillary specialties, ranging from CPCAs to FDSs.

It almost seems on purpose that the investment industry has complicated the landscape with a myriad of accreditations to maintain some air of mystery. There are so many acronyms and designations because the industry's late bloom into a profession coincided with an era of private training. Quite frankly, every private educational body wants a piece of action that comes with developing an accreditation, delivering the educational requirements and insisting on annual membership dues. Admittedly, many accreditations are clearly beneficial, while some offer little or no real value to clients.

When it comes right down to it, you're hiring this individual to manage your investments. The other perks are nice, but keep in mind what services and expertise you're looking for. Currently, the CSI delivers the largest number of professional credentials in Canada, including eight certificate programs, four designations and two fellowships. You can be more comfortable with any of these specialist programs; however, nothing replaces experience.

How many client families do you manage in your practice?

This is less important if the advisor runs a discretionary fee-based practice. If it's not discretionary, the advisor is required to make a phone call to the client every time a trade is transacted. Mathematically speaking, you can figure out pretty quickly that with 500 client families, at five minutes per phone call, this is obviously not practical. Markets can swing dramatically in 42 working hours and if your name is Mr. Zebra, you may have quite a different execution price than Ms. Able. Use your judgment and remember where you likely fit in the pecking order of clients.

Typically, IAs manage approximately 200–300 clients, which may indicate being in charge of upward of 1,000 different securities on the books. Discretionary PMs, on the other hand, can manage a greater number of clients due to the homogeny of their portfolios and the bulk trading platforms. No clients, despite the size of their accounts, are left behind on a trade or change in the portfolio.

Do you provide financial planning? If so, what planning do you offer and are there additional fees for that service?

Not all IAs offer even basic financial planning directly; however, major bank-owned firms and many independent firms offer some form of financial planning, made available through a separate individual on a fee-for-service basis. Simple plans and investment projections are often offered for no charge using straightforward calculation software. Fees charged for financial plans can run from hundreds of dollars to thousands, depending on the complexity of the advice. It's not uncommon for other individuals to be called in to collaborate with the financial planner, including your lawyer and accountant.

Do you prepare an IPS outlining my objectives?

An IPS is a document that your advisor puts together that states your objectives, risk tolerance, assets to be invested and a few other personal details. It should outline what the strategy will be for managing your portfolio and more importantly what it won't be. Conventionally, discretionary PMs have a blueprint or IPS for any pooled portfolios that they manage, describing what they can and cannot invest in and in what proportions. It's a good idea to ask for this document. If you have a portfolio of any description, you should ask for an IPS for your accounts. This will help ensure your advisor understands your needs, and because they're written in black and white, you will have something to which to hold them accountable.

Have you had any regulatory issues?

Here is a list of provincial regulatory websites. They each list licensed investment professionals and any inquiries and disciplinary action taken against any particular person.

B.C. Securities Commission – www.bcsc.bc.ca
Alberta Securities Commission – www.albertasecurities.com
Saskatchewan Financial and Consumer Affairs Authority – www.sfsc.gov.sk.ca
Manitoba Securities Commission – www.msc.gov.mb.ca
Ontario Securities Commission – www.osc.gov.on.ca
Autorité des marchés financiers – www.lautorite.qc.ca
Service Newfoundland and Labrador – www.servicenl.gov.nl.ca/securities/
New Brunswick Securities Commission – www.nbsc-cvmnb.ca/nbsc/
Nova Scotia Securities Commission – www.gov.ns.ca/nssc/
Prince Edward Island Office of the Superintendent of Securities – www.gov.pe.ca/securities/
Yukon Office of Superintendent of Securities – www.community.gov.yk.ca/corp/securities_about.html
Northwest Territories Department of Justice Office of the Superintendent of Securities Registry Northwest Territories – http://www.justice.gov.nt.ca/SecuritiesRegistry/index.shtml
Nunavut – www.gov.nu.ca

Alternatively, you can visit the Canadian Securities Administrators website at www.securities-administrators.ca and perform a National Registration Search or you can generate an IIROC Advisor Report which will outline the background, qualifications and disciplinary information on advisors at IIROC regulated firms.

Do you consider my account to be a large one or a smaller one?

In a transaction-based platform, this will give you some insight into how actively the advisor will be reviewing your portfolio, in particular.

Do you charge fees or commissions?

Questions about fees should be dealt with right off the bat. Answers should be clear, understandable and transparent. Ask about FE, DSC and LSC fees on mutual funds or whether funds are purchased on a no-load or front end zero commission bases. Inquire about the amounts charged on fee-based accounts. Usually larger accounts have a lower percentage charged, so find out what those thresholds are and if you can expect your advisor to reduce your fees when you reach those levels or whether you have to track that. What are the commissions that your broker or IA charges for **commission-based** trades? Are there different fees charged for solicited and non-solicited trades depending on whether you or your advisor came up with the investment idea? Bonds, foreign exchange, treasury bills and other fixed income vehicles have fees in the form of spreads between the buying price and selling price. Ask what those fees look like for the size of trades that you'll be making if your account is commission based.

How are fees and commissions calculated and how often are they charged?

Not wishing to be entirely redundant, please feel free to flip back to chapter 2 on stocks, chapter 3 on bonds, chapter 4 on alternative investments and chapter 5 on pooled investments for details on fees.

What did you do professionally before you became an IA?

Would it surprise you if the IA was formerly a telemarketer or a truck driver? It shouldn't as long as the former profession was legal, of course. It may tell you a little more about the individual and what natural skill sets and experience he adds to his investment style. If he worked on oilrigs for 15 years, he may have particular insight into that sector of the market. I've met successful IAs who were former NHL hockey players. Their sense of dedication has served them well, not to mention their connections with wealthy former teammates and friends. It isn't surprising that those with a background as a professional athlete might similarly be focused in any profession that they pursue.

What is your investment strategy and philosophy?

This hopefully is obvious. This open-ended inquiry will fill in some gaps about how the practitioner sees the investment world and more importantly, how she plans on investing your little golden nest egg.

What is your minimum account size?

Some investment professionals have a minimum investment amount, especially discretionary PMs. Sometimes the IA arbitrarily sets these and sometimes they're constrained by the investment structure at the firm. For example, many **SMA** or full discretionary platforms require a minimum of $200,000 in at least one account. Times are changing though and so are these levels.

If certain **alternative strategies** are part of your portfolio, they may have minimum restrictions, as well. If you are an **accredited investor**, most of these limitations are as low as $5000, but that is not always the case.

Is the firm registered with the provincial securities commission or with IIROC?

According to IIROC's website at www.iiroc.ca, it's the national self-regulatory organization which oversees all investment dealers and trading activity on debt and equity marketplaces in Canada. Created in 2008 through the consolidation of the Investment Dealers Association of Canada and Market Regulation Services Inc., IIROC sets high-quality regulatory and investment industry standards, protects investors and strengthens market integrity while maintaining efficient and competitive **capital markets**. IIROC carries out its regulatory responsibilities through setting and enforcing rules regarding the proficiency, business and financial conduct of dealer firms and their registered employees, and through setting and enforcing market integrity rules regarding trading activity on Canadian equity marketplaces. In addition, each province has a self-regulatory body that governs the actions of investment dealers and their representatives.

The Canadian Investor Protection Fund (CIPF) protects investments, including cash and securities, held at an IIROC-regulated firm in the event that firm becomes insolvent or ceases operations due to bankruptcy.

Are client assets held with a third-party custodian?

It's not necessary to ask this when you deal with an advisor at a schedule A or B bank in Canada, but it's a good question for finding out where your accounts are held with smaller firms and independent agents.

How often are you available to meet with me?

You may wish to meet with your advisor regularly or sporadically. Several factors come to bear on the decision of how frequently to meet. Personal preference, the size of your portfolio and whether your manager has discretion over decisions are key components of determining the answer. A couple, now in their 80s, has been meeting with me each month ever since we began working together. It's obviously an exception and impossible to afford to everyone unless your total number of clients is limited to 140 and you do nothing else. Similarly, not everyone wants to meet that often or even at all. Some clients prefer to manage their accounts over the phone or Internet and speak to their advisor on an ad hoc basis. It's a good idea to be in contact with your advisor at least every year whether you want to or not. You'd be surprised how much can change in the marketplace as well as your own personal situation over 12 months. Also, this will keep you personally connected to your advisor and keeps you top of mind when new ideas or opportunities crop up.

For my investment objectives, what returns should I expect?

What you are looking for is something reasonable. On average, 10-year Government of Canada bonds yielded 7.6% over the 50 years ending in 2011, but those numbers include the 1980s where yields were in the 20% range. Also, remember that as interest rates drop, bond prices rise. When interest rates are near zero, the chance of them rising with a negative effect on bond prices is a more likely picture going forward. The outlier years of the past dramatically affect average calculations. In an environment where inflation is contained within the targeted 2% range and interest rates are in the low single digits, don't use long-term averages to manage future return expectations for bonds and other fixed income products. Besides the wisdom to underestimate rather than overestimate returns is built on common sense.

U.S. **equities** over the last 50 years have returned an average of 9.3% measured by the S&P 500, while the **S&P/TSX** Canadian stock index has an average of 6.2% for the last 20 years.

Keep your expectations in the single digit range and expect your advisor to as well. If she over promises, there's only one side of the bar she will fall on when the actual numbers are reported. Also, you don't want the professional who is stewarding your hard-earned assets to take on undue risks in an effort to meet unrealistic return expectations. That never works out the way you'd like it to.

Will you be dealing with me directly or do you have any associates who will be handling my account? Who is your assistant and what do you expect me to handle directly with your assistant?

Especially in the case of large investment practices that have several team members, certain clients end up dealing with a particular individual within the group. This may be determined by personalities to a certain extent but often, it's driven by the size of your account and the amount of revenue it generates. It may also depend on your relationship with a certain team members or whether you have any specific needs that a specialist on the team deals with directly. Usually, a licensed or unlicensed investment assistant or clerical staff member handles administrative processes for all clients.

Maximizing Your Professional Relationship

> "Practically Investing *is a good title for this book. When Coreen asked me to write a few words of advice for readers I thought the best thing to do would be to share my simple lessons for investing that I have learned over my 25 plus years in the business. As a professional investor I have had the chance to learn these lessons more than once. If you stick to them—which is easier said than done—they will make you money.*
>
> 1. *Only invest with people who are risking their own money alongside you. If they are just collecting a fee, your interests are not aligned.*

2. Don't respond to timelines. If you are being pressured to make a quick decision it's usually because it's not a good one. I have always found that people want your money next week as much as they do this week.
3. Pay serious attention to the details when investing your money. Understand the risks that you are taking and if you want to take them or not. Only you know if you want more risk in your portfolio or less.
4. Cut your losses: 9 times out of 10 taking your first loss is the least expensive thing to do. Burying your head in the sand and hoping things get better is almost always a mistake. Doubling down is ALWAYS a mistake!!
5. Only pay fees for things you can't replicate for less on your own.
6. Keep your head up because investing by design has its good days and bad days.

Good luck."

—Michael W. MacBain, Founder,
East Coast Fund Management Inc.

Intimidation and the Implications of Not Following Advice

The brutal reality is that if your IA calls and you're the one holdout not to take her advice, you'll be left behind. Consider it from the other side of the phone. An IA must speak to each client in order to buy or sell any security. Not everyone will be available to speak so there are timing and connection issues, not to mention the sometimes-lengthy process to arrive at the investment thesis. Then there are those clients who insist on thinking about it; words that make any advisor cringe at the implications of duplicating the effort of contacting this individual again at some point and reiterating the whole sales pitch. With 200–300 families under management in a typical practice, it's nearly impossible to reach everyone within a reasonable time frame even if each and every call connected with the client.

Not only that, but imagine you're the 1 out of 200 phone calls that always needs more time, needs to think about the trade or often refuses the advice. It's purely human nature to travel the path of least resistance for efficiency, if not preservation of sanity. When you beat your head with a hammer, it feels great when you stop. How many phone calls would you expect to receive from a transaction-oriented practitioner if you decline most of their recommended transactions? It's an arduous process to interact with 200 personalities without roadblocks. It is possibly, one of the toughest jobs, sitting down.

Left unmanaged, dozens of rogue, unloved stock positions accumulate with stale sell recommendations. Like the Island of Misfit Toys, these positions become neglected and vaguely monitored. If several of them are sitting in your investment account, you may want to consider hiring someone new. If you aren't happy with the advice you're receiving, it's strong evidence that you're with the wrong IA for you.

Let's flip this story over to the receiving side where clients get some empathy, as well. Abruptly receiving an unexpected phone to make an important, on-the-spot financial decision isn't easy. Most people don't typically make critical decisions swiftly and unfortunately, with the intentional or unintentional pressure put on them, many unilaterally defer to their advisor's instruction. The system isn't ideal on either side of the equation.

> "I got a call from my advisor. He said, 'You have an opportunity to buy Agrium now! It is going to $100 and you need to act now.' I felt under pressure to make a decision without knowing any of the fundamental reasons for the investment. He said that if I don't start trusting him with more aggressive investments I would have to expect lower returns."
> —Lori Renwick, Medical Sales Manager

When time becomes constrained half of the research is left out of the conversation, assuming that it's a well-thought-out investment decision in the first place. When your IA calls, take specific notes to summarize the discussion (see appendix 1) and don't be afraid to ask meaningful questions. Your advisor is there to help you make sound decisions.

The unfortunate part of this discussion is that this model for investment management is far from perfect. It's wrought with issues, not the least of which are inefficiencies; inconsistent investment performance among clients as a result of the timing of when each individual receives the IA's advice; and the risk that some investment positions can fall through the cracks due to simple human capacity. In addition, it can be an intimidating client experience. Not to diminish the excellent professionals who run good practices under this platform, the pragmatism of this approach is difficult to justify.

The Right Amount of Risk

Risk is most commonly described as the potential to lose money but it can be more clearly divided between two distinctions: first as the chance of permanent loss of **capital** and the second as the variability of returns through market **volatility**. The second instance is practically important in the event that you need to sell your investments when the value is lower and the ability for the investor to stomach the roller coaster ride. The disconnection between these two distinctions becomes problematic when you are trying to articulate your **risk tolerance** to the professional stewarding your assets.

The goofy part about risk being synonymous with **volatility** in the second definition is that most people don't mind it when it's profitable. In fact, everyone categorically loves upward **volatility** and the more the better! So when discussing risk, it takes a slight shift in thought from the regular use of the term 'risk' to ensure that you and your IA are on the same page.

The importance for being able to clearly understand your **risk tolerance** is high because this will be the foundation for guiding your **asset allocation** into various classes of investments, as well as the inclusion or prohibition of certain types of securities. What level of **volatility** can you withstand before you start losing sleep at night or chew your fingernails to the quick? Of course you don't want to be subject to those levels of stress, but discomfort with various degrees of **volatility** comes at widely different points for everyone.

Most investment firms offer questionnaires to help determine your risk or **volatility** acceptance level; however, remember that **loss aversion** leading to faulty reasoning may come into play in multiple choice questions like: What level of loss can you withstand in a calendar year: 0%, 10%, 25% or more? It can almost sound like a trick question.

Attempting to quantify subjective qualities that change over time, including **risk tolerance**, is close to futile. Unfortunately, in the absence of any quantifiable approach, the best guess alternative to qualifying **risk tolerance** is the limited option we are left with. In order to find common ground you may want to consider expressing yourself with familiar words to describe what a loss means to you. An experienced IA or PM has witnessed the behaviour of investments through different market conditions and can recommend what will fit with the experience you're seeking. There are a few considerations to keep in mind during this process. All advisors hold preferences and biases and will work with you within their stable of familiarity. Secondly, your **risk tolerance** will limit the suitable set of securities and investments that are available within your range of **volatility** as your acceptance of risk drops. Lastly, your return expectations travel hand in hand with the variety of opportunities you can invest in and your comfort with swings in those investments, generally speaking.

The other point to note is that your **risk tolerance** is *your* **risk tolerance.** It represents what volatility you can tolerate or you may need to tolerate. It does not describe how much risk your RRSP can withstand compared with your margin or other investment accounts. It encompasses the aggregate of your investments because it's about you, not a specific account. Guard against segmenting your portfolio into part-risk and part-safety or holding certain accounts as risk-free and other accounts as riskier. This is an illogical approach as pointed out before. Let your professional divide your securities based on the tax advantage, cash flows and income types among your various accounts and tax shelters to maximize your overall strategy.

Volatility is the set of variable returns that you should expect during normal economic cycles. High levels are when your returns are all over the place. One-year you may earn 12%, the next -18%, followed by 23%. Zero **volatility** is when your returns are consistent, earning (or losing) the exact same return each year regardless of weather it is 1% ever year or 8% ever year. Interestingly, a -5% return year after year also has zero **volatility**.

Permanent loss of **capital** is the risk that an investment or group of investments could become worthless. This is not an **asset allocation** decision among good quality investments but a decision limiting speculative or high-risk securities. Having a low ability to sustain permanent loss of **capital** will prohibit the selection of cowboy investments.

Individuals view risk and their ability to sustain market fluctuations at different times in their life. Here are a few considerations to ponder on the interpretation of risk.

- When the consequences become more severe, the perception of risk changes.
- Emotions can drive the need for fearful retreats by overcompensating on a conservative stance, as much as greed can intervene in thoughtful portfolio construction.
- Your level of knowledge around your investments and your understanding of risk has a direct correlation to how much volatility you're willing to accept. For example, if you understand what is happening at a company or in an economic cycle, you're more willing to tolerate share price fluctuations than if you do not.
- Some personalities are structured to accept more dynamic outcomes than others.
- The fewer your financial constraints, the more comfortable you are with variable returns because there is less immediate dependence on those assets and the fear of loss is tempered.
- Security in your employment and stability in your employment income creates space to tolerate more unpredictability over short periods of time.
- Stability in your relationships and personal circumstances allows latitude to introduce more variability in controlled areas of your financial life.
- Everyone has a saturation point for risk.
- Economic cycles and being bombarded with the news around them changes our perception of risk.
- Motivations behind your investment decisions contribute to how much risk you will accept.
- Your attitude toward money directly influences your acceptance of risk. Do you work to live or live to work?
- Historic events shape your personality, such as growing up during the depression, suffering unrecoverable losses or observing your parents' behaviour around money.
- Your sense of responsibility over investment performance may impact how you view risk.

- People with fewer assets tend to be more risk averse than those with wealth. Interestingly, the more wealth you have, the less risk you need and vice versa.

Whatever your **risk tolerance**, be consistent and feel comfortable. Measure yourself by the sleep factor. If your investments are constantly on your mind, preventing you from getting a good night's rest, you've taken on too much risk.

How Much Do You Know?

Quantifying risk was difficult enough; you also need to assess your investment knowledge. It's to your detriment to overestimate your skill but don't sell yourself short. Ask yourself the following basic questions and rate them on a scale from 1–5 where 1 is zero knowledge, 3 is average and 5 is high proficiency. This is not meant to be scientific but serves only to give you a reference point.

1. I understand the difference between a bond and a stock.
   1   2   3   4   5
2. I feel comfortable determining how to balance a portfolio.
   1   2   3   4   5
3. I know what fees I am being charged on my investments.
   1   2   3   4   5
4. I know the approximate taxation of interest versus dividends and **capital gains.**
   1   2   3   4   5
5. I know approximately what I have made on my portfolio over the last 10 years.
   1   2   3   4   5

This is a short list of questions but if you answered the majority of the questions with 1 or 5, you should give yourself an assessment of no knowledge or high working knowledge, respectively. If you answered somewhere in-between, with a tendency to 3s and 4s, you may want to consider yourself as medium, moderate or average knowledge. Mostly 2s would indicate a somewhat limited knowledge base. Remember that this is highly subjective, but in defence of this approach, the entire topic is highly subjective. There is no standardized process and every investment firm has its own self-assessment or "pick-a-category" checkbox on its client file form to describe where you fall. Keep in mind this is a gradient. Picking a shade between white and black is a marginal framework and is only meant to be a general guide.

Negotiating Fees

You get what you pay for but control the things you can, like taxes and fees. There are several earlier sections that discuss fees, so I won't include a discourse here as well. There are dangers to overpaying as well as underpaying so learn the convention and be realistic about where you fit.

And call your mother; she hasn't heard from you in a while.

Past Performance is Not an Indicator of Future Returns

Chasing past performance is a trap for investors and professionals alike. The competitive lure of backward-looking profits coupled with pressure and guilt to have foreseen this, are too tempting to resist. Far too often it's the best performing PMs and strategies, even asset classes, that are almost never in the top quartile the following year. If you wish to guarantee that you'll underperform, jumping to last year's highest performing investment is statistically the best strategy to pursue, hands down.

Stick to your knitting. Flavour-of-the-month investing and last year's darlings aren't worthy pursuits. Keep your sights on the future. Review your specific objectives outlined in your IPS when sober thoughts prevailed. If you have forward-looking macro views, follow those with conviction.

I Can Lose Money as Well as Anyone and Other Online Techniques

There have been enough long stretches of **bull markets** where a dart and a stock list are the only supplies you need to turn a profit. It's enough to make hobbyists

A **bear market** is measured by a 10% peak to trough (top to bottom) drop in the stock market.

proclaim their omnipotence and swear off paying commissions higher than $12.99. The retreat from the pulpit happens quietly and painfully during a financial crisis or **bear market**.

For those with an interest in investing for themselves, I won't dissuade you, but be mindful that professionals study for years and devote time every minute that the market is open while you're focused on the other important things in your life. It takes years of strategy, experience and concerted energy to develop good investment skills. After all, it's professionally called a practice for a reason.

The truth is there is no perfect solution to investing. Some strategies are simply better than others. Those based on research and discipline are more predictable and profitable over time but they all oscillate and underperform from time to time.

When it comes to investing for yourself, if you're inclined to buy that submarine screen door company that your Uncle Joe recommended at Thanksgiving dinner, at least save yourself the fees of a full-service advisor and educate yourself enough to feel comfortable buying the shares in a discount brokerage account. That is, if no professional can talk you out of it and you have incinerated your IPS.

It's a Good Sign

That nagging feeling has left you. You suddenly realize that you haven't thought about your investments for months. It's a realization that happens when you're in the middle of something else important and the thought jumps into your frontal lobe, bounces off your skull and melts into a smile. You made a good decision. If you don't have that sense after a year or two, keep looking.

References:

www.csi.ca Canadian Securities Institute
www.fpsc.ca Financial Planning Standards Council
www.cfainstitute.org CFA Institute

Appendix 1

Date:_____ Time: _____:_____ am/pm

Investment discussion with:_____
Call made / Call received / Meeting / Email Sent / Email Received

Name of IA: _____ Ph #_____
Investment Firm: _____ Email _____

Recommendation: Buy / Sell
Name of Security: _____
shares/units or face value _____ Price $_____
Commissions or Fees $_____ Total Amount $_____

Reason for the recommendation:
_____
_____

How does it meet my investment objectives?
_____
_____

What are the risks?
_____
_____

I will receive: Prospectus / Offering Memorandum / Research
Annual Report / Quarterly Report / News Release / Other

My instructions: Buy / Sell / Do Nothing
Notes: _____
_____
_____

Note: you can also print a similar form from the Canadian Securities Administrators/
Autorites Canadiennes en valeurs mobilieres website at
www.securities-administrators.ca

Chapter 9

An IPS Will Save Your Bacon

> I like my veggies wrapped in bacon, sprinkled with brown sugar and baked until the sugar is bubbly.
> — Homer Simpson

Despite our best attempts, we are all subject to the human condition. *Thankfully* and *unfortunately*. The benefit of knowing what you are working with is that you can do something about it.

An IPS is the only barrier between sober decisions and joining the emotional bungee jump when severe market swings prevent several nights of sleep in a row. Think of it as a business plan for your investments.

For this discussion, we'll assume that you're using a professional IA but if you invest for yourself, the same principles apply. Just because an IPS is a straightforward concept, don't trick yourself into thinking that it's any less important than the stocks and bonds you plan to buy and sell. Arguably, an investor managing her own portfolio needs an IPS more than one who has an arms length relationship with an IA. We are our own worst enemies. Consider the last time you went on a diet or began a gym membership. Great intentions are easily defined. It's when the normal psychology of being a person fails you that being reminded of your original, well thought out intentions can keep you on track, especially if they are indisputable, having been written down in black and white.

An IPS is also a communication tool. While it ensures that the person you are working with understands what you need and want from your investments, it gives you something to hold him accountable to, insofar as the strategies he employs and the expectations that you've set out with him.

There are key components to include in your investment business plan. Firstly, list the basics including your name, date of birth, residential address, etc. Your age and where you file your taxes are important investment considerations. You may also want to list your legal, tax, lending and insurance professionals for collaboration purposes, each of who play key a role in your overall plan. Provide the names of your children and their birth dates, as they are likely beneficiaries of your estate; your income sources and marginal tax rates; your RRSP and TFSA contribution room availability and strategies to be considered surrounding effective use of those limits. In addition, summarize your balance sheet of assets and liabilities to provide a framework for managing effective use of your **capital**.

From an investment strategy standpoint, start by itemize your past investment experiences and the depth of your investment knowledge. Explain what your anticipated investment time horizon is and dates that you expect to inject or withdraw large sums from your investments: Are you planning to use income from your portfolio to fund your lifestyle? Are you children nearing university age and will be using the funds you've set aside in the RESP? Do you expect an inheritance in the next decade? Do you need a new car, roof or are you planning to buy an investment property? Will you be downsizing your home and adding to your investment portfolio after the kids head off to college?

You get the idea.

This provides your advisor with a perspective on how long investments can reasonably be held in planning around economic cycles and your cash flow needs. Some investments are better to be held longer term than others and can be managed with liability matching in line with your cash requirements, with bonds that mature at those times, for example. Your **asset allocation** (the amount you have in fixed income, equities, **alternative strategies**, cash investments, etc.) is determined by your risk tolerance and market conditions. Write down what quantities you will hold in various types of investments (determined between you and your IA) and what strategies are employed to rebalance those proportions. You may wish to have your portfolio reset tactically on a scheduled bases or when the one asset class becomes too large by a certain percentage, compared to the other allocations.

Devise a risk description in your own words as well as expected return and what levels of volatility you are prepared to tolerate. Risk was discussed in chapter two about equities. Recall that your level of risk can be described in two main ways. Focus your discussion around volatility as the variability of returns instead of taking on investments offering huge returns to offset the risk of the investment failing. Permanent loss of **capital** is a devastating result and these highly risky investments are outside the scope of what most investors are seeking.

There are no rules on exactly how you document any of these components but simply that they are stated so that all of the parties have a clear understanding of what is expected and what to do when conditions change.

Although the investments are specifically the focus of an IPS, there is nothing to say that you cannot include estate planning, retirement planning, tax planning and legal objectives on the document. In that case, you may want to consider details about your will, beneficiaries, powers of attorney, representation agreement, philanthropic intentions; and life, disability, critical illness and long-term care insurance policies in force. Also, record your retirement income objectives, income sources and whether you have any shortfalls or excesses between your plans and the assets that you have to fund them. This may have an impact on the types of investments that are suitable for you. If you have a shortfall, you may need to incorporate additional growth to your strategy or if the reverse is true, your stance may become focused on preservation of **capital** rather than growth.

Last but not least, include a list of service expectations and fees that will be charged. Transparency is tantamount to performance. Let your professional guide you and for your benefit, ensure that there is well-defined agreement about all that he will be doing for you and at what cost.

Most investment professionals will already have an IPS template. Your role is to help fill in the blanks and to ensure that all the information that you want included is part of the document.

It only takes a little forethought to develop an IPS and you will never regret having gone through the exercise.

Conclusion

Final Steps

> A man is not finished when he's defeated.
> He's finished when he quits.
> —*RICHARD M. NIXON*

As a woman, I'm grateful for the processes that allow a spunky gal from Vancouver to make a life in the world of money; glass ceilings and all. As a professional, I believe it behoves us each to learn and challenge each other in practice and theory: an ultimate optimist.

Take a moment to reflect on the wide variety of topics that you ingested. There were a lot of profitable details covered.

If you are interested in finding out more about the future of finance, the CFA Institute's website is the pinnacle authority on industry developments. As the leaders in a movement to breed fairness and integrity across all investment markets globally, you can find a wealth of information about the work they are doing at **www.cfainstitute.org**.

There is one last instruction: take the three details that pop into your mind and write them down on the inside front cover or on one of the blank spot in the first few pages. Consider how you can apply them profitably in your investment life. I'm not going to get philosophical but the best results seem to begin incrementally.

The Wednesday/Friday group that I run with each week also has members who power-walk. We all meet at six in the morning and each group heads out on their journey, meeting back at Gio's coffee shop an hour later. It's a terrific bunch of people with a strong draw but I must admit that during the dark Canadian winters, arguing with the alarm-snooze version of myself to slip off my comfy pink pyjamas, pour myself into Lululemon® running gear and throw myself out into the icy, moonlit morning, is tough.

Last week, I decided to join the walking group instead. I don't really know what stopped me from doing that before but I'm happy that I finally came around to that as an option. We walked seven kilometres in about 45 minutes, which surprised me as much as anything could.

So, back to those three investment details…what's the single most impactful thing you can do right now?

Sometimes you just need to "give it a go" with no attachment to the outcome. Don't prejudge what will happen and put your best sneaker forward.

GLOSSARY

This is a glossary, not a dictionary. It is meant to be helpful in the context of what has been written in this book. More often than not, it is colloquial in nature in order to be approachable and useable in this framework.

Some of it might even be satirical. Or funny. Or both.

absolute returns – The actual numerical return calculated on a portfolio regardless of how much the relative market in which the portfolio is invested, is up or down. This measure is important for hedge funds that endeavour to produce positive returns regardless of changes in the stock market, for example. Also see, relative return.

accredited investor - Generally speaking, accredited investors are either registered industry professionals; a person or a couple with assets of more than $1 million; someone whose income is over $200,000 or over $300,000 when combined with that of a spouse; or a corporation or trust managed by an accredited individual. Some provinces make exceptions to the accredited investor restrictions. In some provinces, non-accredited investors can participate in **OM** investments if they invest $150,000 or if they sign a risk disclosure document warning them that they may lose all of their money.

activist managers – These hedge fund managers invest in shares of a company at the current, sombre market price, step in and fix the problem to theoretically unlock the value of the enterprise, driving the stock price up.

Adjusted Cost Base (ACB) – For tax purposes, this is generally the price you paid for an investment including commissions and transaction costs. If you receive a return of capital payment, this amount will reduce your ACB as it is considered your invested, after-tax money.

after-market liquidity – When an investment doesn't trade on an exchange, as is true of many manufactured investment products, the only way to exit the investment is to find another investor who will buy it from you or wait until the maturity. However, most firms will provide liquidity by buying these investments from you during the term.

all or none – Instructions on a buy order to fill it entirely or not at all.

alpha, alpha returns – It denotes when the outperformance of a portfolio is statistically significant, attributed to the manager's ability rather than by accident. The manager's strategies matter and the returns are not a random accident.

alternative asset classes – An inclusive nomenclature to describe all varieties of hedge fund strategies or private equity as opposed to traditional long only investments in asset classes such as stocks and bonds.

alternative strategies – Similar to alternative asset classes, except may also refer to the way that the strategy is executed. Also see, alternative asset class.

anchoring – This is when you assign a value to something based on information that is irrelevant or random. Reluctance to sell a stock for no other reason than the current price is lower than your purchase price, is an example of how we attach an immaterial value to the stock. Also see, entry level biases.

arbitrage – When a profitable opportunity to buy and sell a similar investment on different markets, at different prices exists.

ask – The price offered to sell shares on the market. In the case of a market order to buy shares, it will fill at the asking or offered price.

asset allocation – An investment strategy to reduce risk by combining various asset classes in one portfolio and placing a certain proportion of the portfolio in each.

Asset Backed Commercial Paper (ABCP) – A short-term debt instrument secured by a physical asset, typically issued by a financial company or bank.

averaging down – A strategy of purchasing more of a security at a lower price formerly thought to be advantageous in reducing your average purchase price. Owning more of something that continues to drop in value is counterintuitive, however.

backwardation – When the contracts to buy a commodity in the future are less than the spot or present value of the commodity. This happens when the market anticipates a drop in the price of the commodity so the future price reflects that.

balanced fund – A mutual fund that holds both stocks and bonds.

BBA, B.Com. or BMgmt– Bachelor of Business Administration, Commerce and Management are undergraduate programs in business as the first level of university. Usually general in nature, it typically covers 4 years of full-time study.

bear market – A 10% peak to trough (top to bottom) drop in the stock market measured by the local index. In Canada, that would be the Standard and Poor's Toronto Stock Index (S&P/TSX).

behavioural finance – A growing study of human cognitive biases and the common propensity to make errors with money and investing.

bellwether stock – The term bellwether refers to the practice of placing a bell around the neck of a castrated ram (a wether) leading his flock of sheep. While out of sight, the sound of the bell is a directive on the whereabouts of the flock. When earning season begins, the bellwether stock is that of the largest (typically industrial) companies who report their earnings. Analysts look to these reports as an indication of how subsequent reports will come in under or over expectations.

beta – The sensitivity of an asset to the price movements of the market. More technically, it is measured mathematically by regression analysis to indicate a securities exposure to systematic risk, being how closely its price movements are related to the market.

bid – The price offered to buy shares on the market. If you have a market order to sell shares, it will fill at the bid.

block trade – Buying or selling a large quantity of a security all at once for one average price, possibly across multiple markets, for multiple accounts.

blue chip stocks – These are the shares of companies that retain a strong reputation regardless of the market conditions. Typically, they're large (market capitalization) and pay a dividend that increases over time.

bond features – The cool contraptions that are part of a bond allowing either the company that issued the bond or the investor who purchased the bond to take action at certain times when it is in their best interest. Perks, really.

bond fund – A pooled mutual fund that holds fixed income investments.

bond indenture – The legal agreement on a fixed income instrument outlining the terms and features of the bond issue.

bottom-up investing – Analysis of investment options from a detailed starting point, including technical analysis and quantitative analysis.

bull market – Steadily rising value of the local stock market index.

CA® – Chartered Accountant.

CAIA® – Chartered Alternative Investment Analyst is a specialization in the hedge fund and alternative investment sector. It's a rigorous set of exams not easily passed.

call option – A contract that grants the owner the right to buy a certain stock at a certain price on or before a certain date. As a bond feature, this gives the corporation the ability to repay the bond prematurely, under certain circumstances. Also see, callable feature.

callable feature – This gives the corporation the ability to repay the bond prematurely, under certain circumstances.

call date – The date outlined in the bond agreement at which the corporation may call a bond.

call value – The specified price at which the corporation may call a bond.

capital – Money, wealth or financial resources.

capital gain or **loss** – Increase or decrease in the total value of your investment. Also see, **realized capital loss**.

capital markets – Any platform hosting publicly traded securities, where investors, speculators, corporations and governments come to offer and trade equity, debt or other securities.

capital structure arbitrage – Where an investor buys a security and shorts a different type of security from the same company for the expressed purpose to take the risk of the company out of the equation and to make a profit. For example, buying the bonds and shorting the common shares of the same company.

cash per share – A negative number shows that the company has borrowed money to finance debt. Generally speaking, the use of leverage by a company that has stable, growing earnings is a way for management to increase the return on shareholders' investments. Cash per share can also be an indicator of financial stability or instability if the company has borrowed too much money in relation to its ability to repay the debt.

CFA® – Chartered Financial Analyst. The charter is granted after the successful completion of all 3 levels of exams and 4 years of relevant employment experience, by the CFA Institute. In Canada, only CIM® and CFA® charterholders may become a Portfolio Manager.

CFP® – Certified Financial Planner is recognized as the central financial planning designation. The CSI regulates financial planning and planners are required to maintain ethical standards and ongoing educational updating.

CGA® – Certified General Accountant.

churn, churning – High turnover in an investment portfolio, assumedly to generate excess commissions, in the absence of meaningful tax benefit or profit.

CIM® – Chartered Investment Manager. It used to be called Canadian Investment Manager, at least that's how my certificate from the Canadian Securities Institute (CSI) reads. This designation allows a professional to invest funds as an Associate PM and then a PM after a 2-year period. A PM can invest funds on a discretionary basis. The only other designation that qualifies for a PM designation is the CFA® charter.

closed end products – These are investment pools manufactured with a finite maturity date. Typically, they trade on the stock market or can be redeemed periodically or at maturity by the manufacturing investment firm.

CLU® – Chartered Life Underwriter specializes in developing effective solutions to manage risk, estate planning and income replacement using insurance products.

CMA® – Certified Management Accountant.

cognitive biases – These are nothing more than tricks and shortcuts that our brains use to help us make quick decisions and be more efficient in our lives. Unfortunately, these pre-fab decision trees don't necessarily add value to the financial outcomes at hand.

commission-based trades, commission-based account – An investment account where each trade generates a commission. This is in contrast to a fee-based account that charges a monthly fee on the total market value of the assets under management.

common share – The equity or stock of a corporation is divided into equal shares and represents a proportional ownership of the company.

comparables – Evaluating similar assets in order to determine the value of one that is not priced. This can be used for pricing real estate, stocks, bonds and other securities but it is heavily relied upon in illiquid markets to determine asset values.

CAGR, pronounced [kay-ger], (as in kegger - a bash at which party-goers drink beer from a keg) is an acronym referring to a company's Compound Annual Growth Rate. It measures how much the earnings of a company are growing over a specific period of time, like 5 or 10 years. It's an indication of the company's health and how well it's managed.

contango – The natural condition where the current spot price is less than the future price of the same commodity.

contingent owner – In the case of a TFSA, you may name your spouse in order that the funds remain in the tax shelter and are assigned to them as the new owner upon your death rather than being paid out in cash.

conversion option, convertibility – An option that is attached to debentures giving the owner the right to switch the bond into a predetermined number of shares at a specific price. The price of the debenture will reflect the value of this option in addition to the value of the bond. Also see, convertible debenture.

convertible debentures – An unsecured bond with an embedded option allowing the bondholder to switch the bond into a predetermined number of shares of the issuing company at a certain price. Also see, conversion option.

corporate fund – When a family of various types of mutual funds is offered through one corporate structure, switching from one strategy to another do not generate a capital gain or loss as there is no disposition of the corporate shares.

counterparty – Is the guy on the other side of the trade. If you are buying, he is selling and vice versa so it is important to feel confident that they will follow through on their promises to fulfill the deal. It isn't when your friends congregate in the kitchen with drinks in their hands, despite some of my friends' beliefs.

coupon adjusted-rate securities (CARS) - Reconstituted bonds manufactured from the components of existing bonds in order to reissue them at par, referred to as CARS or PARS. Also see, principle adjusted-rate securities

coupons – The interest payments on a bond.

CPA® – Chartered Professional Accountant is the new amalgamation of the three separately labeled professional accountant designations, CMA®, CGA® and CA®.

CPCA® – Certified Professional Consultant on Aging is another new designation. It's granted after successfully completing training focused on the aging demographic and their specific needs in areas such as pension information and healthcare.

critical illness insurance (CI) – An insurance contract which will pay the annuitant a predetermined value in the event that they contract a life threatening illness defined under the contract.

CSWP® – Chartered Strategic Wealth Professional is the CSI's answer to the CFP for sophisticated financial planning strategies.

currency hedging – Using derivatives to negate the influences of a foreign currency on an investment.

day-trade – Buying and selling a security within the same trading day.

debentures – Unsecured bonds issued by a corporation.

deep value investment strategies – An investment strategy focused exclusively on extremely undervalued securities on the premise that they will return to normal levels over time, resulting in a profit.

Deferred Sales Charge (DSC) – A fee option to purchase mutual funds where the investor doesn't pay a fee up front but is subject to a declining fee if they withdraw their money within the first 7 years after the investment is made.

defined benefit pension plan – An employer based retirement plan where retirement payments are calculated in advance. Also see, defined contribution pension plan.

defined contribution pension plan – An employer based retirement plan where employee contributions are known but the retirement payments are determined from the portfolio returns and other factors. Also see, defined benefit pension plan.

DEX – A theoretical bond index in Canada representing the prices of over a thousand bond issues to represent general changes in the market.

discount, discounted – The difference between the lower price that a bond trades at and its face value. This happens when the prevailing market interest rates are higher than the bond's coupon rate and is the amount offered by the current bondholder to entice new investors to buy the bond.

discretionary portfolio management/Portfolio Manager – An investment professional who may manage all of the daily decisions on a client's portfolio, as guided by their IPS. They must hold a certain license and have been awarded a CIM or CFA charter.

distressed investors and managers – One who invested in bonds of companies facing default risks or that may be at risk of filing for bankruptcy protection.

diversifying – Spreading your investments among low correlated assets in order to reduce your overall volatility and potential permanent loss of capital.

dividends – The amount of cash flow declared and distributed to shareholders. Dividends from eligible Canadian corporations are taxed more favourably than interest income. In order to receive a dividend, you must be the shareholder of record on the date that a dividend is declared. Usually, dividends are paid on a regular schedule but the board of directors must still officially declare the dividends in advance of each payment. Regardless, it's only surprising when a special dividend is declared or if there's a sudden change in the dividend payment policy of a company.

double exposure – In ETF's, these vehicles use derivatives in order to multiply the daily movement of the underlying investment that it tracks. Due to losses that happen during daily rebalancing, these are meant to be day-traded rather than held overnight.

drawdowns – The peak to trough drop in the value of an investment. It can also refer to the value that a new issue drops on the market as a function of the fees reducing the NAV and the market price reflecting the after-fee value.

duration – The sensitivity of a bond to a change in prevailing interest rates. It's a function of the term to maturity and coupon payments. The longer the duration, the more sensitive it is to a rise or drop in interest rates.

EBITDA – Earnings before interest, tax, depreciation and amortization is used to get a reflection of the earnings of a company from its business activities before the accountants start fooling around with the numbers.

Earnings Per Share (EPS) – are reported after taxes, interest, depreciation and expenses have been deducted from the gross revenues of the business and divided among all of the shares outstanding. This gives a relative amount of earnings attributed to each share outstanding.

earnings season – Ye gay ol' time that happens quarterly when public companies announce their business results. Earnings reports are clumped together over several weeks.

efficient market hypothesis – This theory claims that because information is efficiently digested by all market participants, investors cannot achieve excess returns on a risk adjusted basis over the average market return.

entry-level biases – This irrational behaviour, also called anchoring, is when an investor considers the purchase price as a determinant in whether to keep an investment. Also see, anchoring.

equities – Synonymous with stocks or common shares. Also see, common shares, shares, stock.

equity fund – A mutual fund restricted under a prospectus to investing in common shares.

event driven – In this class of hedge fund, investment managers look to profit from major or sudden events in the market.

excess contribution – Any contribution made to a plan over and above the limits permitted. There is an allowable $2000 over-contribution limit for RRSPs.

exchange-traded fund (ETF) – These are continuously offered pools that are traded on the stock exchange, designed to replicate an index, commodity or portfolio. ETFs are subject to tracking error due to small differences in execution and fees.

exchange-traded note (ETN) – These are continuously offered notes issued by an entity with the expressed purpose to return a value tied to an index, commodity or portfolio. They carry the risk of being a debt instrument of the issuer, but this structure is more suitable for investments that are difficult to replicate or theoretical in nature.

ex-dividend date – In order to receive a dividend, you must be the shareholder on record by the settlement date, which is 3 business days after you buy the shares. If you buy the shares on Monday, June 1, you will be the shareholder of record on Thursday, June 4. In reverse, if the dividend is paid to shareholders of record date Friday, June 5, the ex-dividend date is Wednesday, June 3. If you bought the shares on Wednesday, you would not receive the dividend because the shares would not settle in time.

extrapolation – This is the natural predisposition to more heavily consider your most recent experience in predicting the future.

face value – Original paper version bonds literally had the amount that the bond is worth printed on the front of the page. The face value is the amount that is lent to the company by the investor and is the amount that will be repaid to the investor at the end of the term. It is also referred to as the principle of the bond as well as the par value. Also see, principle, par value.

fair market value – This is where a security trades among many market participants who have considered all information about the investment.

FCA® – Fellow of the Institute of Chartered Accountants.

FCGA® – Fellow of the Certified General Accountants Association.

FCSI® – Fellowship of the CSI is obtained once several Canadian securities licenses are completed, a letter is obtained endorsing the application, a sponsorship is in place by an existing fellow and 7 years of investment experience are completed within the preceding decade.

fee-based account – Any investment account that is set up so that a set monthly management fee is charged as a percentage of the assets in the account rather than a commission charged for each trade made. Typically, the percentage charged is lower for larger sized accounts. Management fees charged on taxable accounts may be deductible for income tax purposes against any income whereas commissions charged can only be used to offset capital gains. There may be trading limits imposed on this account structure to curtail heavy trading abuses and those may be described as a number of transactions per year or the total value of assets bought and sold in a year.

fee class – Mutual funds and other investments may be offered with more than one type of fee structure. In order to keep the various options straight, the issuer associates each with a different class of the same investment.

FDS – Financial Divorce Specialist specializes in, you guessed it, planning for the financial aspects of a divorce. While this area of expertise is relatively new as a formal discipline, the Academy of Financial Divorce Specialists endeavours to form loose regulation around practitioners of this ilk.

Front End (FE) – A fee structure that is negotiated when an investment is made in a mutual fund. This fee is deducted from the investment amount and the investor is not subject to any fees upon redemption of the fund.

fully diluted – The total count of all shares outstanding if every derivative is exercised and the relative number of shares issued (options, warrants, convertible debentures, etc.).

fundamental (qualitative) analysis – There are a few ways of analyzing stocks for investing. Fundamental analysis refers to the process of reviewing the business plans, earnings and other enterprise information to determine valuations, growth and other qualitative aspects of companies.

futures contracts – Investors, speculators and commodity business managers can lock in future prices, including the cost for storage and expected commodity price increases in the short term, by buying or selling standardized contracts on an exchange.

Gross Domestic Product (GDP) – This is the value of all of the goods and services produced within a country's borders over a certain time period including private and public production.

gross up amount – Dividends from eligible Canadian corporations are subject to preferential tax treatment by increasing the amount of dividend claimed (called the gross up amount) and then applying a tax credit.

growth and momentum strategies – These are two popular investment styles that were defined for the qualities of steady earnings growth and momentous earnings growth respectively. They are considered in contrast to a value investment style, which pins investment decisions to the relative value of investments rather than their earnings growth or the speed of their earnings momentum prospects.

hedge fund – An alternative investment strategy that differs from traditional strategies in execution or the securities that they invest in. Usually these funds are only available to accredited investors however, they are sometimes offered under a prospectus or an ETF structure allowing anyone to participate in them.

IA – Investment Advisor, formerly referred to as a stockbroker.

illiquid markets – When there is no one prepared to buy what you are selling, the market is illiquid meaning that you cant turn your investment into cash by selling it.

income trust units – A tax structure formerly popular among enterprises as an alternative to a corporate structure.

Individual Pension Plans IPP – These pension plans are generally designed for self-employed individuals.

initial public offering (IPO) – When a security is issued for the first time to the public.

intrinsic value – This is a mathematical, present value calculation of future estimated earnings or cash flow from operations, in consideration of the tangible assets of a company. There are several methodologies used to calculate this value. The outcome is highly inconsistent among analysts because the estimates for growth rates and methods of calculation can vary wildly among practitioners.

Investment Policy Statement (IPS) – This is used to document your objectives and define the investment approach to manage your portfolios. It is a great communication tool and establishes who you are as an investor and guides your portfolio manager.

issues – What my councillor says prevents me from fulfilling my dreams. Kidding. We refer to issues colloquially as a type of security that was released at a specific time, by a specific company or with specific terms.

junk bonds – Any debt instrument that is rated below BBB, which is also considered to be below investment grade.

lagging indicator – A lagging indicator is some signal that tells you what is going to happen after it already happened. Officially, it's a measurable factor that changes following a modification in an economic trend.

leverage, leveraged – Borrowing creates leverage as the initial invested capital required is less. This is as true when you borrow to invest, as it is for a corporation that borrows to develop its enterprise. Similarly, the use of derivatives increases leverage since a smaller amount of capital is required to create an exponential exposure to some underlying investment. Increasing leverage also increases risk, as the volatility of returns is higher relative to the smaller amount of capital invested and the higher the risk of default.

liability matching – The strategy of arranging payments of interest and dividends or the maturity of a fixed income investment with dates when money is needed to satisfy a disbursement.

limit order – An offer to buy or sell a stock at a specific price.

liquidity – This is the ability to change investments into cash readily. A market is liquid when there are multiple buyers and sellers.

long bull market – A bull market is one where the stock market, measured by the stock exchange index is trending upward. When this trend prevails for a long period of time, it commonly breads complacency and some investors begin to let their guard down and become less fearful and less vigilant as a common behavioural response.

long position, long – When you own or buy a security, you are long the position. Long investors expect the securities to increase in value to produce a profit. Your risk is limited to the amount you invested in the event that the securities drop to zero. A long-only manager refers to Portfolio Managers (PM) who have a limited mandate to only own stocks or bonds, such as a traditional mutual fund manager. In the long-only world, a bear market means losses on the portfolio.

long-only manager – An investment manager who is only permitted to buy securities and is restricted from shorting securities in the portfolio.

long-short hedge fund – This hedge fund strategy attempts to remove or partially remove the effects of the market volatility in general by offsetting securities owned with ones that are shorted in the market. Also see, market neutral.

long-term care insurance – In order to protect individuals from the rising costs of private long-term care during their final years, insurance companies offer an insurance plan that will pay a contractual amount for personal care. The premiums are high for this type of insurance since the likelihood that you will collect it is also high.

loss aversion – The tendency for an individual's fear of losing money to result in irrational decision making.

low correlated, low correlation – When assets behave differently from one another they have a low correlation to each other. By combining low correlated investments, the overall volatility of your investment portfolio is reduced.

Low Sales Charge (LSC) – In an effort to bridge the gap between the front end purchase option and the deferred sales charge option, mutual fund companies developed a hybrid approach where investors can shorten the period that funds are locked-in and not pay a fee to invest in the fund upfront. In practice, many quality investment professionals offer mutual fund purchases on a front-end zero commission fee basis, rendering this and DSC purchase programs ineffectual.

macro – In referring to a hedge fund strategy, the objectives of this type of investment are to capitalize on themes and major trends in investment markets around the world.

managed futures – This trend following hedge fund strategy uses sophisticated computer algorithms to invest long and short in the futures market to make a profit. Typically, these strategies follow multiple futures markets at once.

margin, margined – For arbitrage or other trading strategies between mispriced securities, it's the profitable difference between the two securities. It also refers to an account type in which you may borrow against the value of margin eligible securities held in your portfolio. When you have margined your account, you have borrowed against securities in your account and your account is said to be in margin.

margin calls – For investors who have borrowed against the securities in their investment account and the value of the securities have decreased or become ineligible to be used as security, the account holder must deposit funds to cover the excess margin debt or sell enough securities to cover the shortfall.

market capitalization – Number of shares outstanding multiplied by the current share price. It describes the size of the company or its equity. This is one measure of how liquid a company is or how easy it is to buy or sell the shares.

market neutral, market neutral manager – This hedge fund strategy attempts to remove or partially remove the effects of the market volatility in general but offsetting securities owned with ones that are shorted in the market. Also see, long-short, pair trading.

market order – Offers to sell or buy shares at the current bid or ask price respectively.

matured value – For investments with a due date, this is the expected value of the investment on that date. It's usually predetermined and often called the par value.

MBA – Master of Business Administration is a university graduate degree in business from the faculty of business or management.

mental accounting – When an individual segregates their money into imaginary buckets, treating each bucket separately in terms of risk levels or investment strategy.

merger arbitrage – This event driven, hedge fund strategy is executed by exploiting the difference between two company's securities during a merger, by buying the underpriced one and selling the other to derive a profit once the merger is complete.

Modern Portfolio Theory – Essentially, the theory contends that if you design a portfolio among various investments that behave differently at different times, there is a set of mathematically ideal portfolios that extract the most return for the minimum amount of volatility.

monetize – The act of turning an asset into money (cash) by selling it or liquidating it.

money market instruments – These are short-term fixed income instruments including treasury bills (issued by the federal government), bankers acceptances (issued by banks) and commercial paper (issued by corporations).

moving average – Rolling average price of a stock. Typically, 50-, 100- and 200-day moving averages are considered in technical analysis where lines drawn over various rolling periods intersect, indicating a change in price trends.

MTI® Estate and Trust Professional – These professionals address sophisticated estate planning strategies for protecting wealth and transitioning it to the next generation.

net asset value (NAV) – The value of each unit of a pooled investment is calculated by dividing the market value of all of the investments in the pool, minus any expenses, by the total number of units outstanding.

new issues – When a company raises money in the capital markets, they issue a new security. This can be a new share issue, bonds or debentures. Also see, issue.

no load – This option does not oblige the investor to pay a fee to buy or sell the mutual fund. This option is usually reserved for proprietary mutual funds available at major Canadian banks.

notional value – When using derivatives, this often refers to a principle or theoretical value of a portfolio or other asset.

offering memorandum (OM) – This is a required document given to investors describing details of the investment terms and is used instead of a prospectus. Only accredited investors (or in some provinces non-accredited investors who sign a risk disclosure) may participate in investments offered under this format. Also see, prospectus.

Old Age Security (OAS) – A federally distributed retirement payment to eligible Canadians during their retirement years in order to provide financial security.

options , options contract – These are derivative contracts that are written by investors and traded on the stock exchange. Each contract gives the bearer the right to buy or sell an underlying security at a set price on or before a set date.

orphan and granny company – A colloquial phrase implying that the stock is suitable for those with low risk tolerance.

oscillating markets – When the average stock market level trades up and down within a band level, neither making nor losing progress in the value. There is no trend in the market either upward or downward.

Over-the-Counter (OTC) – Securities that are not listed on a recognized exchange trade over the counter between agreeing counterparties. In the case of bonds, major financial institutions provide liquidity and pricing on bonds sold into and from their private inventories. The over-the-counter equity market is also referred to as the pink sheets and is a trading arena for stocks that cannot or chose not to be listed on a regulated stock exchange.

pair trading – This is a market neutral hedge fund strategy in which the investment manager selects two similar stocks; one to buy long and one to sell short. The intention is to produce a return from the spread in the performance of the two companies while nullifying the effects of the market in general.

par value – For a bond, this is the equivalent to the face value of the bond and means that the bond is trading at 100 cents on the dollar. Also see, face value, principle.

passive investments – Certain ETFs that follow established markets or commodities are considered passive investments since there are no portfolio management decisions being made.

per share – In evaluating a business, its income and assets are conventionally expressed as an amount in relation to the number of shares that it has issued or outstanding.

PFP® – Personal Financial Planner is the designation issued by the Canadian Securities Institute. It's a broad-based program.

Portfolio Manager (PM) – After being awarded a CFA charter or a CIM certificate and 2 years of supervision as an Associate PM, a licenced PM may offer discretionary investment management where they take charge of the day-to-day investment decisions.

Post-Retirement Benefits (PRB) – You may increase your retirement income by making additional contributions, if you're between the ages of 60 and 70, are working and contributing to CPP or receiving CPP or QPP.

premium – In a stock take-over offer, this is the amount over the market price offered by the acquiring company. In reference to a bond, it's the amount that a bond is trading at over the par or matured value of the bond. In terms of an option, the premium is the sticker price you pay to obtain the contract or you receive by selling the contract.

Price to Book ratio (P/B) – The market price of the stock divided by book value per share. This metric measures the relative trading value of the stock compared with the book value of the company.

Price to Cash Flow ratio (P/CF) – Market price of a stock divided by the cash flow from operations. It is a relative measure comparing the cash generated by the company with the price that their shares trade at on the market.

Price to Earnings ratio (P/E) – Market price of the stock divided by earnings of the company per share. The higher the price, the higher the P/E. The higher the earnings, the lower the P/E. A high P/E may be an indication of the shares being overvalued in the market relative to the company's earnings.

Price to Intrinsic Value (P/IV) – Trading price of the stock divided by the intrinsic value of the company. This ratio can be used to illustrate whether the shares of the company are trading too high or too low compared with the intrinsic value. Recall that the intrinsic value is a mathematical calculation based on the present value of future earnings and the assets of the company.

principle – With fixed income, the principle is the face value of the bond upon which the coupon interest is calculated. Also see, face value.

principle adjusted-rate securities - Reconstituted bonds manufactured from the components of existing bonds in order to reissue them at par, referred to as PARS or CARS. Also see, coupon adjusted-rate securities

private debt – Fixed Income bonds that are placed privately with institutional investors. It can also mean bank debt including senior secured notes, which more recently have been packaged and sold to the general public in pooled notes and ETFs. Also see, Senior Secured Loan Funds.

prospectus – The legal document required to be given to every investor prior to making the investment providing details about the investment. It is most often used for mutual funds.

put option – A derivatives contract that grants the owner the right to sell a specific underlying investment, at a specific price, on or before a specific date. To obtain this contract the purchaser pays the writer a premium. Also see, option.

quantitative analysis – This type of analysis uses a multi-factor screen to sort and evaluate stocks. It also may include computer-based trading formulas and algorithms or other screening tools define which securities to buy or sell.

realized capital losses – When you sell an investment that has dropped in value, the amount of the loss is realized for tax purposes in that tax year. It can also be carried back and applied against capital gains that you have claimed in any of the former 3 tax years or carried forward to offset future capital gains indefinitely.

Real Return Bonds (RRB) – The semi-annual interest payments and the capital of on these fixed income investments track the Canadian Consumer Price Index (CPI). This makes the bond effective in maintaining purchasing power as inflation rises. In Canada, the federal government and the province of Quebec issue them.

record date – The date on which a company executes a transaction. Shareholders of record on that date will participate in the reorganization (such as a stock split or reverse split) or a dividend declared, for example.

relative returns - The conventional measure of performance for traditional portfolios. When the stock market drops in value traditional portfolios, including long only mutual funds, feel that they are doing well by dropping in value less than the market.

relative value, relative value manager – In comparing the value of securities within the context of other assets, markets or other goal posts, these managers exploit mispriced securities in order to derive a profit.

residual – The matured value of a bond once the coupons are all stripped off. It is also the principle of the amount lent to the company or government issuing the bond.

retractable feature – This perk for bond investors allows them to request the company to repay their investment early, upon certain terms. This is helpful in the case of rising interest rates when an investor may want to reinvest at higher prevailing rates.

return of capital – When your original invested capital is repaid to you either in an instalment or at maturity. This amount reduces your ACB.

reverse stock split – A share reorganization in which the value of a company's equity is divided among fewer shares.

RFP® – Registered Financial Planner is offered by a privately run organization from the CFP group. The organization separately provides education and self-governance among members.

RHU – Registered Health Underwriter specializes in living health benefits such as disability income replacement.

risk disclosures – A written warning discussing the known risks of an investment.

risk tolerance – When we talk about risk, there are two main reference points. First is the volatility, or variability of returns, and the second is the potential for permanent loss of capital. Assuming that no investor willingly tolerates the latter, risk tolerance refers to your comfort level with the variability of returns in your portfolio, especially when the value of your investment drops.

secondary market – Where securities trade among the general public.

secured – When some asset is used as collateral against a debt obligation.

securities – A term to generally describe a traded financial instrument.

Senior Secured Loan Funds – A diversified portfolio of private debt financing extended by banks to medium and large corporations, usually secured by assets and carrying a floating interest rate. These are generally poor quality and high risk.

Separately Managed Account (SMA) – An investment pool in which each investor directly holds every security individually, with their unique ACB, professionally managed by a PM.

serial autocorrelation – The movement of something compared to itself over several intervals in a repeated pattern . A trend is useful in predicting the future value of a security and is used in trend following investment strategies including managed futures.

settlement – The date after shares are traded (T) when the payment and the shares must be delivered. For common shares, that is the trade date plus 3 trading days (T+3). Mutual funds are T+3. Bonds are T+2. Money market is T+1.

share – The equity of the company is divided among investors/owners in units of shares. Also see, common share, equity, stock.

shares outstanding – The number of shares that are issued by the company and held by investors.

short position, short, shorting – When you borrow shares, sell them hoping that the price will drop, buy the shares back at a lower price and return the shares. When you short a position, you are responsible to pay any dividends declared to the person who is long the position. Shorting has unlimited risk (until you cover the short by buying the shares back) since prices can theoretically continue rising indefinitely.

sinking fund – Setting aside money periodically in order to protect yourself in the future against a disaster (or to retire a debt) may be an alternative to insurance.

small cap – Denotes a small company defined by the size of their market capitalization (the number of shares outstanding multiplied by the market price), sometimes quantified in the neighbourhood of $200million to $1billion.

special situations – In event driven hedge fund strategies, this refers to the unique or sudden events that the manager exploits to make a profit.

speculation – As opposed to investing based on sound reasoning, speculation is a flagrant approach of buying an asset with the hope to gain a profit in the absence of firm evidence or consideration.

split – See, stock split.

spot price – The current market price of a commodity.

Standard and Poor's Toronto Stock Index (S&P/TSX) – The Canadian stock index determined by the level of the market capitalization of the 300 largest, publicly traded companies in the country.

stock – The equity share of a company. Also see, common share, equity, share.

stock market index – A collection of the largest publicly traded stocks intended to represent the entire market. The S&P/TSX is made up of the largest 300 companies weighted by market capitalization, which means that the largest companies influence the index more than the smaller ones. Also see, Standard and Poor's Toronto Stock Index (S&P/TSX).

stock split – When a company decides to multiply the number of shares outstanding without changing the equity in the company. If you hold 300 shares and the shares split on a 2-for-1 basis, you will hold 600 shares with each share worth about half of the value it traded at prior to the reorganization.

stop-loss – An order to sell shares at a specific price. It will then become a market order and fill at whatever bid is available. This type of order can be filled at any price one the stop loss price is triggered. Also see, stop-loss limit.

stop-loss limit – An order to sell shares at a specific price but no lower than a given floor price. Also see, stop-loss.

strategy – A measurable or planned method for investing.

strike price – In option trading, this is the price on the option agreement at which you can execute the trade on the underlying security.

strip bonds – When a bond has all of its semi-annual coupon payments removed, what remains is the principle or residual. It's said to be stripped of its coupons. Also see, zero coupon bonds.

successor annuitant – This is the person designated to become the alternate person on which the life insurance contract, segregated fund or TFSA is based on, usually maintaining the structure of the contract upon the death of the original annuitant.

swaps – An investment vehicle with which institutions exchange one thing for another between each other, under a contract at a future date.

tactical asset allocation – The disciplined approach of taking profits on predetermined periodic dates from investments that have performed well, and investing the excess money in other investments that have not in order to rebalance the amount of capital allocated to each.

tail events – Tail events are those events that are rare. The shape of a normal distribution curve is a hump with two long tails on either side. Two standard deviations from the middle of the hump is the area on the far right or far left, in one of the tails. This area under the curve describes unusual and unpredictable events. For statisticians, it's the area under the curve of a normal distribution, two standard deviations from the mean.

tax loss selling – Selling a security for the expressed purpose to offset a capital gain from another investment in that tax year. Securities may be repurchased after 30 days or an alternate security may be purchased in its place at any time.

technical analysis – Uses numeric market prices, volumes and other data to forecast stock direction and movement. It is a binary, graphical representation of share prices and is used to predict which securities to buy or sell and when.

time value – In calculating derivatives with an expiry date, the premium to purchase it can be broken down into 3 components: the intrinsic value, the volatility and the time value. The more time there is before the expiry, the more chance there is that it could be profitable, the higher the time value is in the cost of buying the derivative.

top-down investing – When your investment perspective is based on thematic or macro viewpoint, it is considered to be an overviewed position.

tracking error – The difference between an ETF's performance and the returns of the investments it endeavours to replicate. Fees, trading costs and timing are the most obvious culprits, but some investments, such as commodities, may not be traded during the same hours as the ETF.

trailing commission, trailers – These are the monthly fees paid to the IA for their role in administering the client drawn from the management expenses charged to the mutual or segregated fund or from a structured investment product.

trusts – A legal tax entity. It is used in estate and tax planning to separate assets from an individual or a corporation.

unsolicited trades – When the account owner requests a trade be executed that was not solicited by the IA.

value trap – Describes companies whose shares have traded at a low market price relative to their earnings (P/E), book value (P/E) or cash flow (P/CF), usually for an extended period of time. Sometimes however, stock prices are cheap because there are underlying reasons that make the company a less savoury investment due to a mature and declining business or poor management, for example.

volatility – This is referred to as the variability of returns. If your portfolio earns 3% every year, you have zero volatility. Similarly if your portfolio drops by -2% every year, you also have zero volatility. If your returns are 3%, 25%, -16%, 7%, -23% in sequential years, your investment has high volatility.

volatility index (VIX) – A measure of volatility in the market derived from the price S&P500 option premiums using the Black-Scholes model.

volume – The number of shares traded on the exchange in one trading day.

warrants – Derivatives issued by a corporation that grant the holder the ability to purchase additional shares of the company, at a specific price, before a specific date.

zero coupon bonds – These bonds are sold at a discount and mature at par or face value. The appreciation in the price is the return on the investment as all of the coupons have been stripped off. Also see, strip bonds.

ABOUT THE AUTHOR

Coreen T. Sol, Chartered Financial Analyst, is a Portfolio Manager with more than 20 years of experience in private wealth management and a passion for inspiring change and altering the way we invest.

Beginning her career as a teller at the Royal Bank of Canada, she worked in a number of personal and corporate positions before managing a small community bank branch in New Westminster, BC. During this time, Coreen was one of the first personal banker licensees in British Columbia to sell mutual funds to bank clients, in the mid-1990's. From here, she went on to become an Investment Advisor at RBC Dominion Securities and, after receiving her CFA® charter in 2003, began managing discretionary portfolios on an industry unique platform.

Today, Coreen administers her private wealth practice through CIBC Wood Gundy. Her work is built on the transparency of individual securities, quantitative models, and bulk trading. In a rapidly changing economic landscape of unpredictable markets and extravagant fees, Coreen hopes to guide and inspire a new league of both private wealth investors and financial professionals. Transforming the way we invest is her mission.

A former professional ballet dancer, Coreen is also an avid yogi, snowboarder, runner and loves to spend time on the golf course. During her downtime, you can most likely find her catching up on her favourite late night talk shows, tending to her expanding vinyl collection, or developing her artistic skills with a variety of paint mediums. Coreen currently lives in Kelowna, British Columbia, with her three children.